# THE PLEASURES OF EATING WELL

## NOURISHING FAVOURITES FROM THE COMO SHAMBHALA KITCHEN

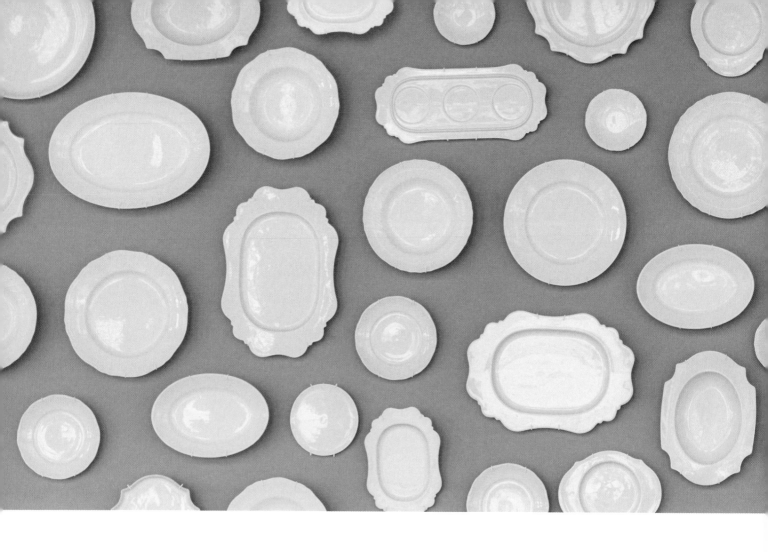

TO ALL THE DEDICATED CHEFS WHO HAVE INSPIRED  ME AND WORKED SO HARD IN THE COMO KITCHENS

PHOTOGRAPHY
BY
LISA LINDER

# THE PLEASURES OF EATING WELL

## NOURISHING FAVOURITES FROM THE COMO SHAMBHALA KITCHEN

COMO SHAMBHALA

CHRISTINA ONG

CLEARVIEW

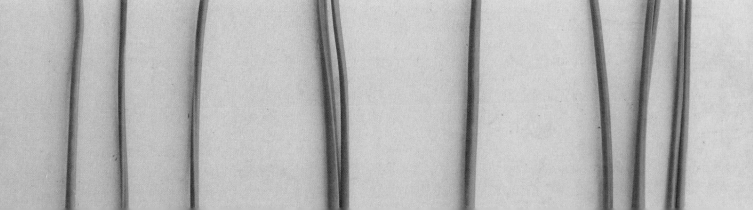

*Contents*

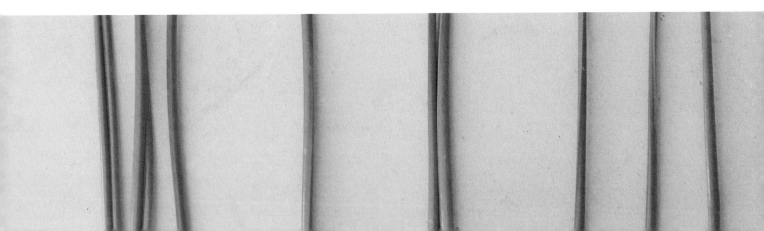

# I have always felt at home in the kitchen. Growing up, I watched my grandmother cook.

It wasn't that she taught me specific recipes, but in watching her, I picked up a passion for food and the pleasure it brings to the family table. She made everything from scratch, with few machines. She made her own rice flour, her own vegetable and chicken stocks. She collected sea kelp to use as a gelling agent, never relying on processed packaged foods. To those experiences I then added numerous trips to Italy – many of them because of my fashion business – where I started to appreciate how simple really good food could be. I learnt how important it was to source the right ingredients: fresh, local, seasonal. I started to eat at The River Café in London, and bit by bit, found I connected with chefs almost more than anyone else. I have always bought cookbooks obsessively. I love markets; I crave contact with ingredients and ideas. But then I firmly believe that if one doesn't enjoy food, it's hard to enjoy life. The pleasures of eating well are built into my DNA.

Still, if there's a single pressure on the way we eat now, it's time, or a lack of it. Everyone has to adapt in the kitchen to accommodate the speed of modern life, especially with the pressures of international travel that affect so many of us. Hence, flexibility is one of the key attractions of COMO Shambhala Cuisine. This book features recipes that can fit into any time of day: a juice, a broth, a salad. The recipes are also suitable for different social circumstances, whether you are eating alone, or among family and friends. Some of the recipes are helpful for recuperating post-illness, or for people who exercise a lot; other dishes will help with a liquid-based detox. There are a few recipes that are admittedly complex, and not for everyone; I have included them in this book because I love the detail that goes into a really special dish, and sometimes the act of working through a more technically challenging recipe has a meditative side to it as well.

What the recipes don't do is fit into one prescriptive way of eating – raw, macrobiotic or otherwise. COMO Shambhala mixes up different approaches with a few common threads, chief among them being avoidance of processed foods, which goes back to my grandmother's earliest inspirations.

Eating well is instinctive; COMO Shambhala Cuisine honours the belief that our bodies tell us all we need to know. Eating well is about energy and flavour, not calorie-counting. Personally, I moderate my meat intake – I find it hard to digest meat when I am on the move – and refined sugars. I try to buy organic, but don't fixate on it. I look instead for foods that have been intelligently farmed, where the meats and vegetables haven't been pumped with hormones and pesticides. I generally prefer light desserts but I certainly don't avoid sweet foods altogether. I juice once in a while, but I wouldn't ever do this instead of eating. I don't particularly like raw – I sometimes think I will be chirping like a bird if I eat any more nuts and seeds – even though 'raw' is a key component of COMO Shambhala Cuisine. But then that's what I mean by flexible. You can take or leave the recipes in this book to suit you, your lifestyle, and the time you have to commit to the kitchen.

This is the first time we have gathered the most popular dishes served at all our COMO Hotels and Resorts in a single book. We've simplified wherever possible for the home cook while retaining a few challenging recipes for those with more confidence in the kitchen. I hope you enjoy it, because cooking the COMO Shambhala way should be nothing but pure, unadulterated pleasure.

*Christina Ong*

COMO Shambhala advocates proactive holistic wellness, combining modern science with ancient healing. A hallmark of COMO Hotels and Resorts, COMO Shambhala marries healthy eating with pleasurable gastronomy, self-directed exercise with expert instruction, massage with greater mental repose, and thought with action. From city centres to island retreats and highland resorts, COMO Shambhala offers massage, yoga, Ayurveda, aromatherapy, Pilates, Tai'Chi, and Qigong and aromatherapy-based hair, skin and bodycare products. Complementing these services is COMO Shambhala Cuisine, the enzyme-rich, healthy and delicious cuisine designed to boost concentration and energy, balance blood sugar levels and cleanse the body from the inside out.

BALI | BHUTAN | BANGKOK | LONDON | MALDIVES | MIAMI BEACH | PERTH | PHUKET | SINGAPORE | TURKS AND CAICOS

"*I firmly believe that if one doesn't enjoy food, it's hard to enjoy life.*" CHRISTINA ONG

# NUTRITIOUS AND DELICIOUS

## THE BENEFITS OF COMO SHAMBHALA CUISINE

Every COMO Shambhala recipe in this book is designed to inspire the palate with memorable flavours. While all are healthy and energising, each has a unique nutrition profile. For easy reference, we have highlighted the particular benefits of each recipe.

## ANTIOXIDANT-RICH

Selenium and vitamins C, E and A (as beta-carotene) possess recognised antioxidant properties to neutralise free radicals and buffer the effects of oxidative stress and damage in the body. Per serving, these recipes provide an excellent source (20 per cent or more of the recommended daily intake) of at least two of these micronutrients. The recipes may also include ingredients with other antioxidant phytonutrients such as carotenoids, flavonoids and polyphenols.

## CALMING

COMO Shambhala's Ayurvedic doctors highlight the 'moist', 'warm' and 'lubricating' characteristics of these recipes to help restore balance to the system and pacify the 'doshas'. The emphasis on whole grains and complex carbohydrates supports the production of serotonin, a neurotransmitter with a soothing effect. All are antioxidant-rich and include sources of anti-inflammatory omega-3 fatty acids, which counteract the effects of chronic stress and anxiety on the body.

## CLEANSING

These recipes remove sources of irritation or inflammation from the diet while nutritionally stimulating the body's detoxification systems that eliminate impurities. All are antioxidant-rich, vegan, gluten-free and contain no refined grains, added sugars or sweeteners.

## DIGESTIVE SUPPORT

These recipes are suitable for individuals wishing to improve gastrointestinal regularity and alleviate occasional symptoms of gas, bloating, indigestion and generalised discomfort. Per serving, these recipes are high in total dietary fibre, providing 5 or more grams of combined soluble and insoluble fibres. Selected ingredients may offer prebiotic and probiotic benefits to nourish and maintain microflora beneficial to the gut.

## ENERGISING

These fibre-rich, high-protein recipes (5 grams or more serving) fuel active muscles, stabilise blood sugar levels and provide sustained energy for anyone adhering to a fitness regimen. Per serving, these recipes provide 20 per cent or more of the recommended intake of at least two B vitamins, which are valuable to proper metabolic function. Likewise, all recipes are antioxidant-rich and contain sources of anti-inflammatory omega-3 fatty acids to help replenish nutrients and accelerate tissue recovery.

## HIGH-PROTEIN

These recipes support individuals requiring or electively choosing a high-protein diet. Per serving, they fulfil 20 per cent of the recommended daily value of protein (10 or more grams). Recipes may incorporate animal-based or complementary plant-based sources of protein to ensure a comprehensive range of all essential amino acids.

## HEART HEALTHY

These recipes promote optimal functioning of the vasculature supporting the cardiac system and the brain. While not low in total dietary fat, all possess a desirable overall lipid profile – low in saturated fats (3 grams or less per serving), low in cholesterol (20mg or less per serving), and free of all trans-fatty acids – while offering heart-healthy monounsaturated and anti-inflammatory omega-3 fatty acids. The recipes are naturally low in sodium (140mg or less per serving) and often exclude added sugars, sweeteners and refined grains.

# IMMUNE-BOOSTING

These recipes are ideal for strengthening and maintaining the body's natural defences. All selections are high-protein, antioxidant-rich, and provide 20 per cent or more of the recommended daily intake of zinc — a trace mineral vital to tissue healing and the development and functioning of immune cells. Some ingredients in these recipes may also feature prebiotic and probiotic properties to foster a healthy immune response.

# MINERAL-RICH

Per serving, these recipes provide 20 per cent or more of the recommended daily intakes (RDIs) of two or more essential minerals — including major minerals (such as calcium, phosphorus, magnesium and potassium) and trace minerals (such as iron, zinc, selenium, copper and chromium).

# REJUVENATING

These recipes are all rich in antioxidants, vitamins and minerals. The recipes exclude added sugars to prevent fluctuations in energy and mental acuity. All contain sources of omega-3 and monounsaturated fatty acids to counteract inflammation, lubricate the cells of the brain and central nervous system, and nourish the hair, skin and nails.

# SMART CARBOHYDRATE

The ingredients in these recipes emphasise naturally occurring carbohydrates such as those found in whole grains, legumes, fruits, vegetables, nuts and seeds. All recipes are high in total dietary fibre (providing 5 grams or more per serving) and are free of refined grains and any added sweeteners. These selections are useful for individuals routinely monitoring blood sugar levels or following low glycaemic index diets.

# VITAMIN-RICH

Per serving, these recipes offer 20 per cent or more of the recommended daily intakes (RDIs) of two or more essential vitamins — including both water-soluble vitamins (C and B vitamins) and lipid soluble vitamins (A, D, E and K).

The validated nutritional claims of each recipe have been based on a per serving analysis comparable to the industry 'RACC' standard (regular amounts customarily consumed). The quantity of salt in most recipes is described as 'to taste'. If you are following a sodium-restricted diet, modify this step by omitting the salt completely, or keeping to below the 140mg or less per serving.

In addition to these nutritional benefits, many of our recipes also adhere to dietary and preparation principles that many of our guests follow. We believe that everyone deserves flavour and variety in every meal, special requirements notwithstanding.

# GLUTEN-FREE

These recipes are free of wheat, rye, barley and any cross-breeds or by-products containing traces of these grains — and meet international gluten-free standards. These recipes are suitable for individuals avoiding gluten due to personal preference, intolerance or a diagnosed allergy. Some of the recipes do contain fish sauce or tamari soy. If you are observing a gluten-free diet, please ensure that your sauces are certified wheat-free and gluten-free by the manufacturer.

# RAW

These recipes uphold 'Raw' or 'Living Food' philosophies, which prohibit cooking above 40–46°C/104–115°F. The recipes employ low temperature culinary techniques such as dehydrating, soaking, sprouting, cold-pressed juicing and fermenting in order to preserve naturally-occurring enzymes, phytochemicals, vitamins, minerals, amino acids and essential oils. These recipes emphasise fresh fruits, vegetables, seeds, nuts, legumes and whole grains.

# VEGAN

These recipes are suitable for individuals who adhere to a strict vegan diet. They exclude meat, poultry, fish, shellfish, dairy and egg and other animal-derived ingredients. These selections emphasise plant-based sources of nutrition, including fruits, vegetables, legumes, grains, nuts and seeds.

For ease of reference, we have listed the recipes under each nutrition profile or dietary principle in the Index, which starts on page 300.

COOKING
NOTES

**1.** Ingredients indicated with (G) are further described in the Glossary starting on page 296.

**2.** We recommend weighing ingredients (ingredients are listed in grams and ounces). The cup equivalents are provided for your convenience.

**3.** Please stick with one measurement, standard, metric or imperial, when measuring, by weight or volume.

**4.** All spoon measurements, unless otherwise indicated, are level. We have used standard 5ml teaspoons and 15ml tablespoons. Australian standard tablespoons are 20ml; for Australian readers, please use 3 teaspoons per tablespoon.

**5.** Eggs are large and weigh approximately 60g/2½oz.

**6.** Some recipes include raw or lightly cooked eggs, meat and fish. These should be avoided by the elderly, infants, pregnant women, convalescents and anyone with an impaired immune system.

**7.** All fruits and vegetables are assumed to be medium in size, unless specified as small or large.

**8.** Cooking times are for guidance only and based on conventional ovens. For fan or convection ovens, follow the manufacturer's instructions concerning the oven temperature. Check cakes 10 minutes before the given time.

**9.** 'Season' means to season with sea salt and freshly ground black pepper. 'To Taste' directions allow flexibility for readers concerned about their sodium levels.

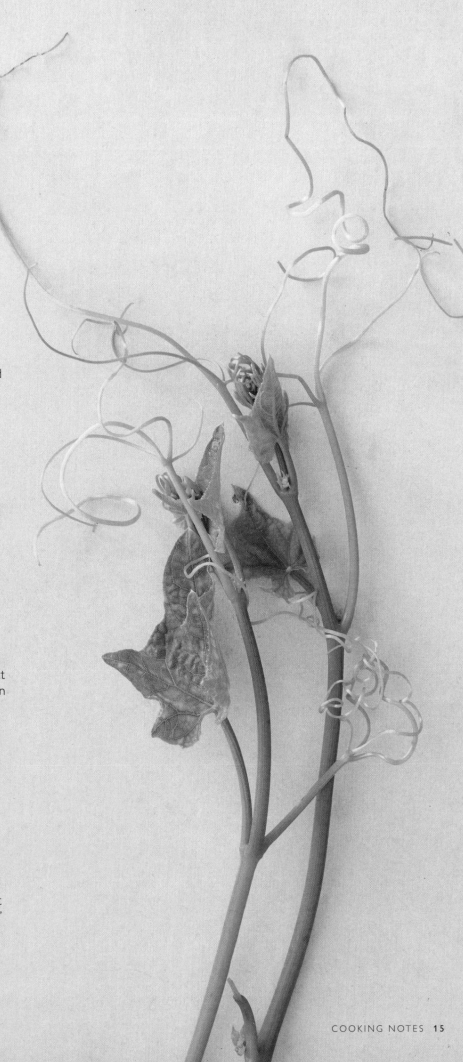

# Breakfast

CHAPTER 1

Breakfast is vital to kickstart your metabolism – so yes, the adage is true: breakfast is the most important meal of the day and worst meal to skip. It's vital to take time over this meal. Ensure you're consuming something fresh, and above all, rehydrate, with juice or a fruit salad. If you want to eat something more substantial, take heed of the recipes containing protein, which will keep you feeling full. Nuts and seeds are also important, and are best eaten in the morning, because they take time to digest. Flaxseed is a favourite in our kitchens; indeed it would be hard to find a food that contains a higher soluble and insoluble fibre content.

Of course not everything in this chapter makes sense to prepare on a daily basis – the buckwheat pancakes (page 35) and Maldivian egg curry (page 48) are two special occasion dishes – but it is easy to poach an egg and whizz up a 'Green Goddess' sauce (page 42). You can also go into the time-poor working week fully prepared, focusing on recipes with a longer shelf life: the 'toast' (page 32), muesli (page 26) and granola crunch (page 25), among them.

As to the milks we recommend for our COMO Shambhala cereals, it really comes down to personal preference. Some avoid cow's milk; rice milk has the thinnest consistency, and the least flavour. Store-bought nut milk can contain a lot of emulsifying agents, which stops it from splitting. So if you can't find a good-quality nut milk, make your own (page 267) or use soy milk, but that's an acquired taste.

Most of all, enjoy your first meal of the day. These recipes are versatile; they allow you to experiment and explore. The young coconut porridge (page 30), for instance, can be mixed with any fruit in season, wherever you are in the world.

*Everything about this breakfast salad comes together on the plate, in look and taste. Bali's ripe papayas – packed with anti-parasitic enzymes – are sweet, with a brilliant vibrant colour. Kiwis help rehydrate your body and contain a boost of vitamin C.*

Vitamin-Rich | Mineral-Rich | Heart Healthy | Digestive Support | Raw | Gluten-Free | Vegan

# KIWI, PAPAYA
# AND LONGAN SALAD WITH
# LEMONGRASS SYRUP

### SERVES 4

### LEMONGRASS SYRUP
6 LEMONGRASS STALKS, TOPS TRIMMED

150G/5OZ (½ CUP) COCONUT NECTAR
OR AGAVE NECTAR (G)

1 TABLESPOON LIME JUICE

### KIWI, PAPAYA AND LONGAN SALAD
½ RIPE RED PAPAYA

8 KIWI FRUIT, PEELED AND CUT INTO 4 ROUNDS

360G/12OZ (3 CUPS) LONGANS, PEELED,
SEEDED AND CUT IN HALF

### TO SERVE
5G/¼OZ (¼ CUP) MINT LEAVES

2 LEMONGRASS STALKS, TOPS AND OUTER
LAYERS REMOVED, FINELY SLICED

To make the lemongrass syrup, put the lemongrass stalks through a juice extractor and catch the juice in a jug (you should have 50ml/scant ¼ cup juice). Add the coconut nectar and lime juice and mix well. Cover and refrigerate until ready to use.

To make the kiwi, papaya and longan salad, cut the papaya into quarters lengthwise, peel, then cut into 1½cm/ ½ inch wedges. Arrange the papaya, kiwi and longans on a serving platter.

To serve, pour the chilled lemongrass syrup over the fruit and decorate with mint and sliced lemongrass.

**Note:** If longans are unavailable, use blueberries instead.

*Thailand's mangoes and pineapples are so exceptional, we try to tinker with them as little as possible. This salad is a celebration of these raw ingredients – with just a very slight twist from the addition of the passionfruit syrup.*

Vitamin-Rich | Mineral-Rich | Antioxidant-Rich | Heart Healthy | Digestive Support | Raw | Gluten-Free | Vegan

# MANGO, PINEAPPLE AND BLUEBERRY SALAD WITH PASSIONFRUIT SYRUP

## SERVES 4

### PASSIONFRUIT SYRUP
100G/3½OZ (⅓ CUP) COCONUT NECTAR OR AGAVE NECTAR (G)
80ML (⅓ CUP) PASSIONFRUIT JUICE
80ML (⅓ CUP) PASSIONFRUIT PULP
2 TABLESPOONS LIME JUICE

### FRUIT SALAD
2 RIPE MANGOES
1 SMALL PINEAPPLE
75G/3OZ (½ CUP) BLUEBERRIES
45G/1⅔OZ (⅓ CUP) YOUNG COCONUT MEAT, CUT INTO TRIANGLES

### TO SERVE
5G/¼OZ (¼ CUP) THAI BASIL LEAVES AND BUDS

For the passionfruit syrup, combine the coconut nectar and passionfruit juice in a small saucepan, bring to the boil and reduce by half. Remove from the heat and stir in the passionfruit pulp and lime juice. Cover and refrigerate until ready to serve.

To make the fruit salad, remove the skin from the mangoes then cut the cheeks into wedges. Peel and core the pineapple and cut into wedges. Place the mango, pineapple, blueberries and coconut on a serving platter.

To serve, pour 125ml (½ cup) of the chilled passionfruit syrup over the fruit and scatter with the Thai basil leaves and buds.

# TROPICAL FRUIT, NUT AND SEED GRANOLA CRUNCH WITH VANILLA BEAN YOGHURT

MAKES 700G/1LB 9OZ (6 CUPS) GRANOLA

SERVES 4

This gluten-free, mineral- and nutrient-rich granola screams summer with its bright colours. It is also versatile, and can be eaten as a snack or cereal with milk. If necessary, a soy-based or fermented coconut yoghurt can be substituted for the Greek-style yoghurt. The granola can be stored in an airtight container for up to a fortnight.

Vitamin-Rich | Mineral-Rich | Antioxidant-Rich | High-Protein | Immune-Boosting | Digestive Support | Rejuvenating | Energising | Gluten-Free

## NUT AND SEED GRANOLA CRUNCH

300G/10½OZ (1½ CUPS) PUMPKIN SEEDS

110G/4OZ (¾ CUP) SUNFLOWER SEEDS

240G/8½OZ (1½ CUPS) BLANCHED
WHOLE ALMONDS

140G/5OZ (1 CUP) RAW MACADAMIA NUTS

150G/5OZ (1 CUP) RAW CASHEWS

90G/3OZ (½ CUP) DRIED PAPAYA,
CUT INTO 8MM/⅓ INCH STRIPS

35G/1½OZ (¼ CUP) DRIED APRICOTS,
CUT INTO 8MM/⅓ INCH STRIPS

35G/1½OZ (¼ CUP) DRIED PINEAPPLE, CHOPPED

2 TABLESPOONS FRESHLY SQUEEZED
ORANGE JUICE

2 TABLESPOONS FRESHLY SQUEEZED LEMON JUICE

85G/3OZ (¼ CUP) RAW HONEY

¼ TEASPOON VANILLA EXTRACT

½ TEASPOON ORANGE BLOSSOM WATER

¼ RIPE MANGO, CHOPPED

1 BANANA, PEELED AND SLICED

1 PEAR, GRATED WITH SKIN ON

75G/3OZ (SCANT 1 CUP)
FRESHLY GRATED COCONUT

2 ORANGES, ZEST ONLY, FINELY GRATED

1 TEASPOON GROUND GINGER

1 PINCH SEA SALT

## VANILLA BEAN YOGHURT

1 VANILLA BEAN (POD)

480ML (2 CUPS) LOW-FAT GREEK-STYLE YOGHURT

## MANGO PURÉE

½ RIPE MANGO, DICED

2 TEASPOONS COCONUT NECTAR
OR AGAVE NECTAR (G)

## TO SERVE

75G/2¾OZ (½ CUP) BLUEBERRIES

¼ MANGO, PEELED AND CUT INTO 8 THIN SLICES

1 BANANA, PEELED, SLICED IN HALF
LENGTHWISE AND CUT INTO WEDGES

2 TABLESPOONS BABY MINT LEAVES
(OR REGULAR MINT)

To make the granola, place the pumpkin seeds, sunflower seeds, almonds, macadamias and cashews in a large bowl, cover with water and soak for 2 hours. Drain and rinse the seeds and nuts, then place in a food processor. Using the pulse button, mix until coarsely chopped then transfer to a large bowl.

Place the dried papaya, apricots and pineapple in a bowl, cover with warm water and soak for 1 hour. Drain and add to the nut mixture. With a blender, combine the orange and lemon juices, honey, vanilla extract, orange blossom water, mango and banana until it is a purée. Add this to the nut mixture and mix well. Add the pear, coconut, orange zest, ground ginger and sea salt and mix in to combine.

Place the mixture on Teflex or non-stick sheets on dehydrator trays. Using your fingers, pinch the mixture into small mounds and dry at 48°C/118°F for 12 hours. Turn the granola over and dry for another 12 hours at the same temperature. Remove from the dehydrator, cool to room temperature and store in an airtight container. Alternatively, dry in an oven heated on its lowest setting.

For the vanilla bean yoghurt, split the vanilla bean in half lengthwise and scrape out the seeds. Stir the vanilla seeds into the yoghurt, then cover and refrigerate for at least 30 minutes to allow the flavours to infuse.

To make the mango purée, place the mango with the nectar in a blender and mix until puréed. Set aside.

To serve, you need 70g/3oz (½ cup) of granola per portion. Place 2 tablespoons of mango purée in the bottom of 4 serving glasses and top with 60ml (¼ cup) of vanilla yoghurt. Scatter with half of the nut and seed granola crunch and the blueberries. Then top with the remaining yoghurt, and layer with the mango purée and granola crunch. Finish with sliced mango, banana wedges and mint leaves.

*This muesli, developed ten years ago at COMO Parrot Cay, is still a favourite. The apple and pear go particularly well together, balancing sweet and sharp. You can, however, use any combination you like. The important thing is not to scrimp on the fruit, which gives this dish life.*

Vitamin-Rich | Mineral-Rich | Antioxidant-Rich | High-Protein | Digestive Support | Smart Carbohydrate | Cleansing | Raw | Gluten-Free | Vegan

# NUT, SEED AND DRIED FRUIT MUESLI WITH FRESH APPLE AND PEAR

### SERVES 4

**MUESLI**

450G/1LB (3 CUPS) RAW CASHEWS, ROUGHLY CHOPPED

320G/11OZ (2 CUPS) RAW ALMONDS WITH SKIN, ROUGHLY CHOPPED

75G/3OZ (½ CUP) SUNFLOWER SEEDS, ROUGHLY CHOPPED

100G/3½OZ (½ CUP) PUMPKIN SEEDS, ROUGHLY CHOPPED

65G/2½OZ (¾ CUP) FRESHLY GRATED COCONUT

70G/2½OZ (½ CUP) DRIED CRANBERRIES

100G/3½OZ (⅔ CUP) CHOPPED DRIED APRICOTS

75G/3OZ (½ CUP) RAISINS

1 TEASPOON GROUND NUTMEG

2 TEASPOONS GROUND CINNAMON

1 PINCH SEA SALT, OR TO TASTE

**TO SERVE**

1 GREEN APPLE

1 GREEN PEAR

1 TABLESPOON FLAXSEED MEAL

1½ TABLESPOONS BABY MINT LEAVES (OR REGULAR MINT)

800ML (3⅓ CUPS) CHILLED ALMOND NUT MILK (SEE BASICS PAGE 267)

To make the muesli, combine all the nuts, seeds and coconut in a large bowl and mix well to combine. Spread the ingredients over dehydrator trays and dry at 48°C/118°F for about 12 hours, or until dry and crunchy. Alternatively, dry in an oven heated on its lowest setting. Transfer to a large bowl and cool slightly. Add the dried fruit, nutmeg, cinnamon and sea salt and toss well to combine. Store in an airtight container (it will keep for up to 2 weeks).

To serve, spoon 85g/3oz (⅔ cup) of muesli into each bowl. Grate the apple and pear into a bowl and mix together, then spoon over the muesli. Sprinkle with the flaxseed meal and scatter with baby mint leaves. Serve with the chilled almond nut milk on the side.

**Note:** This recipe makes about 12 portions of muesli, which can be stored in an airtight container for up to 2 weeks.

This porridge is a great alternative to traditional versions. Quinoa is a delicious seed-like grain, full of phytonutrients and antioxidants that can help lower your blood sugar levels. It is also a great source of complete protein. The pears cook out nicely in the porridge and add another texture to the dish - use the firmer varieties, not Nashi or Asian pears - while the dried fruits bring sweetness.

Vitamin-Rich | Mineral-Rich | Antioxidant-Rich | High-Protein | Digestive Support
Smart Carbohydrate | Cleansing | Rejuvenating | Calming | Gluten-Free | Vegan

# QUINOA, PEAR AND DRIED CRANBERRY PORRIDGE WITH ALMOND NUT MILK

### SERVES 4

### QUINOA AND PEAR PORRIDGE

750ML (3 CUPS) ALMOND NUT MILK
(SEE BASICS PAGE 267) (OR SOY OR RICE MILK)

2 PINCHES GROUND CINNAMON

1 PINCH SALT

320G/11½OZ (2 CUPS) COOKED QUINOA
(SEE BASICS PAGE 286)

2 PEARS, PEELED, CORED AND DICED

2 TABLESPOONS BLACK RAISINS

2 TABLESPOONS DRIED CRANBERRIES

### TO SERVE

½ BEURRÉ BOSC OR KAISER PEAR, GRATED

2 TABLESPOONS TOASTED WHOLE ALMONDS

2 PINCHES GROUND CINNAMON

250ML (1 CUP) CHILLED ALMOND NUT MILK
(SEE BASICS PAGE 267)

1 PINCH SEA SALT, OR TO TASTE

To make the quinoa and pear porridge, combine the almond nut milk, cinnamon, salt and 250ml (1 cup) water in a small saucepan. Heat until warmed through then add the cooked quinoa and diced pear. Bring to the boil then reduce the heat and simmer, stirring occasionally for about 15 minutes, or until the liquid has reduced by half. Add the raisins and cranberries and cook for a further 5 minutes, or until the porridge is warm and the desired consistency.

To serve, spoon the porridge into serving bowls, top with the grated pear and sprinkle with almonds and ground cinnamon. Serve the chilled almond nut milk on the side.

This is a porridge truly packed with goodness. The coconut water is lauded for its low-calorie, high-electrolyte properties, while the coconut meat can help improve the body's immune system and anti-inflammatory responses. Achieving an oatmeal-like consistency is all about how you blend the young coconut meat and water with the almonds. It needs to be done on the lowest speed; if blended too quickly it will end up as a purée.

Vitamin-Rich | Mineral-Rich | Antioxidant-Rich | High-Protein | Digestive Support | Rejuvenating | Raw | Gluten-Free | Vegan

# YOUNG COCONUT, ALMOND AND CINNAMON-SCENTED PORRIDGE

**SERVES 4**

### PORRIDGE
320G/11OZ (3 CUPS) WHOLE FLAKED ALMONDS
125ML (½ CUP) YOUNG COCONUT WATER
290G/10OZ (2 CUPS) YOUNG COCONUT MEAT
1 TABLESPOON COCONUT NECTAR
OR AGAVE NECTAR (G)
½ VANILLA BEAN (POD), SPLIT LENGTHWISE
AND SEEDS SCRAPED OUT
1 PINCH SEA SALT

### SPICED COCONUT WATER
125ML (½ CUP) YOUNG COCONUT WATER
1 PINCH GROUND CINNAMON
1 TABLESPOON COCONUT NECTAR
OR AGAVE NECTAR (G)

### TO SERVE
35G/1½OZ (¼ CUP) YOUNG COCONUT MEAT,
CUT JULIENNE
70G/2½OZ (¼ CUP) RED PAPAYA, DICED
1 BANANA, PEELED AND SLICED 3MM/⅛ INCH THICK
8 STRAWBERRIES, CUT INTO QUARTERS
2 PINCHES GROUND CINNAMON

To make the porridge, place the almonds in a bowl, cover with water and soak for 12 hours. Drain and rinse the almonds, then place them in a blender with the coconut water. Using the pulse button, blend until the nuts are coarsely chopped. Add the coconut meat, coconut nectar, vanilla seeds and sea salt and pulse until you have a coarse, porridge-like consistency.

To make the spiced coconut water, combine the coconut water with ground cinnamon and nectar, mixing well. Cover and refrigerate until ready to serve.

To serve, combine the coconut meat with the papaya, banana and strawberries. Drizzle with the coconut water and toss gently to combine. Spoon the almond porridge into chilled bowls and top with the dressed fruit. Finish with a sprinkling of ground cinnamon.

*This is a favourite breakfast dish, first developed at COMO Parrot Cay. The 'toast' contains a good dose of flaxseed, which is packed with omega-3 and 6. On its own, the 'toast' keeps in an airtight container for a week.*

Vitamin-Rich | Mineral-Rich | Antioxidant-Rich | High-Protein | Heart Healthy | Digestive Support
Smart Carbohydrate | Cleansing | Rejuvenating | Energising | Raw | Gluten-Free | Vegan

# 'REAL TOAST'
# WITH AVOCADO CRUSH,
# HEIRLOOM TOMATOES
# AND CUCUMBER

### SERVES 4

**'REAL TOAST'**

400G/14OZ (2½ CUPS) BLANCHED WHOLE ALMONDS

60G/2½OZ (⅓ CUP) FLAXSEEDS

65G/2½OZ (½ CUP) SUNFLOWER SEEDS

½ LARGE RED BELL PEPPER (CAPSICUM)

½ LARGE YELLOW BELL PEPPER (CAPSICUM)

1 TELEGRAPH CUCUMBER

2 CARROTS, PEELED

1 RED APPLE

4 CLOVES GARLIC, FINELY CHOPPED

SEA SALT AND GROUND WHITE PEPPER, TO TASTE

**TO SERVE**

250ML (1 CUP) AVOCADO CRUSH (SEE BASICS PAGE 270)

2 HEIRLOOM TOMATOES, SLICED OR VINE-RIPENED TOMATOES

½ TELEGRAPH CUCUMBER, CUT INTO RIBBONS ON A TURNING SLICER OR THINLY SLICED ON A MANDOLIN

14G/½OZ (½ CUP) MIXED HERBS SUCH AS FLAT-LEAF PARSLEY, BABY BASIL AND DILL

2 TABLESPOONS LEMON DRESSING (SEE BASICS PAGE 278)

For the 'real toast', place the almonds, flaxseeds and sunflower seeds in separate bowls, cover with water and soak for 2 hours. Put the peppers, cucumber, carrot and apple through a juice extractor for the vegetable pulp (you will need 300g/10½oz, or 2 cups, of pulp). Catch the juice in a jug, which can be drunk separately as a vegetable juice. Transfer the pulp to a food processor and add the garlic, seasoning with sea salt and a grind of white pepper. Drain and rinse the almonds and seeds and add to the food processor bowl. Process, scraping down the sides of bowl occasionally until a coarse paste forms. Check the seasoning and adjust as necessary.

Transfer the mix to a bowl. Take 90ml (⅓ cup) of the mixture and shape into a 6x12cm/2x5 inch rectangle that is 8mm/⅓ inch thick on a Teflex or non-stick sheet on a dehydrator tray. Repeat with the remaining mixture. Place in the dehydrator and dry at 48°C/118°F for 8 hours then turn the pieces over and dry for a further 8 hours. Cool and store in an airtight container. Alternatively, dry in an oven heated on its lowest setting.

To serve, spread a heaped spoonful of avocado crush on a slice of the 'real toast' and top with 3 to 4 slices of tomato and 1 to 2 cucumber ribbons, followed by the herbs tossed with the lemon dressing. Serve immediately.

# SPICED BUCKWHEAT PANCAKES WITH CANDIED BUTTERNUT PUMPKIN AND ORANGE SYRUP

**SERVES 4**

*This recipe was devised for COMO Uma in Paro, Bhutan. In days past, buckwheat was considered the poor man's food, grown only in non-rice growing areas, especially at high altitudes. In this recipe, however, the buckwheat flour works beautifully with the spice, orange and pumpkin purée. The folding of the egg whites through the mixture at the end makes the pancakes light. This is well worth the effort for a special breakfast.*

Vitamin-Rich | Mineral-Rich | Antioxidant-Rich | High-Protein | Immune-Boosting | Digestive Support | Calming | Energising | Gluten-Free

## CANDIED BUTTERNUT PUMPKIN

250ML (1CUP) FRESHLY SQUEEZED ORANGE JUICE, STRAINED

1 ORANGE, ZEST ONLY

340G/12OZ (1 CUP) RAW HONEY

600G/1LB 5OZ PEELED BUTTERNUT PUMPKIN, CUT INTO 16 1CM/½ INCH THICK WEDGES

## BUTTERNUT PUMPKIN CREAM

220G/8OZ (1 CUP) ROAST BUTTERNUT PUMPKIN PURÉE (SEE BASICS PAGE 272)

60ML (¼ CUP) LOW-FAT GREEK-STYLE YOGHURT

2½ TABLESPOONS RAW HONEY

## BUCKWHEAT PANCAKES

140G/5OZ (1 CUP) BUCKWHEAT FLOUR

60G/2½OZ (¼ CUP) POWDERED COCONUT PALM SUGAR (OR ORGANIC BROWN SUGAR) (G)

1½ TEASPOONS BAKING POWDER

½ TEASPOON BAKING SODA (BICARBONATE OF SODA)

1 TEASPOON GROUND CINNAMON

½ TEASPOON FRESHLY GRATED NUTMEG

1 ORANGE, ZEST ONLY, FINELY GRATED

1 PINCH SEA SALT, OR TO TASTE

230ML (JUST UNDER 1 CUP) SOY MILK

3 EGGS, SEPARATED

100G/3½OZ (½ CUP) ROAST BUTTERNUT PUMPKIN PURÉE (SEE BASICS PAGE 272)

1 TEASPOON VANILLA EXTRACT

SUNFLOWER OIL, FOR COOKING

## TO SERVE

1 ORANGE, PEELED AND THINLY SLICED (PITH REMOVED)

1 TABLESPOON PUMPKIN SEEDS

4 ORANGE OR GOLDEN NASTURTIUM FLOWERS, IF AVAILABLE

To make the candied butternut pumpkin, place the orange juice, orange zest, honey and 250ml (1 cup) water in a deep saucepan. Bring to the boil and stir to dissolve the honey, then add the butternut pumpkin pieces. Return to the boil, then reduce the heat and simmer for 25 to 30 minutes, or until the butternut pumpkin is tender and the sauce is slightly thickened. Transfer the butternut pumpkin to a plate then remove the sauce from the heat and allow to cool.

To make the butternut pumpkin cream, combine the roasted butternut pumpkin purée, yoghurt and honey in a bowl and mix well. Cover and refrigerate until ready to use.

To make the buckwheat pancakes, mix the dry ingredients together in a bowl. In a separate bowl, mix the soy milk, egg yolks, butternut pumpkin purée, vanilla and orange zest and whisk until smooth.

Slowly pour the wet ingredients into the dry ingredients, whisking constantly until smooth. In a clean bowl, whisk the egg whites until soft peaks form. Using a large rubber spatula, fold one-third of egg whites gently into the batter to loosen, then fold in the remaining egg whites until incorporated. Cover and refrigerate for 20 minutes.

Heat 2 blini pans, or place 2 ring moulds, each 12cm/5 inches across, in a large frying pan and brush with a little sunflower oil. Add 100ml (scant ½ cup) of the pancake mix to each pan (or ring) and cook over a medium heat until bubbles appear on the surface. Turn over and cook until golden brown on the other side. Transfer to a plate and keep warm. Repeat with the remaining pancake batter.

To serve, warm the candied butternut pumpkin over a low heat. For each serving, place a hot pancake on a warmed plate, top each with a slice of orange and 2 pieces of candied butternut pumpkin, and repeat this with another pancake. Finish with a quenelle of butternut pumpkin cream and drizzle candied butternut pumpkin syrup over the stack. Scatter with pumpkin seeds and flowers.

*The lemon zest in the pancake batter is a winner; it really lifts the dish and I love the smooth, rich texture of the maple cream resulting from the blended young coconut and cashews.*

Vitamin-Rich | Mineral-Rich | Antioxidant-Rich | High-Protein | Digestive Support | Rejuvenating | Energising

# LEMON-SCENTED PANCAKES WITH BANANA, BERRIES AND CASHEW MAPLE CREAM

### SERVES 6

**PASSIONFRUIT SYRUP**

125ML (½ CUP) MAPLE SYRUP
125ML (½ CUP) PASSIONFRUIT JUICE
125ML (½ CUP) PASSIONFRUIT PULP
60ML (¼ CUP) LIME JUICE

**MAPLE CREAM**

140G/5OZ (1 CUP) RAW CASHEWS
125G/4½OZ (½ CUP) SLICED YOUNG COCONUT MEAT
160G/5½OZ (¼ CUP) MAPLE SYRUP
2 TABLESPOONS CACAO BUTTER (G)
2 TEASPOONS VANILLA EXTRACT
¼ TEASPOON GROUND CINNAMON

**WHOLEMEAL PANCAKES**

125G/4½OZ (¾ CUP) WHOLEMEAL FLOUR
100G/3½OZ (⅔ CUP) UNBLEACHED FLOUR
20G/¾OZ (SCANT ¼ CUP) WHEATGERM
60G/2½OZ (¼ CUP) POWDERED COCONUT PALM SUGAR (OR ORGANIC BROWN SUGAR) (G)
1½ TEASPOONS BAKING POWDER
½ TEASPOON BAKING SODA (BICARBONATE OF SODA)
1 LEMON, ZEST ONLY, FINELY GRATED
1 PINCH SEA SALT, OR TO TASTE
2 EGGS, SEPARATED
75ML (¾ CUP) SUNFLOWER OIL, PLUS EXTRA FOR COOKING
375ML (1½ CUPS) ALMOND NUT MILK (SEE BASICS PAGE 267)

**TO SERVE**

370G/12½OZ (1½ CUPS) BLUEBERRIES
3 WHOLE BANANAS, PEELED, CUT IN HALF LENGTHWISE AND THEN CROSSWISE
9 STRAWBERRIES, CUT IN HALF
12 VIOLA HERB OR OTHER EDIBLE FLOWERS (OPTIONAL)

For the passionfruit syrup, place the maple syrup and passionfruit juice in a small saucepan. Bring to the boil and cook until reduced by half. Remove from the heat and stir in the passionfruit pulp and lime juice. Cool slightly, cover and refrigerate until ready to use.

To make the maple cream, place the cashews in a bowl, cover with water and leave to stand for 2 hours. Drain and rinse, then place in a blender with the remaining ingredients. Blend until well combined and the consistency is smooth. Cover and refrigerate until ready to use.

To make the wholemeal pancakes, mix the dry ingredients together in a bowl. In a separate bowl, whisk the egg yolks, oil and milk together. Slowly pour the wet ingredients into the dry ingredients, whisking until smooth.

In a clean bowl, whisk the egg whites until soft peaks form. Using a large rubber spatula, fold one-third of the egg whites into the batter to loosen the mixture, then gently fold in the remaining egg whites until incorporated. Cover and leave to stand in the fridge for 20 minutes.

Heat 2 blini pans, or place 2 ring moulds, each 12cm/5 inches across, in a large frying pan and brush with a little sunflower oil. Add 100ml (scant ½ cup) of the pancake mix to each pan (or ring) and cook over a medium heat until bubbles appear on the surface. Turn over and cook until golden brown on the other side. Transfer to a plate and keep warm. Repeat with the remaining pancake batter.

To serve, add the blueberries to the passionfruit syrup in a small saucepan and heat gently until warmed through. Place one wholemeal pancake in the centre of each plate and top with a piece of banana and half the berries. Spoon the passionfruit syrup over each pancake, scatter with the herb flowers, if liked, then finish with a quenelle of maple cream.

*This waffle recipe was devised in 2003 for COMO Metropolitan in Bangkok. The waffles are very filling, as the mix also contains bananas. They're even more delicious when there's plenty of banana cream and maple sauce to mop up. The fresh cranberry purée balances the sweetness.*

Mineral-Rich | Antioxidant-Rich | High-Protein | Immune-Boosting | Energising

# BANANA WHOLEMEAL WAFFLES WITH DRIED APRICOT AND CRANBERRY SAUCE

**SERVES 4**

### BANANA SAUCE
1½ RIPE BANANAS, PEELED AND CHOPPED
75G/3OZ (⅓ CUP) SILKEN TOFU, CHOPPED
1½ TABLESPOONS SOY MILK
1½ TABLESPOONS RAW HONEY
2 TEASPOONS LEMON JUICE

### DRIED APRICOT AND CRANBERRY SAUCE
60G/2½OZ (½ CUP) FROZEN CRANBERRIES, THAWED
65G/2½OZ (½ CUP) DRIED CRANBERRIES
160G/5½OZ (½ CUP) MAPLE SYRUP
4CM/1½ INCH STRIP OF ORANGE PEEL, PITH REMOVED AND CUT JULIENNE
8 DRIED APRICOTS, DICED

### BANANA WHOLEMEAL WAFFLES
2 RIPE BANANAS, ROUGHLY CHOPPED
1½ TEASPOONS SUNFLOWER OIL
180ML (¾ CUP) SOY MILK
1 TEASPOON VANILLA EXTRACT
160G/5½OZ (1 CUP) WHOLEMEAL FLOUR
75G/3OZ (½ CUP) ALL-PURPOSE (PLAIN) FLOUR
1 TABLESPOON BAKING POWDER
1 PINCH SEA SALT, OR TO TASTE
4 EGG WHITES

### TO SERVE
4 SMALL RIPE BANANAS, PEELED AND CUT IN HALF LENGTHWISE
12 PIECES OF WHOLE WALNUTS, BROKEN IN HALF
12 SMALL SPRIGS OF BABY MINT LEAVES (OR REGULAR MINT)

To make the banana sauce, place the bananas, tofu, soy milk and honey in a blender, mixing until smooth. Add the lemon juice to taste and blend further to combine.

For the dried apricot and cranberry sauce, blend the thawed cranberries with 180ml (¾ cup) water until puréed, then pass through a sieve into a saucepan. Add the remaining ingredients, bring to the boil then reduce the heat and simmer for 8 to 10 minutes, or until slightly thickened. The sauce will thicken further on standing (the dried fruit absorbs the liquid).

To make the banana waffles, combine the bananas, oil, soy milk and vanilla in a bowl and whisk to a thick paste. Sift the dry ingredients into a separate bowl, add the sea salt and mix until they are combined. Add to the banana mixture in 3 batches, stirring well. In a clean bowl, whisk the egg whites until soft peaks form. Using a large rubber spatula, fold one-third of the egg whites into the batter to gently loosen the mixture, then fold in the remaining egg whites until incorporated. Cover and refrigerate for 20 minutes.

Heat a waffle maker and add 250ml (1 cup) of batter to the machine. Close the lid and cook for about 5 minutes, or until golden. Keep the machine warm and repeat with the remaining batter.

To serve, spoon the banana sauce into the centre of each plate, spreading it with the back of a spoon to make a 15cm/6 inch circle. Place half a waffle just off centre on the sauce. Top each waffle with half a banana and a spoonful of cranberry sauce, then repeat this layering with the other half. Scatter with walnuts and mint leaves, and serve immediately.

*This dish was created for COMO Shambhala Estate in Bali, as a healthy alternative to the traditional potato-based rösti. The batter is used sparingly and only to bind the zucchini and onion mix.*

Vitamin-Rich | Mineral-Rich | Antioxidant-Rich | High-Protein | Rejuvenating | Calming

# ZUCCHINI RÖSTI WITH SMOKED SALMON, DILL AND LEMON-SCENTED COTTAGE CHEESE

### SERVES 4

**LEMON-SCENTED COTTAGE CHEESE**
200G/7OZ (1 CUP) COTTAGE CHEESE
½ TEASPOON LEMON ZEST, FINELY GRATED
2 TEASPOONS LEMON JUICE

**ZUCCHINI RÖSTI**
2 LARGE ZUCCHINI (COURGETTES)
2 TABLESPOONS CHOPPED DILL
1 SMALL BROWN ONION,
CUT IN HALF AND THINLY SLICED
30G/1OZ/4 TABLESPOONS WHOLEMEAL FLOUR
¼ TEASPOON BAKING POWDER
2 EGGS, LIGHTLY BEATEN
SEA SALT AND FRESHLY GROUND
WHITE PEPPER, TO TASTE
2 TABLESPOONS SUNFLOWER OIL

**TO SERVE**
1 LARGE ZUCCHINI (COURGETTE), SLICED INTO
3MM/⅛ INCH RIBBONS ON A MANDOLIN
1 TABLESPOON LEMON DRESSING
(SEE BASICS PAGE 278)
180G/6OZ (8 SLICES) SMOKED SALMON
1 TABLESPOON DILL TIPS
¼ LEMON, THINLY SLICED AND
CUT INTO WEDGES

For the lemon-scented cottage cheese, combine the cottage cheese with the lemon zest and juice. Cover and refrigerate until ready to serve.

To make the zucchini rösti, cut the zucchini into 2cm/¾ inch lengths then, using a mandolin, cut into thick julienne strips. Combine the zucchini with the dill and onion in a bowl. In a separate bowl, mix the flour and baking powder. Add the lightly beaten eggs and whisk until combined, then season with sea salt and a grind of white pepper. Heat 2 blini pans and add just enough of the batter to the zucchini mixture to bind it together. Place 180ml (¾ cup) of mixture to each pan and cook over a medium heat for about 4 minutes, or until golden brown. Turn the rösti over and cook for a further 4 minutes, or until golden. Place on a plate lined with paper towel and keep warm. Repeat with the remaining rösti mixture and sunflower oil. If you don't have blini pans, use 2 ring moulds, each 10cm/4 inches across, in a large frying pan, the base brushed with a little sunflower oil.

To serve, place each rösti on a warmed serving plate. Dress the zucchini ribbons with the lemon dressing, then place on top of each rösti. Lay the smoked salmon over the zucchini and scatter with dill tips and lemon slices. Finish with a spoonful of the lemon-scented cottage cheese and a good grind of white pepper.

**Note:** Do not let the rösti mixture stand for more than 10 minutes after combining the ingredients before cooking; the water will leach out of the zucchini, oversoftening the zucchini and thinning down the mix.

*This dish is an easy way to start the day, and is full of goodness. Calorie for calorie, green vegetables (especially the leafy varieties) contain the most concentrated source of nutrition of any food. The 'Green Goddess' sauce makes this dish really special.*

Vitamin-Rich | Antioxidant-Rich | High-Protein | Calming | Gluten-Free

# SEASONAL GREENS WITH POACHED EGG AND 'GREEN GODDESS' SAUCE

### SERVES 4

**'GREEN GODDESS' SAUCE**

20G/¾OZ (½ CUP) TARRAGON LEAVES

15G/½OZ (½ CUP) CHIVES, CUT INTO 2CM/¾ INCH LENGTHS

20G/¾OZ (½ CUP) CHERVIL LEAVES

7.5G/¼OZ (½ CUP) FLAT-LEAF PARSLEY LEAVES

10G/⅓OZ (½ CUP) BASIL LEAVES

1 CLOVE GARLIC, SLICED

1 LEMON, PEELED

1 TABLESPOON FRESHLY SQUEEZED LEMON JUICE

1 AVOCADO, PEELED, STONED AND ROUGHLY CHOPPED

SEA SALT AND GROUND WHITE PEPPER, TO TASTE

125ML (½ CUP) SOY MILK

1 TABLESPOON EXTRA-VIRGIN OLIVE OIL

**SEASONAL GREENS AND POACHED EGGS**

1 TEASPOON WHITE VINEGAR

SALT AND GROUND WHITE PEPPER, TO TASTE

4 EGGS

8 GREEN ASPARAGUS SPEARS, WOODY BASE TRIMMED AND BASE OF STALKS PEELED

20 BABY GREEN BEANS, TAILED

12 STEMS BROCCOLINI, WOODY BASE TRIMMED AND STEMS PEELED

12 KALE OR CHARD LEAVES, CLEANED AND STEMS REMOVED

2 TABLESPOONS LEMON DRESSING (SEE BASICS PAGE 278)

To make the 'Green Goddess' sauce, roughly chop the herbs. Place all of the ingredients in the blender, except the soy milk and olive oil. Blend to a smooth consistency. With the motor running, gradually add the soy milk and oil to produce a thick sauce – thick enough to achieve a napping consistency that evenly coats the back of a spoon. Check the seasoning and adjust as necessary.

For the seasonal greens and poached eggs, bring a large saucepan of water to the boil. Fill another saucepan of water with 12cm/4¾ inches of water, add the vinegar and a pinch of salt and bring to the boil. When the water is boiling in both pans, crack the eggs into 4 cups, reduce the heat on the vinegared water to almost boiling and stir in a clockwise motion. Carefully add the eggs one at a time and set the timer for 4 minutes. When cooked, carefully remove the eggs from the water with a slotted spoon and drain on a paper towel.

While the eggs are poaching, blanch the asparagus, beans and broccolini in boiling water for 45 seconds, or until just beginning to soften. Remove with a slotted spoon, drain on a paper towel then place in a bowl. Add the kale to the boiling water and cook for 2 to 3 minutes, then drain and carefully squeeze some of the water out. Add the kale to the bowl of other vegetables, then add the lemon dressing, season with sea salt and a grind of white pepper and toss gently to combine.

To serve, place the kale in the centre of the serving plates and arrange the seasonal greens over the top. Place the poached eggs on the greens and spoon over 1 tablespoon of 'Green Goddess' sauce. Serve immediately.

*This is a great vegan breakfast dish, our ode to Tex-Mex. The spicy pepper and roast tomato mix is critical for flavour. If you require more fibre, add some cooked kidney beans into the scrambled tofu.*

Vitamin-Rich | Mineral-Rich | Antioxidant-Rich | High-Protein | Heart Healthy | Digestive Support | Rejuvenating | Calming | Energising | Gluten-Free | Vegan

# SCRAMBLED TOFU
# WITH
# BRAISED SPICED PEPPERS,
# SWEETCORN
# AND AVOCADO

**SERVES 4**

### SPICED PEPPERS

4 LARGE VINE-RIPENED TOMATOES
2 SMALL RED BELL PEPPERS (CAPSICUM)
2 SMALL GREEN BELL PEPPERS (CAPSICUM)
1 TABLESPOON EXTRA-VIRGIN OLIVE OIL
1 SMALL ONION, THINLY SLICED
SEA SALT, TO TASTE
1 TABLESPOON GROUND CUMIN
½ TEASPOON PAPRIKA
2 PINCHES GROUND TURMERIC
2 PINCHES GROUND CAYENNE PEPPER

### SWEETCORN, AVOCADO AND GEM LETTUCE SALAD

SUGAR, TO TASTE
1 LARGE CORN COB
1 AVOCADO, PEELED, STONED AND CUT INTO WEDGES
8 CHERRY TOMATOES, SLICED INTO 5MM/¼ INCH ROUNDS
1 BABY GEM LETTUCE, LEAVES SEPARATED, WASHED, SPUN AND CUT INTO POINTS
2 TABLESPOONS LEMON DRESSING (SEE BASICS PAGE 278)

### SCRAMBLED TOFU

260G/9OZ FIRM TOFU, ROUGHLY CHOPPED TO RESEMBLE SCRAMBLED EGGS
8 SPRING ONIONS (SCALLIONS), SLICED INTO ROUNDS

### TO SERVE

4G/⅛OZ (¼ CUP) CORIANDER (CILANTRO) LEAVES
2 TABLESPOONS SPICY SEED MIX (SEE BASICS PAGE 292)

To make the spiced peppers, preheat the oven to 160°C/320°F. Place the tomatoes in the oven for 30–40 minutes until they are soft. Push the tomatoes through a sieve into a bowl, using a ladle to extract all the juice. Cut the tops and bottoms from the peppers, and reserve the trimmings. Remove the seeds and discard, then cut the peppers into julienne strips. Push the pepper trimmings through a juice extractor, catching the liquid in a jug.

In a non-stick pan, heat the oil and add the onion and peppers. Season with salt and cook, stirring occasionally, over a low to medium heat for about 15 minutes, or until the ingredients are soft and sweet. Add all the spices and cook, stirring frequently for 2 more minutes, or until fragrant. Add the pepper and roasted tomato juice, increase the heat, bring to the boil then reduce the heat to a simmer and cook for about 10 to 15 minutes, or until the liquid has reduced to about three-quarters but is not dry. Remove from the heat.

For the sweetcorn, avocado and lettuce salad, bring a saucepan of water to the boil, season with salt and sugar and cook the corn cob in simmering water for 10 minutes before draining. Using a sharp knife, cut the kernels from the cob in long shards and leave to cool. Just before serving, combine the cooled corn shards, avocado, cherry tomatoes and lettuce in a bowl, drizzle with the lemon dressing and toss gently to combine.

To make the scrambled tofu, heat a large non-stick frying pan over a high heat. Add the chopped tofu and cook until the tofu is almost dry. Add the spiced pepper mix and cook for a further 3 minutes. Add the spring onions and remove from the heat.

To serve, spoon the tofu onto serving plates, top with the dressed salad, scatter with coriander leaves and sprinkle with the spicy seed mix.

**Note:** To reduce food waste, we use the pepper trimmings in the sauce. If you don't have a juicer, you can omit this step. It will still be delicious; just bump up the amount of roast tomatoes.

"Every culture begins the day with its own flavours. For our two Maldivian resorts, COMO Cocoa Island and COMO Maalifushi, we drew upon the warming curries that kickstart the day for fishermen." CHRISTINA ONG

# MALDIVIAN CURRY WITH SOFT-COOKED EGG, VEGETABLES AND ROSHI

**SERVES 4**

### ROSHI

365G/13OZ (JUST UNDER 2½ CUPS) PLAIN (ALL-PURPOSE) FLOUR

1 TEASPOON SEA SALT

2½ TABLESPOONS SUNFLOWER OIL

### MALDIVIAN CURRY BASE

1 TABLESPOON SUNFLOWER OIL

¼ TEASPOON BROWN MUSTARD SEEDS

6 FRESH CURRY LEAVES

¼ TEASPOON CUMIN SEEDS

5 PODS CARDAMOM, SPLIT AND BRUISED

1 ONION, THINLY SLICED

3 CM/1¼ INCH PIECE GINGER, PEELED AND CUT JULIENNE

3 GARLIC CLOVES, ROUGHLY CHOPPED

¼ TEASPOON GROUND TURMERIC

¼ TEASPOON CHILLI POWDER

¼ TEASPOON GROUND CORIANDER

5 LARGE VINE-RIPENED TOMATOES FINELY CHOPPED

30CM/12 INCH PIECE PANDANUS LEAF, RAKED AND TIED (IF AVAILABLE) (G)

400ML (1⅔ CUPS) FRESH COCONUT MILK (SEE BASICS PAGE 266)

### CURRY GARNISH

4 EGGS

1 SMALL SWEET POTATO, PEELED AND CUT INTO 5CM/2 INCH BATONS

4 SNAKE BEANS OR LONG GREEN BEANS, CUT INTO 5CM/2 INCH LENGTHS

8 BABY CARROTS, PEELED AND CUT INTO 5CM/2 INCH BATONS

FRESHLY SQUEEZED LIME JUICE, TO TASTE

### TUNA COCONUT SAMBAL

185G/6½OZ CANNED TUNA IN OIL, DRAINED

½ SMALL RED ONION, DICED

2 TABLESPOONS FRESHLY SQUEEZED LIME JUICE

1 SMALL GREEN CHILLI, CHOPPED

7.5G/¼OZ (½ CUP) CORIANDER (CILANTRO) LEAVES, CHOPPED

100G/3½OZ (1 CUP) FRESHLY GRATED COCONUT

SEA SALT, TO TASTE

### TO SERVE

4G/1/8OZ (¼ CUP) CORIANDER (CILANTRO) LEAVES

1½CM/½ INCH PIECE GINGER, PEELED AND CUT JULIENNE

12 CURRY LEAVES, SHALLOW-FRIED IN OIL

To make the roshi, combine the flour, salt and oil in a bowl. Gradually stir in 160ml (⅔ cup) of water, ensuring that only just enough is added to make a pliable dough. Turn the dough onto a lightly floured surface and knead for 5 to 8 minutes, or until smooth. Allow the dough to rest for 10 minutes before dividing into 12 equal portions. Roll out each portion on a lightly floured surface until very thin.

Heat a flat grill or heavy-based frying pan over a medium heat. When hot, place a roshi in the pan and cook for about 1 minute, or until bubbles appear on the surface, then turn over and cook for a further 30 to 45 seconds until lightly coloured but not crisp. Roll into a cigar shape, cover with a cloth and keep warm until serving.

To make the Maldivian curry base, heat a heavy-based pot over a medium to high heat. Add the oil and, just before it begins to smoke, add the mustard seeds. and cook until they begin to pop. Add the curry leaves, cumin seeds, cardamom, onion, ginger and garlic. Season with salt then reduce the heat to medium and cook until the onion is soft. Add the turmeric, chilli powder and ground coriander and cook for a further 3 to 4 minutes. Stir in the tomatoes and pandanus leaf and cook until the tomatoes have slightly softened. Add the coconut milk, bring to the boil then reduce the heat and simmer, stirring occasionally, for 25 to 30 minutes.

To make the curry garnish, place the eggs in a small saucepan, cover with cold water and bring to a simmer. Cook for 3 minutes. Remove from the heat, drain and plunge into iced water to stop the cooking process before peeling very gently. Place the sweet potato in a saucepan and cover with cold water. Bring to the boil then reduce the heat and cook until tender before draining.

Bring another saucepan of water to the boil, add the snake beans and cook for 30 seconds. Remove them with a slotted spoon and refresh under cold running water. Add the carrots to the same boiling water and blanch for 1 minute, or until just tender.

Heat the curry base and coconut milk in a saucepan over a medium heat. Add the eggs and vegetables, bring to the boil then reduce the heat to a simmer. Cover with a lid and cook for 4 to 5 minutes, or until completely warmed through and the eggs are just set through. Season with the lime juice.

To make the tuna coconut sambal, combine all the ingredients in a bowl just before serving, seasoning with salt.

To serve, spoon the curry into 4 warmed bowls and scatter with the coriander leaves, ginger julienne and fried curry leaves. Serve accompanied by warm roshi and tuna coconut sambal.

# Soups

CHAPTER 2

In the late nineties, we started offering week-long yoga retreats at COMO Parrot Cay in the Turks and Caicos. The role of the soup became more prominent as part of a liquid detox served alongside our juices. As the COMO Shambhala philosophy developed, we started to introduce a wider range of soups to deliver specific nutritional benefits – especially for those on our various wellness programmes at COMO Shambhala Estate in Bali. Now our 'Green Goddess' soup (page 74) has an almost cult reputation – it is our most popular 'raw' soup.

Our 'raw' soups – served cold or room temperature – tend to be avoided by our Ayurvedic doctors, who focus on the warming features of hot soups. All soups, however, are very effective at giving your digestive system a break. Clear soups have always had a history of healing in Asia, especially good quality stocks as in the Chinese Herb and Black Chicken Tonic Soup (page 54). Invest time and passion in this stage, and it changes everything.

The other favourite ingredient in the COMO Shambhala kitchen is Tomato Jam (page 290). All the flavours are intensified to bring a vegetable soup alive. Another tip: with soups, it is critical to sweat out the garlic, onions and ginger until they are soft and sweet. And don't be afraid of storing soups. The Chinese black chicken soup (page 54), tomato soup (page 56) and lentil soup (page 58) can all be stored in the fridge for a few days.

*This version of a traditional Chinese tonic soup was devised for COMO Metropolitan in Bangkok. The soup is made with black chicken, also known as Silkie chicken. Black chicken tastes sweeter and is thought to nourish the 'yin' of the kidneys and liver and bring down fevers.*

Vitamin-Rich | Antioxidant-Rich | High-Protein | Calming

# CHINESE HERB AND
# BLACK CHICKEN TONIC SOUP

**SERVES 6**

### CHICKEN TONIC SOUP

1½KG/3LB WHOLE BLACK CHICKEN (G)
(OR ORGANIC FREE-RANGE CHICKEN)

4CM/1½ INCH PIECE GINGER, PEELED AND SLICED

6 CLOVES GARLIC, SLICED

5 CORIANDER (CILANTRO) ROOTS,
CLEANED, SCRAPED AND BRUISED (OR 10 STEMS)

3 STAR ANISE

2 CINNAMON QUILLS

4 STRIPS DRIED ORANGE PEEL

2 PANDANUS LEAVES, EACH TIED IN A KNOT
(IF AVAILABLE) (G)

60G/2½OZ (¼ CUP) POWDERED COCONUT
PALM SUGAR (OR ORGANIC BROWN SUGAR) (G)

2½ TABLESPOONS TAMARI SOY

½ STALK CELERY, THICKLY SLICED

½ SMALL ONION, SLICED

½ SMALL LEEK (GREEN PART ONLY),
THICKLY SLICED

½ BUNCH SPRING ONIONS (SCALLIONS),
GREEN TOPS ONLY, PLUS 6 SLICED INTO ROUNDS

½ PORTION CHINESE MEDICINE MIX (G)

125ML (½ CUP) SHAOXING WINE

1 TABLESPOON SESAME OIL

1 CHAYOTE

### TO SERVE

1 PANDANUS LEAF, TIED IN A KNOT (G)

12 BRAISED SHIITAKE MUSHROOMS, CUT 1CM/½
INCH THICK SLICES (SEE BASICS PAGE 275)

6 STRIPS DRIED ORANGE PEEL

6 STAR ANISE

100G/3½OZ (½ CUP) BLACK WOOD EAR MUSHROOMS,
CUT INTO LARGE PIECES, IF AVAILABLE

18 DRIED WOLFBERRIES (GOJI) BERRIES

1 WHITE-COOKED CHICKEN
(SEE BASICS PAGE 294)

6 KALE LEAVES, CUT INTO 7CM/2¾ INCH LENGTHS

4G/⅛OZ (¼ CUP) CORIANDER
(CILANTRO) LEAVES

½ TEASPOON SESAME OIL

4 CHINESE CELERY LEAVES, CUT JULIENNE

GROUND WHITE PEPPER

For the chicken tonic soup, remove the wing tips and feet from the chicken, followed by the backbone and discard. Cut the limbs and the breast into smaller pieces and place all the chicken pieces in a large stockpot.

Add the remaining ingredients for the chicken tonic soup to the stockpot, except the chayote. Cover with 4 litres (8 cups) cold water, or enough to cover the ingredients by 10cm/ 4 inches and bring to the boil. Reduce the heat and simmer for 2 hours, regularly skimming the surface to remove any scum.

Peel the chayote, halve it, remove the core and cut each half into 6 wedges. Add the chayote to the pot and simmer for a further 30 minutes. Remove the pot from the heat, skim the surface, remove the chayote and set aside. Strain the stock through a fine chinois or sieve and discard the solids.

To serve, combine the chicken stock with the pandanus leaf, shiitake mushrooms, orange peel, star anise, black fungi, wolfberries, white-cooked chicken and chayote and cook over a medium heat until warmed through. Bring a separate saucepan of water to the boil. Add the kale and blanch for 1 minute before removing with a slotted spoon and dividing among warmed bowls.

Discard the pandanus leaf, then ladle the soup into the bowls, taking care to distribute the chicken, herbs and spices evenly. Scatter with the coriander leaves. Add a drop of sesame oil to each bowl and a grind of white pepper. Scatter with Chinese celery leaves and serve immediately.

**Note:** Chinese medicine shops sell pre-mixed packets for soup containing ingredients such as dried longans, wolfberries, liquorice root, ginseng, rhizoma and Chinese angelica root.

At our flagship COMO Shambhala Estate in Bali, we offer an extensive variety of vegetarian soups, and this is a crowd-pleaser. Roasting the tomatoes gives depth of flavour as does the addition of tomato jam.

Vitamin-Rich | Mineral-Rich | Antioxidant-Rich | High-Protein | Immune-Boosting | Digestive Support | Calming | Energising | Gluten-Free

# MOROCCAN
# ROAST TOMATO SOUP

**SERVES 4**

### ROAST TOMATO SOUP

2½KG/5LB 9OZ VINE-RIPENED TOMATOES, CORES REMOVED

2 TABLESPOONS OLIVE OIL

1 LARGE ONION, FINELY CHOPPED

1½CM/¾ INCH PIECE GINGER, PEELED AND FINELY CHOPPED

4 CLOVES GARLIC, FINELY CHOPPED

1 SMALL LEEK, WHITE PART ONLY, FINELY CHOPPED

1 FRESH RED CHILLI, SEEDED AND FINELY CHOPPED

SEA SALT, TO TASTE

1 TEASPOON GROUND TURMERIC

2 TEASPOONS GROUND CORIANDER

2 TEASPOONS GROUND CUMIN

1 TEASPOON GROUND GINGER

2 TABLESPOONS RAW HONEY

2 TABLESPOONS TOMATO JAM (SEE BASICS PAGE 290)

2 TEASPOONS PRESERVED LEMON, FINELY CHOPPED (SEE BASICS PAGE 294)

2 TABLESPOONS FRESHLY SQUEEZED ORANGE JUICE

1 TABLESPOON FRESHLY SQUEEZED LEMON JUICE

1.2 LITRES (5 CUPS) VEGETABLE STOCK (SEE BASICS PAGE 269)

### TO SERVE

180G/6OZ (1 CUP) COOKED RED KIDNEY BEANS

100G/3½OZ (4 CUPS) SPINACH LEAVES, WASHED

4G/⅛OZ (¼ CUP) CORIANDER (CILANTRO) LEAVES

5G/¼OZ (¼ CUP) MINT LEAVES

1 TABLESPOON TOASTED WHOLE ALMONDS

To make the roast tomato soup, preheat the oven to 180°C/350°F. Place the tomatoes in a roasting pan and bake for 30 minutes, or until softened. Cool to room temperature then slip off the tomato skins.

Heat the oil in a saucepan over a low heat then add the onion, ginger, garlic, leek and chilli. Season with sea salt and cook gently, stirring occasionally, for about 20 minutes, or until the vegetables are softened and lightly caramelised. Add the spices and cook, stirring for about 3 minutes, or until fragrant. Next, add the honey, tomato jam, preserved lemon, and the orange and lemon juices and cook for a further 2 minutes. Add the roasted tomatoes and cook for 15 minutes, or until the liquid has reduced.

Stir in the stock, cover with a cartouche (see Glossary on page 296) and bring to the boil. Reduce the heat and cook for a further 30 to 40 minutes until thickened. When cooked, pass half of the soup through a mouli grater or food mill into a clean saucepan, add the remaining soup to the saucepan and bring to the boil with the kidney beans and spinach. Cook for a further 2 minutes then check the seasoning and adjust as necessary.

To serve, pour the soup into warmed bowls before scattering with herbs and almonds.

Vitamin-Rich | Mineral-Rich | Antioxidant-Rich | Heart Healthy | Digestive Support | Rejuvenating | Calming | Gluten-Free

# SPICED LENTIL SOUP WITH HARISSA YOGHURT

### SERVES 6

**SPICED LENTIL SOUP**

90G/3OZ (½ CUP) PUY LENTILS

2 TABLESPOONS OLIVE OIL

I ONION, FINELY DICED

3 CLOVES GARLIC, FINELY CHOPPED

1½CM/¾ INCH PIECE GINGER, PEELED AND FINELY CHOPPED

2 STALKS CELERY, PEELED AND FINELY DICED

I BABY FENNEL BULB, TRIMMED, CORED AND FINELY DICED

I RED BELL PEPPER (CAPSICUM), FINELY DICED

½ SMALL LEEK, WHITE PART ONLY, FINELY DICED

SEA SALT AND GROUND WHITE PEPPER, TO TASTE

4 VINE-RIPENED TOMATOES, BLANCHED, REFRESHED, PEELED, SEEDED AND FINELY DICED

½ TEASPOON GROUND TURMERIC

I TEASPOON GROUND CINNAMON

I TEASPOON GROUND CUMIN

I TEASPOON GROUND GINGER

50G/2OZ (¼ CUP) HARISSA (SEE BASICS PAGE 282)

50G/2OZ (¼ CUP) TOMATO JAM (SEE BASICS PAGE 290)

I TABLESPOON RAW HONEY

1.2 LITRES (5 CUPS) VEGETABLE STOCK (SEE BASICS PAGE 269)

350G/12OZ PEELED PUMPKIN, FINELY DICED

**TO SERVE**

50G/2OZ (2 CUPS) SPINACH LEAVES, TORN

125ML (½ CUP) HARISSA YOGHURT (SEE BASICS PAGE 282)

To make the spiced lentil soup, place the lentils in a saucepan and cover with cold water. Bring to the boil before draining and rinsing, then set aside.

Heat a large saucepan over a low to medium heat and add the olive oil. When hot, add the onion, garlic, ginger, celery, fennel, pepper and leek. Season with sea salt and cook over a low heat, stirring occasionally for about 15 minutes, or until soft and sweet. Add the tomatoes, lentils and spices, increase the heat to medium and cook for 3 minutes. Stir in the harissa, tomato jam and honey and cook for a further 3 minutes. Pour in the stock and bring to the boil, then reduce the heat, cover with a cartouche (see Glossary on page 296) and simmer for 20 minutes. Add the pumpkin to the soup, cover again with the cartouche and simmer for a further 25 minutes, or until the pumpkin is tender.

To serve, bring the soup to the boil, add the spinach and heat until just wilted. Check the seasoning and adjust as necessary. Ladle the soup into warmed bowls and top with a spoonful of harissa yoghurt.

"In the valleys of Bhutan, where we have two hotels, the food grown in the fields tastes different to anywhere else I know. The vegetables are bursting with the Earth's true flavours." CHRISTINA ONG

*Beetroot grown in Bhutan, where COMO has two Uma lodges, have a sweet earthy flavour. Roasting them first helps to intensify this taste. The addition of cumin, crumbled goat curd and dill seems like a natural combination, adding a real depth of flavour.*

Vitamin-Rich | Mineral-Rich | Digestive Support | Gluten-Free

# ROAST BEETROOT AND CUMIN SOUP WITH GOAT CURD

## SERVES 6

### ROAST BEETROOT

1KG/2¼LB BEETROOT, TOPS REMOVED, WASHED AND SCRUBBED

2 TABLESPOONS RAW APPLE CIDER VINEGAR

2 TABLESPOONS ORGANIC BROWN SUGAR

1 TABLESPOON OLIVE OIL

### SOUP

2 TABLESPOONS OLIVE OIL

1 LARGE ONION, SLICED

2 LEEKS, WHITE PART ONLY, SLICED

4 CLOVES GARLIC, SLICED

SEA SALT AND CRACKED WHITE PEPPER, TO TASTE

2 TABLESPOONS GROUND CUMIN

2 POTATOES, PEELED AND DICED INTO 2CM/¾ INCH PIECES

60ML (¼ CUP) RAW APPLE CIDER VINEGAR

110G/4OZ (⅓ CUP) RAW HONEY

1.5 LITRES (6 CUPS) VEGETABLE STOCK (SEE BASICS PAGE 269)

### TO SERVE

150G/5OZ FRESH ORGANIC GOAT CURD

6G/¼OZ (¼ CUP) BABY BEETROOT LEAVES, BABY SPINACH OR BABY CHARD

10G/⅓OZ (¼ CUP) DILL LEAVES

To roast the beetroot, preheat the oven to 180°C/350°F. Place a large sheet of foil on a work surface, top this with a sheet of baking paper, then put the beetroot in the centre. Drizzle the beetroot with the vinegar, sugar and olive oil. Bring the sides of the foil in to form a parcel, then place on an oven tray and roast for 1½ to 2 hours, or until tender when tested with a skewer. Remove from the oven, and when the beetroot is cool enough to handle, peel and dice into large chunks.

To make the soup, heat the olive oil in a saucepan over a low heat. When hot, add the onion, leeks, garlic and sea salt and cook, stirring occasionally, for 15 minutes, or until sweet and tender. Stir in the cumin and cook for 3 minutes until fragrant. Add the potatoes and cook for a further 5 minutes, then add the vinegar, honey and diced roast beetroot. Stir in the vegetable stock and cover with a cartouche (see Glossary on page 296). Bring to the boil then reduce the heat and simmer for 45 minutes. Transfer to a blender and blitz until smooth. Check the seasoning and adjust as necessary, then return to a clean saucepan.

To serve, heat the soup then pour into warmed bowls, top with a spoonful of goat curd and scatter over baby beetroot leaves and dill.

*This soup has a smooth, silky texture and is sure to become a firm favourite in your household. The sweetcorn in Thailand is outstanding in both flavour and colour. The spicy seed mix is an optional extra, but complements the sweetcorn and basil beautifully.*

Vitamin-Rich | Mineral-Rich | Antioxidant-Rich | Heart Healthy | Digestive Support | Rejuvenating | Calming | Gluten-Free | Vegan

# SWEETCORN AND BASIL-INFUSED SOUP WITH SPICED SEEDS

**SERVES 4**

### SWEETCORN SOUP
2 TABLESPOONS OLIVE OIL

2 ONIONS, SLICED

3 CLOVES GARLIC, SLICED

3 CM/1¼ INCH PIECE GINGER, PEELED AND CUT JULIENNE

SEA SALT AND GROUND WHITE PEPPER, TO TASTE

6 CORN COBS

2 TABLESPOONS POWDERED COCONUT PALM SUGAR (OR ORGANIC BROWN SUGAR) (G)

2 LITRES (8 CUPS) VEGETABLE STOCK (SEE BASICS PAGE 269)

6 STEMS BASIL

### TO SERVE
½ ROASTED RED BELL PEPPER (CAPSICUM), CUT JULIENNE (SEE BASICS PAGE 276)

85G/3OZ (½ CUP) COOKED CORN KERNELS, RESERVED FROM THE SOUP BEFORE BLENDING

1 TABLESPOON SPICY SEED MIX, (SEE BASICS PAGE 292)

BABY ITALIAN BASIL, LEAVES AND BUDS (OR REGULAR BASIL)

To make the soup, heat a saucepan over a low heat and warm enough olive oil to just cover the base. When hot, add the onions, garlic, ginger and season with sea salt and cook, stirring occasionally for 15 to 20 minutes, or until sweet and soft.

Cut the corn off the cobs and add the kernels to the saucepan, cooking for a further 5 minutes, or until softened. Add the sugar and stock and bring to the boil, then reduce the heat and simmer for 45 minutes. Remove from the heat and add the basil, leaving to stand for 20 minutes to allow the basil to infuse into the liquid. Remove and discard the basil and reserve ½ cup of corn kernels for serving. Transfer the soup to a blender. Blend until smooth, then strain into a saucepan.

To serve, bring the soup to the boil. Check the seasoning and adjust as necessary. Pour the soup into warmed bowls, then top with the roasted red bell pepper and reserved corn kernels. Scatter with the spiced seed mix and finish with the basil leaves and buds.

**Note:** Before blending the soup, make sure you remove the basil, which should only be used to infuse the soup with flavour.

*The secret to the brilliant depth in this soup is the tomato jam, so take the time to make your own. It's a substantial one-dish meal — especially with the addition of barley — which holds up well when made in advance. The herb pistou, however, is best when freshly made just before serving. Garnish with lots of freshly-plucked herbs from the garden.*

Vitamin-Rich | Mineral-Rich | Antioxidant-Rich | Heart Healthy | Digestive Support | Smart Carbohydrate | Rejuvenating | Calming | Gluten-Free | Vegan

# GARDEN VEGETABLE
# AND
# BARLEY SOUP
# WITH HERB PISTOU

### SERVES 6

**GARDEN VEGETABLE SOUP**

2 TABLESPOONS OLIVE OIL

2 ZUCCHINI (COURGETTES), QUARTERED
LENGTHWISE, SEEDED AND DICED

1 RED BELL PEPPER (CAPSICUM), DICED

1 YELLOW BELL PEPPER (CAPSICUM), DICED

2 PENCIL OR BABY LEEKS (WHITE PART ONLY),
SLICED INTO 1CM/½ INCH LENGTHS

1 SMALL ONION, DICED

2 CARROTS, DICED

2 CELERY STALKS, DICED

4 GARLIC CLOVES, FINELY CHOPPED

2 BABY FENNEL BULBS, TRIMMED,
CORED AND DICED

SEA SALT AND FRESHLY CRACKED
BLACK PEPPER, TO TASTE

100G/3½OZ (½ CUP) TOMATO JAM
(SEE BASICS PAGE 290)

130G/4½OZ (⅔ CUP) BARLEY, WASHED

1.2 LITRES (5 CUPS) VEGETABLE STOCK
(SEE BASICS PAGE 269)

1 LARGE BOUQUET GARNI (THYME, BAY, PARSLEY)

**HERB PISTOU**

2 CLOVES GARLIC, SLICED

SEA SALT AND GROUND WHITE PEPPER

10G/⅓OZ (½ CUP) BASIL LEAVES

7.5G/¼OZ (½ CUP) FLAT-LEAF PARSLEY LEAVES

20G/¾OZ (½ CUP) TARRAGON LEAVES

20G/¾OZ (½ CUP) CHERVIL LEAVES

2 TABLESPOONS EXTRA-VIRGIN OLIVE OIL

**TO SERVE**

14G/½OZ (½ CUP) OF MIXED PICKED HERB LEAVES,
INCLUDING BASIL, CHERVIL,
FLAT-LEAF PARSLEY AND TARRAGON

For the vegetable soup, heat the olive oil in a large saucepan, add all the vegetables and season with sea salt. Cover and cook over a low to medium heat, stirring occasionally for about 12 minutes, or until the vegetables are softened but not coloured. Stir in the tomato jam and barley, then pour in the vegetable stock to cover. Bring to the boil then reduce the heat and simmer for 20 minutes. Add the bouquet garni and cook for a further 25 minutes, or until the vegetables and barley are tender. Discard the bouquet garni and check the seasoning, adjusting as necessary.

To make the herb pistou, place the sliced garlic with a pinch of sea salt in a mortar and pound with the pestle. Add the herbs and pound into the paste. Stir in the olive oil and season with a grind of white pepper.

To serve, pour the soup into warmed bowls, top with a small quenelle of the herb pistou and scatter with mixed herbs. Finish with a grind of white pepper.

*This is a popular soup at COMO Parrot Cay. The combination of zucchini, apple and fennel works perfectly, with the grated zucchini adding crunch to each mouthful. If you're not serving it immediately, preserve the colour of the soup by placing the bowl in an ice bath after blending.*

Vitamin-Rich | Mineral-Rich | Heart Healthy | Digestive Support | Smart Carbohydrate | Gluten-Free | Vegan

# ZUCCHINI, APPLE AND FENNEL SOUP

**SERVES 6**

### ZUCCHINI SOUP

60ML (¼ CUP) OLIVE OIL

1 LARGE ONION, SLICED

4 CLOVES GARLIC

3 BABY FENNEL BULBS, TRIMMED, CORED AND SHAVED ON A MANDOLIN

SEA SALT, TO TASTE

3 ZUCCHINI (COURGETTES), QUARTERED LENGTHWISE, SEEDED AND DICED

1.2 LITRES (5 CUPS) VEGETABLE STOCK (SEE BASICS PAGE 269)

2 SMALL GRANNY SMITH APPLES, PEELED, CORED AND SLICED

20G/¾OZ (1 CUP) BASIL LEAVES

### TO SERVE

1 ZUCCHINI (COURGETTE), GRATED

2 ZUCCHINI (COURGETTE) FLOWERS, PETALS PLUCKED

To make the zucchini soup, heat the olive oil in a large saucepan over a low heat. When hot, add the onion, garlic and fennel. Season with salt and cook for 15 minutes, or until the vegetables are soft and translucent. Increase the heat to medium, add the diced zucchini and cook for a further 5 minutes. Add the stock and bring to the boil, then reduce the heat to a simmer and cover with a cartouche (see Glossary on page 296). Cook for 30 minutes then add the apples before replacing the cartouche and cooking for a further 15 minutes. Remove the saucepan from the heat and add the basil, leaving to stand for 15 minutes to allow the flavours to infuse into the liquid. Remove and discard the basil, then transfer the soup to a blender and blend until smooth.

To serve, bring the soup to the boil in a saucepan, add the grated zucchini and return to the boil. Check the seasoning and adjust as necessary. Ladle into warmed bowls and scatter with the zucchini flowers.

*This gluten-free, raw soup is a true crowd-pleaser. The recipe is very similar to traditional gazpacho, but without the bread. Ensure you make a smooth paste with the onion, garlic and nuts first as the right texture is harder to achieve after adding the liquids.*

Vitamin-Rich | Mineral-Rich | Antioxidant-Rich | Rejuvenating | Raw | Gluten-Free | Vegan

# CHILLED ALMOND AND GREEN GRAPE GAZPACHO

**SERVES 4**

### GRAPE GRANITA
330G/11½OZ (2 CUPS) SEEDLESS GREEN GRAPES
2 TABLESPOONS RAW APPLE CIDER VINEGAR
1 TABLESPOON AGAVE NECTAR (G)

### ALMOND AND GRAPE GAZPACHO
500G/1LB 1OZ (3 CUPS) SEEDLESS GREEN GRAPES
½ RED ONION, SLICED
3 CLOVES GARLIC, SLICED
80G/3OZ (½ CUP) PINE NUTS
70G/2½OZ (½ CUP) FLAKED ALMONDS
250–300G/9–10½OZ (3 CUPS) ICE CUBES
60ML (¼ CUP) RAW APPLE CIDER VINEGAR
60G/2½OZ (3 CUPS) BASIL LEAVES
SEA SALT AND GROUND WHITE PEPPER, TO TASTE
60ML (¼ CUP) EXTRA-VIRGIN OLIVE OIL

### TO SERVE
12 SEEDLESS GREEN GRAPES, SLICED INTO ROUNDS
¼ SMALL RED ONION, SLICED LENGTHWISE
5G/¼OZ (¼ CUP) BABY BASIL LEAVES
(OR REGULAR BASIL)
2 TEASPOONS PINE NUTS

To make the grape granita, put the grapes through a juice extractor, catching the juice in a jug (you should get about 250ml, or 1 cup, of juice). Strain the juice and combine with the vinegar, agave nectar and 60ml (¼ cup) water, mixing well. Pour into a shallow freezerproof container, cover and freeze for 4 to 6 hours, or until the mix is frozen. Scrape the frozen mixture with a fork to create ice crystals and return to the freezer until ready to serve.

For the almond and grape gazpacho, place the grapes, onion, garlic and nuts in a blender and blend until finely chopped. Add the ice cubes, apple cider vinegar and basil and blend until combined. Season with sea salt and a grind of white pepper then slowly pour in the extra-virgin olive oil until fully combined. Strain the mixture into a container, cover and refrigerate until ready to serve.

To serve, pour the soup into chilled bowls, top each with a spoonful of granita and scatter with sliced grapes, red onion, basil leaves and pine nuts.

**Note:** Don't make the soup too far in advance as the vinegar content dulls the colour over time. The granita, on the other hand, can be stored in the fridge for up to a month.

*This soup—another raw favourite full of goodness—is great for hot climates. The base is coconut water, which is rehydrating with its high electrolyte properties. Butternut pumpkin is a powerful source of fibre, especially when eaten raw and puréed, while the spiced cashews add crunch and texture. Make up a big batch of cashews; they are perfect for snacking and will store in an airtight container for up to a month.*

Vitamin-Rich | Mineral-Rich | Antioxidant-Rich | Digestive Support | Rejuvenating | Raw

# CHILLED BUTTERNUT PUMPKIN, APPLE AND YOUNG COCONUT SOUP

### SERVES 4

**CHILLED BUTTERNUT PUMPKIN SOUP**

2 GRANNY SMITH APPLES

350G/12OZ BUTTERNUT PUMPKIN, PEELED AND DICED

1½ STALKS CELERY, SLICED

5 SUN-DRIED TOMATOES, SOAKED IN WARM WATER FOR 20 MINUTES, THEN DRAINED

75G/3OZ (½ CUP) YOUNG COCONUT MEAT

500ML (2 CUPS) YOUNG COCONUT WATER

1 TABLESPOON MISO PASTE

1 TABLESPOON RAW TAHINI

2 TABLESPOONS EXTRA-VIRGIN OLIVE OIL

1.5CM/½ INCH PIECE GINGER, PEELED AND SLICED

2 CLOVES GARLIC, SLICED

1 TEASPOON RAW HONEY

1 TABLESPOON RAW APPLE CIDER VINEGAR

3 TEASPOONS FRESHLY SQUEEZED LEMON JUICE

1 TEASPOON MADRAS CURRY POWDER

1 FRESH LONG RED CHILLI, SEEDED AND SLICED

2 TEASPOONS TAMARI SOY

5 LARGE BASIL LEAVES

SEA SALT, TO TASTE

**TO SERVE**

35G/1½OZ (¼ CUP) YOUNG COCONUT MEAT, CUT INTO 5CM/2 INCH JULIENNE STRIPS

60G/2½OZ (½ CUP) BUTTERNUT PUMPKIN CURLS (MADE ON THE TURNING SLICER AND TORN INTO LENGTHS) OR CUT INTO 7CM/2¾ INCH JULIENNE STRIPS

2 TABLESPOONS SPICED CASHEWS (SEE BASICS PAGE 293)

5G/¼OZ (¼ CUP) BABY THAI BASIL LEAVES (OR REGULAR BASIL)

2 TEASPOONS LEMON JUICE

To make the butternut pumpkin soup, put the Granny Smith apples through a juice extractor, and catch the juice in a jug (you should get about 250ml, or 1 cup, of juice). Place the juice and remaining ingredients in a blender and blend until smooth. Strain into a container, cover and refrigerate until ready to serve.

To serve, toss the coconut julienne, pumpkin curls, spiced cashews and basil leaves together in a bowl. Season with the lemon juice to taste. Pour the soup into chilled bowls and place a spoonful of pumpkin salad in the middle of each bowl and serve.

*This is a perennial favourite — packed full of iron from both the greens and the seaweed. We first started serving this soup during summer yoga retreats in Bhutan, where watercress grows rampant and has a lovely mild peppery taste.*

Vitamin-Rich | Mineral-Rich | Antioxidant-Rich | Digestive Support | Rejuvenating | Raw | Gluten-Free

# CHILLED 'GREEN GODDESS' SOUP

### SERVES 4

**'GREEN GODDESS' SOUP**
1 SMALL ONION, SLICED
2 CLOVES GARLIC
60G/2½OZ (2½ CUPS) ENGLISH SPINACH
250G/9OZ (7 CUPS) WATERCRESS
55G/2OZ (2 FIRMLY PACKED CUPS) BASIL LEAVES
40G/1½OZ (2 FIRMLY PACKED CUPS) FLAT-LEAF PARSLEY LEAVES
250ML (1 CUP) YOUNG COCONUT WATER
SEA SALT AND GROUND WHITE PEPPER, TO TASTE
3 TEASPOONS RAW HONEY
50ML (SCANT ¼ CUP OR 2 FL OZ) LEMON JUICE

**TO SERVE**
125ML (½ CUP) AVOCADO CRUSH (SEE BASICS PAGE 270)
20G/¾OZ (¼ CUP) SOAKED HIJIKI SEAWEED OR SEA SPAGHETTI (SEE BASICS PAGE 292)
9G/⅓OZ (¼ CUP) WATERCRESS LEAVES

To make the 'Green Goddess' soup, place the onion, garlic, spinach, watercress, herbs and coconut water in a blender and blend until smooth. Season with sea salt and a grind of white pepper, then add the honey and lemon juice. (If the soup is being made ahead of time, store in a fridge without adding the lemon juice until the time of serving.) Blend to combine.

To serve, pour the soup into chilled bowls. Top with a quenelle of avocado crush and scatter with seaweed and watercress leaves.

*This tasty raw soup is light and summery, with a smooth texture from the avocado. The orange zest and ginger bring extraordinary depth.*

Vitamin-Rich | Antioxidant-Rich | Digestive Support | Smart Carbohydrate | Cleansing | Raw | Gluten-Free | Vegan

# CHILLED CREAMY AVOCADO, MISO AND ORANGE SOUP

**SERVES 4**

### AVOCADO AND MISO SOUP

2 LARGE VINE-RIPENED TOMATOES, DICED

1 AVOCADO, PEELED, STONED AND CUT INTO WEDGES

250ML (1 CUP) YOUNG COCONUT WATER

750ML (3 CUPS) CARROT JUICE

50ML (SCANT ¼ CUP OR 2 FL OZ) FRESHLY SQUEEZED LEMON JUICE

2 TABLESPOONS WHITE MISO PASTE

1 TABLESPOON CHOPPED GINGER

1 CLOVE GARLIC, SLICED

3 TEASPOONS FINELY GRATED ORANGE ZEST

### TO SERVE

8 CHERRY TOMATOES, SLICED INTO 5MM/¼ INCH ROUNDS

2 TABLESPOONS SLICED SPRING ONIONS (SCALLIONS)

4G/⅛OZ (¼ CUP) FLAT-LEAF PARSLEY LEAVES

1½ TABLESPOONS FRESHLY SQUEEZED ORANGE JUICE

SEA SALT AND GROUND WHITE PEPPER, TO TASTE

4 TEASPOONS PUMPKIN SEEDS

2 TEASPOONS PUMPKIN SEED OIL

To make the avocado and miso soup, place all the ingredients and 60ml (¼ cup) water in a blender and blend until smooth. Transfer to a container, cover and chill in the fridge until ready to serve.

To serve, combine the tomatoes, spring onions and parsley leaves in a bowl, add the orange juice, season with sea salt and a grind of white pepper and toss to combine. Pour the soup into chilled bowls, place the salad in the centre of each bowl and sprinkle with pumpkin seeds and a drizzle of pumpkin seed oil.

# Salads

CHAPTER 3

You can't hide anything with a salad. It is food in its most naked form. For this reason, take pride in your ingredients, shop as locally and seasonally as possible – roots, shoots and fine herbs in spring, for instance. Where available, buy organic, though certifications vary so dramatically from country by country. Freshness is key.

Many salad ingredients can be kept in cold storage for a while, but do pick and serve salad leaves and herbs as quickly as possible. We use blanching a great deal, locking in the chlorophyll (the rich green colour) and nutritional benefits by immediately chilling the ingredient in iced water.

All the salad dressings in these recipes store really well, and use minimum amounts of oil and salt (salt also draws water out of salad leaves, making them wilt). Some dressings work across all salads, such as the Lemon Dressing (page 278), and the Orange Blossom Dressing (page 279). The COMO Shambhala bestsellers are the Ginger-Miso Dressing (page 82) and Rainbow Slaw Dressing (page 278).

If certain ingredients listed in these recipes aren't available, simply think what role that ingredient plays in the salad and how it might be substituted. For broad beans, for instance, use edamame. For asparagus, you can always use green beans. And if heirloom tomatoes aren't available, substitute with a selection of the best that the season has to offer.

*This salad is elegant, easy to prepare and rich in enzymes. Ensure you cook the green vegetables in a large pot of boiling salted water and have an ice bath ready and waiting when they're done. The dressing is delicious and always a good one to have to hand.*

Vitamin-Rich | Mineral-Rich | Antioxidant-Rich | Heart Healthy | Digestive Support | Gluten-Free | Vegan

# GARDEN GREENS, LEAVES AND SEED SALAD WITH AVOCADO AND GINGER-MISO DRESSING

## SERVES 4

### GINGER-MISO DRESSING

60ML (¼ CUP) RAW APPLE CIDER VINEGAR

2 TABLESPOONS MISO PASTE

1 TABLESPOON RAW TAHINI

1 CLOVE GARLIC, GRATED

2 TABLESPOONS AGAVE NECTAR (G)

1 LEMON, JUICED

2CM/¾ INCH PIECE GINGER, PEELED AND GRATED

60ML (¼ CUP) EXTRA-VIRGIN OLIVE OIL

### SALAD

8 GREEN ASPARAGUS SPEARS, BASE TRIMMED

12 BABY GREEN BEANS, ENDS REMOVED

4 BABY ZUCCHINI (COURGETTES), TOPS TRIMMED

4 STEMS BROCCOLINI, ENDS TRIMMED AND BASES PEELED

16 SNOW PEAS (MANGETOUT) TRIMMED

¼ SMALL FENNEL BULB, THINLY SLICED ON A MANDOLIN AND PLACED IN ICED WATER

7.5G/¼OZ (½ CUP) FLAT-LEAF PARSLEY LEAVES

1 GEM LETTUCE, LEAVES SEPARATED

1 BELGIAN ENDIVE (CHICORY), LEAVES SEPARATED AND CUT INTO WEDGES

½ AVOCADO, PEELED AND CUT INTO 4 LENGTHS

### TO SERVE

1 TABLESPOON SUNFLOWER SEEDS

1 TABLESPOON PUMPKIN SEEDS

30G/1½OZ (1 CUP) SUNFLOWER SEED SPROUTS OR ALFALFA SPROUTS

To make the ginger-miso dressing, put all the ingredients, except the olive oil in a blender, add 60ml (¼ cup) water and blend to a fine purée. With the motor running, gradually add the oil until emulsified.

For the salad, prepare a bowl of iced water and bring a large saucepan of water to the boil. Season with salt and blanch the asparagus, beans, zucchini, broccolini and snow peas for 45 seconds. Remove the vegetables with a slotted spoon and refresh in iced water before draining.

To serve, place the cooked green vegetables in a large bowl and dress with 3 tablespoons of the ginger-miso dressing until coated. In a separate bowl, mix the fennel, parsley, lettuce and Belgian endive and dress with 1½ tablespoons of dressing. Divide the dressed green vegetables and avocado among serving bowls, then top with the dressed leaves. Finish by scattering the sunflower and pumpkin seeds over each salad and top with the sprouts.

*Orange is one of the most versatile salad ingredients. You could replace the artichokes with roasted baby beetroot. This salad works best as one large salad to be shared, accompanying grilled or steamed fish or chicken, or even with the Moroccan-Spiced Vegetable and Tempeh Curry (page 136).*

Vitamin-Rich | Mineral-Rich | Antioxidant-Rich | High-Protein | Digestive Support | Rejuvenating | Gluten-Free | Vegan

# BLOOD ORANGE, ARTICHOKE AND BROAD BEAN SALAD WITH SHAVED FENNEL, ALMONDS AND ORANGE BLOSSOM DRESSING

### SERVES 4

### ORANGE BLOSSOM DRESSING

250ML (1 CUP) FRESHLY SQUEEZED BLOOD ORANGE JUICE, STRAINED

1 TABLESPOON COCONUT NECTAR OR AGAVE NECTAR (G)

60ML (¼ CUP) EXTRA-VIRGIN OLIVE OIL

½ TEASPOON ORANGE BLOSSOM WATER

2 TABLESPOONS RAW APPLE CIDER VINEGAR

SEA SALT AND GROUND WHITE PEPPER, TO TASTE

### ARTICHOKE SALAD

55G/2OZ (½ CUP) BROAD (FAVA) BEANS, BLANCHED, REFRESHED, PODDED AND PEELED

16 BABY GREEN BEANS, CUT IN HALF

8 BABY GLOBE ARTICHOKES, COOKED À LA GRECQUE (SEE BASICS PAGE 270)

¼ RED ONION, THINLY SLICED LENGTHWISE

20 NIÇOISE OLIVES, PITTED

2 TEASPOONS SALTED CAPERS, WASHED AND DRAINED

### TO SERVE

1 BLOOD ORANGE OR NAVEL ORANGE

10G/⅓OZ (¼ CUP) DILL LEAVES

5G/¼OZ (¼ CUP) MINT LEAVES

25G/1OZ (1 CUP) BABY ROCKET (ARUGULA) (OR REGULAR ROCKET)

¼ SMALL FENNEL BULB, THINLY SLICED ON A MANDOLIN

1 RED RADISH, THINLY SLICED ON A MANDOLIN

25G/1OZ (¼ CUP) FLAKED ALMONDS, TOASTED

4 ORANGE OR YELLOW MARIGOLD OR NASTURTIUM FLOWERS, IF AVAILABLE

To make the orange blossom dressing, place the orange juice and coconut nectar in a saucepan. Bring to the boil, reduce the heat and simmer until reduced to 125ml (½ cup). Remove the pan from the heat and whisk in the extra-virgin oil, orange blossom water and vinegar. Season with sea salt and a grind of white pepper. Leave to cool.

To make the salad, bring a pot of water to the boil and season with salt. Blanch the broad beans and baby beans for 45 seconds. Remove the vegetables with a slotted spoon and refresh in iced water before draining. Combine the vegetables, olives and capers in a bowl and toss through with 2 tablespoons of orange blossom dressing just before serving.

To serve, cut all peel and pith from the orange and thinly slice crosswise into rounds, discarding any seeds. Place slices overlapping in a circle on a large platter, drizzle with a little dressing, and then place the dressed artichoke salad in the centre of the oranges. Combine the herbs, rocket, fennel and radish in a bowl, season and toss with 2 tablespoons of dressing. Place on top of the salad and finish with the nuts and petals.

# SALAD OF ROOTS, SHOOTS AND FINE HERBS WITH HAZELNUTS

**SERVES 4**

This salad works well as a light and satisfying lunch. The salad gets depth and substance from the braised celeriac and nutty overtones from the Jerusalem artichokes. The fennel and apple purée bring everything together. Good quality bottled globe artichokes can be substituted if fresh artichokes are not available.

Vitamin-Rich | Mineral-Rich | Antioxidant-Rich | High-Protein | Digestive Support | Rejuvenating | Gluten-Free | Vegan

### BRAISED FENNEL AND CELERIAC

¼ FENNEL BULB, CUT INTO 4 WEDGES (EACH 2CM/¾ INCH THICK)

¼ LARGE CELERIAC, PEELED AND CUT INTO WEDGES (EACH 2CM/¾ INCH THICK)

500ML (2 CUPS) À LA GRECQUE STOCK, (SEE BASICS PAGE 269)

4 SPRIGS THYME

### FENNEL AND APPLE PURÉE

3 BABY FENNEL BULBS, CORE REMOVED AND THINLY SLICED ON A MANDOLIN

SEA SALT, TO TASTE

2 GREEN APPLES, PEELED, CUT INTO QUARTERS, CORED AND THINLY SLICED ON A MANDOLIN

2 STAR ANISE

1 TABLESPOON EXTRA-VIRGIN OLIVE OIL

### VINAIGRETTE

90G/3OZ (⅓ CUP) AGAVE NECTAR (G)

60ML (¼ CUP) RAW APPLE CIDER VINEGAR

80ML (⅓ CUP) RAW RED WINE VINEGAR

180ML (¾ CUP) OLIVE OIL

60ML (¼ CUP) EXTRA-VIRGIN OLIVE OIL

2 CLOVES GARLIC, SLICED

SEA SALT AND GROUND WHITE PEPPER, TO TASTE

### SALAD

20 BABY GREEN BEANS, TAILED

12 GREEN ASPARAGUS SPEARS, WOODY ENDS TRIMMED AND BASE OF STEMS PEELED

55G/2OZ (½ CUP) BROAD (FAVA) BEANS, BLANCHED, REFRESHED, PODDED AND PEELED

1 TEASPOON SUGAR

12 WHITE ASPARAGUS SPEARS, WOODY ENDS TRIMMED AND STEMS PEELED

4 WHOLE GLOBE ARTICHOKES, COOKED À LA GRECQUE THEN CUT IN HALF (SEE BASICS PAGE 270)

1 RECIPE ROAST JERUSALEM ARTICHOKES, CUT IN HALF (SEE BASICS PAGE 274)

### TO SERVE

20G/¾OZ (1 CUP) WASHED BABY FRISÉE (OR REGULAR FRISÉE)

28G/1OZ (1 CUP) WASHED MIXED HERBS, SUCH AS FLAT-LEAF PARSLEY, DILL, TARRAGON AND CHERVIL

¼ FENNEL BULB, THINLY SLICED ON A MANDOLIN THEN PUT IN A BOWL OF ICED WATER

2 TABLESPOONS LIGHTLY TOASTED HAZELNUTS, CHOPPED

For the braised fennel and celeriac, preheat the oven to 160°C/320°F. Place the fennel and celeriac on separate roasting trays lined with baking paper, cover each with à la Grecque stock and add 2 thyme sprigs. Place a piece of baking paper on top and cover the trays with foil. Cook in the oven for 35 to 45 minutes, or until tender. Remove from the stock and cool.

To make the fennel and apple purée, heat a large wide saucepan and add the fennel. Season to taste with sea salt, cover with 250ml (1 cup) water and cook over a medium to high heat for 15 minutes, or until softened. Add the apple and star anise then cover and cook for a further 5 minutes. Discard the star anise and transfer the mixture to a blender. Add the extra-virgin olive oil and blend until smooth. Set aside.

To make the herb vinaigrette, whisk the agave nectar and both vinegars together in a bowl, then gradually whisk in the oils. Place the garlic with a pinch of sea salt in a mortar and pound with the pestle to a paste. Add the garlic to the dressing and whisk well before seasoning with sea salt and a grind of white pepper.

To make the salad, bring a pot of water to the boil and season with salt. Blanch the beans and green asparagus for 45 seconds. Remove the vegetables with a slotted spoon and refresh in iced water before draining.

Bring another pot of water to the boil, add ½ teaspoon of sea salt and the sugar, then add the white asparagus and cook for 10 to 12 minutes, or until tender. Drain and allow to cool. Place both the green and white asparagus in a bowl and dress with 1 tablespoon of the vinaigrette. Combine the remaining ingredients in another bowl and dress with 60ml (¼ cup) of the vinaigrette.

To serve, place a large tablespoon of fennel purée into the centre of each plate, then smooth it around with the back of the spoon into a half moon. Top with the lightly dressed salad ingredients, followed by the dressed mixed herbs, frisée and shaved fennel. Garnish with the chopped hazelnuts.

*This hearty salad is great for sharing. The black beans, corn and avocado are a nod to Tex-Mex. This salad also works well with grilled fish or chicken.*

Vitamin-Rich | Mineral-Rich | Antioxidant-Rich | Heart Healthy | Digestive Support | Rejuvenating | Gluten-Free | Vegan

# AVOCADO AND SWEETCORN SALAD WITH BLACK BEANS AND QUINOA, CUMIN AND OREGANO VINAIGRETTE

### SERVES 4

### CUMIN AND OREGANO VINAIGRETTE

½ CLOVE GARLIC, SLICED

1¼ TEASPOONS GROUND CUMIN

1 SPRIG OREGANO, LEAVES ONLY, CHOPPED

SEA SALT AND CRACKED WHITE PEPPER, TO TASTE

60ML (¼ CUP) RAW RED WINE VINEGAR

2 TABLESPOONS AGAVE NECTAR (G)

1 TABLESPOON LIME JUICE

60ML (¼ CUP) EXTRA-VIRGIN OLIVE OIL

### QUINOA AND BLACK BEAN SALAD

1 COOKED CORN COB (SEE BASICS PAGE 272)

1 GREEN BELL PEPPER (CAPSICUM), SEEDED AND DICED

80G/3OZ (½ CUP) COOKED QUINOA (SEE BASICS PAGE 286)

¼ SMALL RED ONION, DICED

½ SMALL TELEGRAPH CUCUMBER, CUT IN HALF LENGTHWISE, SEEDED AND SLICED

90G/3OZ (½ CUP) COOKED BLACK BEANS (SEE BASICS PAGE 288)

1 FRESH LONG RED CHILLI, THINLY SLICED INTO ROUNDS

1 AVOCADO, PEELED AND CUT INTO WEDGES

### TO SERVE

¼ BUTTERNUT PUMPKIN, PEELED AND CUT INTO CURLS ON A TURNING SLICER

7.5G/¼OZ (½ CUP) FLAT-LEAF PARSLEY LEAVES, ROUGHLY CHOPPED

4G/⅛OZ (¼ CUP) CORIANDER (CILANTRO) LEAVES, ROUGHLY CHOPPED

40G/1½OZ (½ CUP) SOAKED HIJIKI SEAWEED OR SEA SPAGHETTI (SEE BASICS PAGE 292)

35G/1¼OZ (1 CUP) WATERCRESS LEAVES

4 TABLESPOONS SUNFLOWER SEEDS

To make the vinaigrette, place the garlic, cumin and oregano in a mortar and use the pestle to pound to a paste, seasoning with salt. Transfer the paste to a bowl and whisk in the vinegar, agave nectar and lime juice until combined. Gradually whisk in the olive oil and season with a grind of white pepper.

To serve, remove the corn from the cob by cutting downwards to produce long shards. Place the green pepper, quinoa, onion, cucumber, black beans and chilli in a bowl and dress with 2 tablespoons of the vinaigrette. Toss gently to combine and leave to marinate for 5 to 10 minutes. Arrange the salad down the centre of 4 serving plates and top with corn shards and avocado wedges.

Place the butternut pumpkin, herbs, seaweed and watercress in a bowl and dress with 2 tablespoons of the vinaigrette. Toss gently to combine, arrange over the salad and finish with a good sprinkling of sunflower seeds.

*This salad has been on the COMO Shambhala menu since the beginning. Wild rice has a nuttiness and retains some bite after cooking. This dish works well as a lunchtime main course or for a shared table. Use gluten-free Tamari if you are avoiding gluten.*

Vitamin-Rich | Mineral-Rich | Antioxidant-Rich | High-Protein | Immune-Boosting | Digestive Support | Rejuvenating | Energising | Gluten-Free | Vegan

# WILD RICE AND SEED SALAD WITH TAHINI AND TAMARI DRESSING, AND BEETROOT AND APPLE RELISH

**SERVES 4**

### TAHINI AND TAMARI DRESSING
60ML (¼ CUP) RAW TAHINI
60ML (¼ CUP) TAMARI SOY
1 CLOVE GARLIC, SLICED
1CM/½ INCH PIECE GINGER, PEELED AND SLICED
1 TABLESPOON STRAINED LEMON JUICE
1 TABLESPOON AGAVE NECTAR (G)
125ML (½ CUP) EXTRA-VIRGIN OLIVE OIL

### WILD RICE AND SEED SALAD
300G/10½OZ (1½ CUP) WILD RICE
120G/4½OZ PEELED BUTTERNUT PUMPKIN, CUT JULIENNE
1 RED BELL PEPPER (CAPSICUM), SEEDED AND CUT JULIENNE
¼ RED ONION, SLICED LENGTHWISE
80G/3OZ (1 CUP) SHREDDED RED CABBAGE
80G/3OZ (1 CUP) BEAN SPROUTS
160G/5½OZ (2 CUPS) SHREDDED CHINESE CABBAGE
60G/2OZ (2 CUPS) SHREDDED SPINACH LEAVES
7.5G/¼OZ (½ CUP) FLAT-LEAF PARSLEY LEAVES
2 TABLESPOONS SUNFLOWER SEEDS
2 TABLESPOONS PUMPKIN SEEDS
2 COOKED CORN COBS (SEE BASICS PAGE 272), CUT INTO LONG SHARDS

### BEETROOT AND APPLE RELISH
1 LARGE BEETROOT, PEELED AND CUT INTO SPAGHETTI ON A TURNING SLICER OR CUT JULIENNE
1 GREEN APPLE, PEELED AND CUT INTO SPAGHETTI ON A TURNING SLICER OR CUT JULIENNE
1 TABLESPOON RAW APPLE CIDER VINEGAR
1 TEASPOON COCONUT OR AGAVE NECTAR (G)
SEA SALT, TO TASTE

To make the tahini and tamari dressing, place the tahini, tamari, garlic and ginger in a blender and blend until combined. Add 60ml (¼ cup) water, the lemon juice and agave nectar and blend further. With the blender running, gradually add the olive oil until combined and emulsified.

For the wild rice and seed salad, bring 2 litres (8 cups) water to the boil and stir in the wild rice. Reduce the heat and simmer, covered, for 40 to 45 minutes, or just until the kernels puff open. Uncover, fluff with a fork and simmer for a further 5 minutes. Drain off any excess liquid and transfer to a bowl to cool slightly before use. Add the remaining ingredients, except the corn shards, and toss through with 6 tablespoons of the dressing. Check the seasoning and adjust as necessary.

To make the beetroot and apple relish, place all the ingredients together in a bowl, season with sea salt and gently toss together.

To serve, spoon a third of the rice salad among 4 bowls, top with one-third of corn and repeat, layering twice more and finishing with corn shards. Top the rice salad with beetroot relish and spoon the dressing over and around the plate. Serve warm or at room temperature but never chilled as the rice hardens in the fridge.

*Curly kale has a great texture, which holds perfectly when dressed in salads. It is the 'queen of greens', packed full of iron, antioxidants, fibre and sulphur. At COMO Parrot Cay, where this a popular menu item, guests love the combination of fresh vegetables and the Japanese-inspired dressing.*

Vitamin-Rich | Mineral-Rich | Antioxidant-Rich | High-Protein | Digestive Support | Rejuvenating | Energising | Raw | Vegan

# CURLY KALE SALAD WITH MARINATED SHIITAKES, HIJIKI, SPROUTS AND SEEDS WITH ORANGE SOY DRESSING

**SERVES 4**

### ORANGE SOY DRESSING

250ML (1 CUP) FRESHLY SQUEEZED ORANGE JUICE, STRAINED

60ML (¼ CUP) TAMARI SOY

2 TABLESPOONS AGAVE NECTAR (G)

2½ TABLESPOONS RAW APPLE CIDER VINEGAR

½ TEASPOON CHILLI FLAKES

60ML (¼ CUP) OLIVE OIL

1 TABLESPOON SESAME OIL

SEA SALT AND GROUND WHITE PEPPER, TO TASTE

### SALAD

150G/5OZ BUTTERNUT PUMPKIN, PEELED AND CUT JULIENNE

5CM/2 INCH PIECE PEELED DAIKON, CUT JULIENNE

½ SMALL CUCUMBER, CUT IN HALF LENGTHWISE, SEEDED AND CUT JULIENNE

1 TABLESPOON SLICED RED ONION

4G/⅛OZ (¼ CUP) FLAT-LEAF PARSLEY

160G/5½OZ (2 CUPS) SOAKED HIJIKI SEAWEED OR SEA SPAGHETTI (SEE BASICS PAGE 292)

### TO SERVE

2 HEADS OF CURLY KALE, LEAVES PULLED FROM THE BASE, STEMS REMOVED AND CUT INTO 6CM/2½ INCH PIECES

8 MARINATED SHIITAKE MUSHROOMS, SLICED 8MM/⅓ INCH THICK (SEE BASICS PAGE 275)

50G/2OZ (½ CUP) SNOW PEA (MANGETOUT) SPROUTS OR SUNFLOWER SPROUTS

2 RED RADISHES, SLICED

2 TEASPOONS PUMPKIN SEEDS

2 TEASPOONS TOASTED SESAME SEEDS

To make the orange soy dressing, place the orange juice, tamari, agave nectar, vinegar and chilli flakes in a blender and blend for 2 minutes, or until well combined. With the blender still running, gradually add the oils. Season with sea salt and a grind of white pepper.

For the salad, combine the julienned vegetables, onion, parsley and drained seaweed in a bowl, add 60ml (¼ cup) orange soy dressing and toss to combine.

To serve, toss the kale with 2 teaspoons of the orange soy dressing and divide among serving plates. Spoon the salad over the kale and scatter with sliced mushrooms. Finish with the shoots, radishes and a sprinkling of pumpkin and sesame seeds. Serve immediately.

**Note:** Any kale can be substituted, including the Chinese or Tuscan (cavolo nero) varieties.

# YOUNG COCONUT AND
# VEGETABLE NOODLE SALAD WITH
# TAMARIND DRESSING AND
# AN ALMOND AND CHILLI SAUCE

### SERVES 4

*This salad was created for the COMO Shambhala menu at COMO Parrot Cay in 2002. An immediate hit with the guests, the salad is now considered a resort classic. Young coconut meat gives the salad a great texture. The almond-chilli sauce adds creaminess while the spiced cashews give crunch. Use gluten-free tamari soy if you are avoiding gluten in your diet.*

Vitamin-Rich | Mineral-Rich | Antioxidant-Rich | Digestive Support | Rejuvenating | Raw | Gluten-Free

### ALMOND AND CHILLI SAUCE

100G/3½OZ (1¼ CUPS) FLAKED ALMONDS

2CM/¾ INCH PIECE GINGER, SLICED

2 CLOVES GARLIC, SLICED

2 FRESH LONG RED CHILLIES, SPLIT LENGTHWISE, SEEDED AND ROUGHLY CHOPPED

60ML (¼ CUP) LEMON JUICE

2 TABLESPOONS RAW HONEY

2 TABLESPOONS TAMARI SOY

60ML (¼ CUP) EXTRA-VIRGIN OLIVE OIL

### TAMARIND DRESSING

180ML (⅔ CUP) TAMARIND WATER (SEE BASICS PAGE 291)

2 TABLESPOONS AGAVE NECTAR (G)

2 TABLESPOONS TAMARI SOY

½ CLOVE GARLIC, SLICED

½ FRESH LONG RED CHILLIES, SPLIT LENGTHWISE, SEEDED AND SLICED

1 CORIANDER (CILANTRO) ROOT, CLEANED, SCRAPED AND SLICED (OR 2 STEMS)

60ML (¼ CUP) OLIVE OIL

### COCONUT AND VEGETABLE SALAD

½ ZUCCHINI (COURGETTE)

½ CARROT

1 GREEN APPLE

½ TELEGRAPH CUCUMBER

½ RED BELL PEPPER (CAPSICUM), CUT INTO QUARTERS AND SEEDED

150G/5OZ (1 CUP) YOUNG COCONUT MEAT, CUT JULIENNE

¼ RED ONION, THINLY SLICED

28G/1OZ (1 CUP) MIXED HERBS SUCH AS THAI BASIL, MINT AND CORIANDER (CILANTRO) LEAVES

### TO SERVE

40G/1½OZ (½ CUP) BEAN SPROUTS

1 LONG RED CHILLI, SPLIT LENGTHWISE, SEEDED AND CUT JULIENNE

65G/2½OZ (¼ CUP) SPICED CASHEWS (SEE BASICS PAGE 293)

To make the almond and chilli sauce, place the almonds in a bowl, cover with water and soak for 1 hour before draining and rinsing. Place the almonds, 80ml (⅓ cup) water and the remaining ingredients in a blender and blend until smooth.

For the tamarind dressing, place all the ingredients in a blender and blend until combined.

To make the salad, use a turning slicer to cut the zucchini, carrot, apple and cucumber into spaghetti, or cut into 7cm/ 2¾ inch long julienne strips. In a bowl, combine with the red pepper, young coconut, onion and 60ml (¼ cup) of tamarind dressing. Toss through two-thirds of the herbs.

To serve, use a large tablespoon of the almond and chilli sauce to make a quenelle and place it on each plate. Position the dressed salad in the centre of the plate and scatter with the bean sprouts, shallots, chilli and remaining mixed herbs. Finish with the chopped spiced cashews and serve immediately.

You will be surprised how good the raw version of this classic dish tastes, and just how similar the flavours are, despite a completely different set of ingredients. This Caesar dressing gets its creaminess from the young coconut meat and soaked cashews, which are used to substitute the classic egg-based mayonnaise. Use gluten-free liquid aminos or Tamari soy if you are avoiding gluten in your diet.

Vitamin-Rich | Mineral-Rich | Antioxidant-Rich | Digestive Support | Smart Carbohydrate | Cleansing | Rejuvenating | Raw | Gluten-Free | Vegan

# CAESAR SALAD
# WITH
# MACADAMIA NUT 'CHEESE',
# AVOCADO AND
# CREAMY YOUNG COCONUT
# DRESSING

### SERVES 4

### MACADAMIA NUT 'CHEESE'
280G/10OZ (2 CUPS) MACADAMIA NUTS
2 TEASPOONS CHOPPED GARLIC
2½ TABLESPOONS LEMON JUICE

### CAESAR DRESSING
115G/4OZ (¾ CUP) RAW CASHEWS
75G/3OZ (½ CUP) YOUNG COCONUT MEAT
½ CLOVE GARLIC, FINELY CHOPPED
1½ TABLESPOONS LEMON JUICE
1 TABLESPOON RAW APPLE CIDER VINEGAR
1 TEASPOON WHITE MISO PASTE
½ TEASPOON LIQUID AMINOS OR TAMARI SOY (G)
¼ TEASPOON TABASCO SAUCE
½ TEASPOON SEA SALT, OR TO TASTE

### SALAD
4 BABY GEM LETTUCE, BASES REMOVED
1½ TABLESPOONS SALTED BABY CAPERS, WASHED AND DRAINED
1 AVOCADO, PEELED, STONED, QUARTERED THEN CUT INTO SMALL WEDGES

To make the macadamia nut 'cheese', place all the ingredients in a blender and blend to a smooth paste. Scoop the mixture onto a Teflex or non-stick sheet on a dehydrator tray and smooth evenly until 3mm/⅛ inch thick. Dehydrate at 48°C/118°F for 4 hours, turn over and dry for a further 4 hours. Remove, cool and break into shards that resemble Parmesan shavings. Store in an airtight container for up to a week.

To make the Caesar dressing, place the cashews in a bowl, cover with water and soak for 2 hours before draining and rinsing. Place the cashews and remaining ingredients in a blender and blend until smooth. Thin with a little water if necessary.

For the salad, trim the lettuce into points and place in a bowl with the capers and avocado. Add half of the Caesar dressing (or to taste) and toss well to coat the lettuce leaves.

To serve, arrange the salad in 4 bowls, layering the macadamia nut 'cheese' and the avocado between the wedges of lettuce.

**Note:** This dressing also goes well with vegetable crudités.

*This recipe celebrates tomatoes in season; use the best you can find. Marinating helps to bring out their flavour. The passionfruit juice gives the salad dressing a great zing. Just don't make it too spicy, or the dressing will distract from the tomato flavour.*

Vitamin-Rich | Mineral-Rich | Antioxidant-Rich | Heart Healthy | Rejuvenating | Raw | Gluten-Free | Vegan

# HEIRLOOM TOMATO CEVICHE WITH PALM HEART, AND SPICY TOMATO DRESSING

### SERVES 4

### SPICY TOMATO DRESSING
3 VINE-RIPENED TOMATOES, ROUGHLY CHOPPED
60ML (¼ CUP) LIME JUICE, STRAINED
1 TABLESPOON AGAVE NECTAR (G)
2 PIECES CORIANDER (CILANTRO) ROOTS, CLEANED, SCRAPED AND BRUISED (OR 4 STEMS)
2 CLOVES GARLIC, BRUISED
¼ TEASPOON TABASCO SAUCE
2 TABLESPOONS PASSIONFRUIT JUICE
1 TEASPOON SEA SALT, TO TASTE
60ML (¼ CUP) EXTRA-VIRGIN OLIVE OIL

### SALAD
2 HEIRLOOM GREEN ZEBRA-STRIPED TOMATOES, CUT INTO EIGHTHS
2 YELLOW HEIRLOOM TOMATOES, SLICED
2 ROMA TOMATOES, SLICED CROSSWISE
¼ SMALL RED ONION, SLICED LENGTHWISE
1 FRESH LONG RED CHILLI, SPLIT LENGTHWISE, SEEDED AND CUT JULIENNE
1 BABY GEM LETTUCE, LEAVES SEPARATED AND TRIMMED INTO POINTS
4 SPRING ONIONS (SCALLIONS), CUT JULIENNE
2 SMALL PALM HEARTS, THINLY SLICED
4G/⅛OZ (¼ CUP) FLAT-LEAF PARSLEY LEAVES
4G/⅛OZ (¼ CUP) CORIANDER (CILANTRO) LEAVES

To make the spicy tomato dressing, combine all the ingredients, except the olive oil and salt, in a bowl. Add the sea salt and leave to stand, covered, for 30 minutes to allow the flavours to develop. Push through a sieve into a bowl, using a ladle to push through the tomatoes to extract all the juice (you need about 300ml, or 1¼ cups, juice). Next, gradually whisk in the olive oil.

For the salad, combine the tomatoes, red onion and chilli in a bowl. Add 60ml (¼ cup) of the spicy tomato dressing and stand for 5 minutes.

To serve, toss the lettuce with 2 tablespoons of the dressing, coating well. Place 2 lettuce leaves in each of 4 bowls and spoon over half the tomato salad. Scatter the salad with half of the spring onions, palm hearts and herbs, repeating the layering once more. Drizzle the salad with a little more dressing and serve immediately.

*This bottomless bowl of vegetables is a rainbow of raw goodness. Serve the delicious mustard and apple cider dressing on the side. This is a great salad to eat when breaking a fast; just serve a half portion.*

Vitamin-Rich | Mineral-Rich | Antioxidant-Rich | Digestive Support | Rejuvenating | Raw | Vegan

# OUR BIG RAW SALAD
## WITH
## DIJON MUSTARD
## AND APPLE CIDER
## VINAIGRETTE

### SERVES 4

### RAW SALAD

160G/5½OZ (2 CUPS) SHREDDED RED CABBAGE

160G/5½OZ (2 CUPS) SHREDDED CHINESE WHITE CABBAGE

¼ RED ONION, SLICED LENGTHWISE

1 ZUCCHINI (COURGETTE), CUT INTO SPAGHETTI ON A TURNING SLICER OR CUT JULIENNE

240G/8½OZ PEELED BUTTERNUT PUMPKIN, PEELED, CUT INTO SPAGHETTI ON A TURNING SLICER OR CUT JULIENNE

7.5G/¼OZ (½ CUP) FLAT-LEAF PARSLEY LEAVES

2 BABY GEM LETTUCE, BASE REMOVED AND CUT INTO 3CM/1¼ INCH LENGTHS

½ TELEGRAPH CUCUMBER, CUT IN HALF LENGTHWISE, SEEDED AND SLICED

4 LARGE CHERRY TOMATOES, SLICED

4 STEMS BROCCOLINI, TRIMMED, BASE PEELED

1 AVOCADO, PEELED, STONED AND QUARTERED

½ LARGE BEETROOT, PEELED, CUT INTO SPAGHETTI ON A TURNING SLICER OR CUT JULIENNE

### TO SERVE

4 LARGE BUTTON MUSHROOMS, PEELED AND THINLY SLICED

30G/1½OZ (1 CUP) ALFALFA SPROUTS

2 TABLESPOONS HEMP SEEDS OR CHIA SEEDS

250ML (1 CUP) RAINBOW SLAW DRESSING (SEE BASICS PAGE 278)

For the raw salad, mix the cabbages and onion in a bowl. In another bowl, mix the zucchini, pumpkin and parsley. Divide the lettuce among 4 bowls and cover with the cabbage mixture and then the pumpkin and zucchini mix. Top with a layer of the cucumber, tomatoes, broccolini and avocado, then finish with a tangle of beetroot.

To serve, scatter over the sliced mushrooms, alfalfa sprouts and hemp seeds, placing the rainbow slaw dressing on the side.

"At COMO Shambhala Estate and COMO Uma in Ubud, sourcing locally is a joy. Family farms, carefully cultivated for generations, produce exceptional rice, nuts, fruit, vegetables, spices and coffee." CHRISTINA ONG

*This salad exemplifies how good fresh food really can be. Indonesian Tempeh is a great source of protein, and is featured regularly on our menus in Bali.*

Vitamin-Rich | Mineral-Rich | Antioxidant-Rich | High-Protein | Immune-Boosting | Digestive Support | Rejuvenating | Energising | Vegan

# GADO-GADO
# WITH CASHEW DRESSING
# AND
# CRISPY TEMPEH

**SERVES 4**

### CRISPY TEMPEH
240G/8½OZ PIECE TEMPEH
1½ TABLESPOONS SWEET SOY
½ TEASPOON RAW APPLE CIDER VINEGAR
½ TEASPOON TAMARI SOY

### RAW CASHEW DRESSING
150G/5OZ (1 CUP) RAW CASHEWS
2 TABLESPOONS TAMARI SOY
2½ TABLESPOONS BROWN SUGAR
1 TABLESPOON SUNFLOWER OIL

### SALAD
4 STEMS BROCCOLINI TRIMMED INTO SMALL FLORETS, STEMS CUT INTO 2CM/¾ INCH LENGTHS
4 BABY CARROTS, PEELED AND THINLY SLICED
5CM/2 INCH PIECE DAIKON, PEELED AND THINLY SLICED
4 SNAKE BEANS OR LONG GREEN BEANS, CUT INTO 2CM/¾ INCH LENGTHS
½ ZUCCHINI (COURGETTE), CUT IN HALF LENGTHWISE AND SLICED
12 SUGAR SNAP PEAS, ENDS TRIMMED
½ TELEGRAPH CUCUMBER CUT IN HALF LENGTHWISE, SEEDED AND SLICED
65G/2½OZ (¼ CUP) SPICED CASHEWS (SEE BASICS PAGE 293)
¼ JICAMA, PEELED AND CUT INTO SMALL WEDGES (OR HEART OF PALM)
2 CHINESE CABBAGE LEAVES, THINLY SLICED CROSSWISE
¼ SMALL RED ONION, SLICED LENGTHWISE
2 KAFFIR LIME LEAVES, THINLY SLICED

### TO SERVE
BANANA LEAVES (OPTIONAL)
4 SPRING ONIONS (SCALLIONS), CUT JULIENNE
40G/1½OZ (½ CUP) BEAN SPROUTS
4G/⅛OZ (¼ CUP) CORIANDER (CILANTRO) LEAVES

To make the crispy tempeh, cut the block of tempeh in half lengthwise, then cut this into 5mm/¼ inch thick slices. Combine the sweet soy, cider vinegar and tamari in a large bowl. Add the sliced tempeh and toss to coat in the sauces. Place the tempeh on a Teflex or non-stick sheet and dry in a dehydrator at 48°C/118°F for 3 hours, then turn over and dry for a further 2 hours. Remove from the dehydrator, cool and store in an airtight container for 3 days.

To make the cashew dressing, place the cashews in a bowl, cover with water and soak for 2 hours before draining and rinsing. Place the cashews and the remaining ingredients, except the sunflower oil, in a blender. Add 60ml (¼ cup) water and blend to a fine purée. With the motor running, gradually add the oil and blend until combined. If necessary, add more water to thin the dressing.

To make the salad, place the broccolini, carrots, daikon, beans, zucchini and sugar snap peas in a bowl. Cover with boiling water and stand for 2 minutes. Drain and refresh the ingredients in iced water. Combine the remaining ingredients in a bowl, add the drained blanched vegetables and toss well.

To serve, mix the salad with 180ml (¾ cup) of the cashew dressing and tempeh. Divide the dressed salad among banana leaf-topped plates and scatter with the spring onions, bean sprouts and coriander leaves.

**Note:** Omit the tempeh if you cannot find it. Add some more spiced cashews for crunch. This dressing also works well with vegetable crudités, or can be used in place of peanut butter on toast or crackers.

# Vegetables

CHAPTER 4

Vegetables form the heart of COMO Shambhala Cuisine. In this chapter you'll find a large number of crowd-pleasers, including a healthy dose of COMO Shambhala's much-loved raw recipes. The preparations are well worth the effort, even when they include a dehydrating process. On that point: a dehydrator is a really good investment for any home cook. It has endless uses, including making healthy homemade snacks: root vegetable and kale chips, dehydrated fresh fruits and nut mixes, and fruit leathers. With nuts, however, you must soak, then chop or blend before you start the dehydrating process. Soaking unlocks enzyme inhibitors and releases the nutritional benefits (these benefits, however, are mitigated if you dehydrate at a temperature higher than 46°C/115°F).

Many of these recipes can be part-prepared in advance. This includes the vegetable and maki rolls (pages 110–115), which make a great addition to a small buffet lunch or dinner. They also work well as canapés. The curry bases also hold well, and can be made a day in advance. You can use any vegetables you like for these recipes; just choose what's in season, putting together combinations that marry well in terms of texture and flavour. The 7-grain vegetable burgers (page 131) freeze well. A few other notes: once the flaxseed crackers, pizza or flatbreads have been assembled, they are best served straightaway, as they tend to soften quickly once they are dressed and garnished.

There are couple of recipes in this chapter that contain tempeh. If it's hard to come by, then substitute with a firm organic tofu. You can also use a protein such as chicken or fish.

*The best thing about these rolls is that they can be made in advance – they make great canapés or substantial appetisers. You will need a bamboo sushi mat for this recipe. Use gluten-free tamari soy if you are avoiding gluten in your diet.*

Vitamin-Rich | Mineral-Rich | Antioxidant-Rich | High-Protein | Immune-Boosting | Digestive Support
Smart Carbohydrate | Cleansing | Rejuvenating | Energising | Raw | Gluten-Free | Vegan

# JICAMA, MARINATED SHIITAKE AND AVOCADO SUMMER ROLLS WITH TAMARI AND ORANGE DIPPING SAUCE

### SERVES 6

### TAMARI AND ORANGE DIPPING SAUCE

60ML (¼ CUP) FRESHLY SQUEEZED ORANGE JUICE, STRAINED

60ML (¼ CUP) TAMARI SOY

60ML (¼ CUP) RAW APPLE CIDER VINEGAR

I TEASPOON SESAME OIL

¼ TEASPOON GINGER, FINELY GRATED

### JICAMA 'RICE'

230G/8OZ (1½ CUPS) PINE NUTS

690G/1LB 8OZ (6 CUPS) JICAMA OR YAM BEAN, PEELED, SLICED AND FINELY CHOPPED TO RESEMBLE A GRAIN OF RICE

### SUMMER ROLLS

6 LARGE RICE PAPER WRAPPERS

6 SHEETS TOASTED SEAWEED (YAKI NORI)

20G/¾OZ (1 CUP) MIZUNA, TRIMMED (OR ROCKET/ARUGULA)

I AVOCADO, PEELED, STONED AND CUT INTO 1CM/½ INCH WEDGES

I LEBANESE OR ENGLISH CUCUMBER, ENDS TRIMMED, HALVED AND CUT JULIENNE

I RECIPE MARINATED SHIITAKES, SLICED (SEE BASICS PAGE 275)

80G/3OZ (1¼ CUPS) ENOKI MUSHROOM, BASES REMOVED AND BROKEN INTO BRANCHES

50G/2OZ (½ CUP) SNOW PEA (MANGETOUT) SPROUTS (OR SUNFLOWER SPROUTS)

### TO SERVE

4 SPRING ONIONS (SCALLIONS), CUT JULIENNE

For the tamari and orange dipping sauce, place all the ingredients in a bowl and combine.

To make the jicama 'rice', pound the pine nuts in a mortar with a pestle until a paste forms. Add the pine nut paste to the chopped jicama along with 2 tablespoons of the tamari and orange dipping sauce. Mix well.

To make the summer rolls, soak a rice paper wrapper in warm water for 10 to 20 seconds until softened and pliable. Place the rice wrapper on a bamboo sushi mat, then top with a sheet of nori, shiny-side down. Spread 250ml (1 cup) of the jicama mix over the lower half of the nori sheet. Top with 3 mizuna leaves, 3 slices of avocado, 3 to 4 pieces of cucumber, 6 slices of shiitake mushroom, a scattering of enoki mushrooms and finish with a few snow pea sprouts. Carefully roll up into a firm roll, using the sushi mat as a guide.

To serve, cut each summer roll into 6 round slices just before serving. Scatter with sliced spring onions and serve with the tamari and orange dipping sauce on the side.

# SPICED GREEN PAPAYA, MIXED NUT AND VEGGIE ROLLS WITH TAMARIND AND LEMONGRASS DIPPING SAUCE

**SERVES 4**

*This is another great raw food snack or appetiser, with the unique Thai flavour from the fresh herbs and spices. You will need a bamboo sushi mat to make this recipe. If you are avoiding gluten in your diet, use gluten-free Tamari soy.*

Vitamin-Rich | Mineral-Rich | Antioxidant-Rich | High-Protein | Rejuvenating | Energising | Raw | Gluten-Free

### PAPAYA AND MIXED NUT FILLING

40G/1½OZ (½ CUP) FLAKED ALMONDS

70G/2½OZ (½ CUP) RAW MACADAMIA NUTS

100G/3½OZ (1 CUP) GREEN PAPAYA, CHOPPED

2 TABLESPOONS FRESHLY SQUEEZED LEMON JUICE

20G/¾OZ (1 CUP) THAI BASIL LEAVES, CHOPPED

7.5G/¼OZ (½ CUP) CORIANDER (CILANTRO) LEAVES, CHOPPED

¼ RED ONION, FINELY DICED

2CM/¾ INCH PIECE GINGER, PEELED AND FINELY CHOPPED

½ TEASPOON TAMARI SOY

2 TEASPOONS RAW HONEY

2 PINCHES CAYENNE PEPPER

SEA SALT AND GROUND WHITE PEPPER, TO TASTE

### TAMARIND AND LEMONGRASS DIPPING SAUCE

2 CORIANDER (CILANTRO) ROOTS, CLEANED, SCRAPED AND SLICED (OR 4 STEMS)

1 SMALL FRESH RED CHILLI, SLICED

1 CLOVE GARLIC, SLICED

SEA SALT, TO TASTE

3 STALKS LEMONGRASS, TOPS AND OUTER LAYERS REMOVED, FINELY CHOPPED

2 TABLESPOONS ORGANIC THAI PALM SUGAR (G)

80ML (⅓ CUP) TAMARI SOY

250ML (1 CUP) TAMARIND WATER (SEE BASICS PAGE 291)

2 TEASPOONS LIME JUICE

1 TABLESPOON CHOPPED CORIANDER (CILANTRO)

### VEGGIE ROLLS

2 TELEGRAPH CUCUMBERS

1 GREEN MANGO, PEELED AND CUT JULIENNE

¼ DAIKON, PEELED AND CUT JULIENNE

25G/1OZ (¼ CUP) SNOW PEA (MANGETOUT) SPROUTS (OR SUNFLOWER SPROUTS)

20G/¾OZ (1 CUP) THAI SWEET BASIL LEAVES

16 CORIANDER (CILANTRO) STEMS, EACH 8CM/3 INCHES LONG

1 LONG RED CHILLI, SPLIT LENGTHWISE, SEEDED AND CUT JULIENNE

### TO SERVE

4 BANANA LEAF SQUARES (OPTIONAL)

8 SPRIGS THAI SWEET BASIL

To make the papaya and nut filling, place the almonds and macadamia nuts in a bowl and cover with water. Soak the nuts for 2 hours, then drain and rinse. Place the nuts in a food processor with the remaining ingredients and mix until coarsely chopped. Season with sea salt and white pepper. Transfer the mixture to a bowl, cover and refrigerate until ready to use.

To make the tamarind and lemongrass dipping sauce, place the coriander root, chilli and garlic in a mortar, add a pinch of sea salt and pound with the pestle until a coarse paste forms. Add the lemongrass and pound lightly to bruise. Stir in the palm sugar, tamari, tamarind water and lime juice. Add the chopped coriander leaves just before serving.

For the veggie rolls, use a mandolin and slice the cucumbers lengthwise, leaving them 3mm/⅛ inch thick. For this recipe, you will need 32 strips of cucumber. Place 4 slices of cucumber on the bamboo sushi mat so they overlap each other, laying them lengthwise away from you.

Spread 4 tablespoons (¼ cup) of the papaya and the nut filling over the lower half of the cucumber strips. Place a quarter of the mango, daikon, sprouts, basil, coriander stems and chilli over the nut filling. Using the sushi mat as a guide, roll the cucumber over the filling to form a firm cylinder. Repeat with the remaining cucumber, nut filling and vegetables.

To serve, place a banana leaf square, if using, on a serving plate, cut the cucumber rolls in half on the diagonal and place on the leaf. Scatter the plate with basil and serve the tamarind and lemongrass dipping sauce on the side.

*This recipe was devised for COMO Cocoa Island in the Maldives where Indian flavours reign. The filling is great to have on hand for a healthy snack; it keeps well in the fridge. These maki rolls are full of goodness— packed with nuts, seeds and cauliflower. Use gluten-free liquid aminos or Tamari soy if you're avoiding gluten.*

Vitamin-Rich | Mineral-Rich | Antioxidant-Rich | Heart Healthy | Rejuvenating | Raw | Gluten-Free

### SPICED NUT FILLING

45G/1¾OZ (½ CUP) WALNUT HALVES

80G/3OZ (1 CUP) FLAKED ALMONDS

45G/1⅔OZ (¼ CUP) PUMPKIN SEEDS

35G/1½OZ (¼ CUP) SUNFLOWER SEEDS

75G/3OZ (½ CUP) RAISINS, SOAKED IN A CUP OF EARL GREY TEA

2 SMALL RED SHALLOTS, FINELY CHOPPED

1 CLOVE GARLIC, FINELY CHOPPED

3CM/1¼ INCH PIECE GINGER, PEELED AND FINELY GRATED

2 TABLESPOONS LIQUID AMINOS OR TAMARI SOY (G)

2 TEASPOONS CURRY POWDER

1 TABLESPOON COCONUT NECTAR OR AGAVE NECTAR (G)

5G/¼OZ (¼ CUP) MINT LEAVES, CHOPPED

4G/⅛OZ (¼ CUP) CORIANDER LEAVES (CILANTRO), CHOPPED

150G/5OZ (1 CUP) CAULIFLOWER FLORETS, CHOPPED

### TAMARIND DIPPING SAUCE

180ML (¾ CUP) TAMARIND WATER (SEE BASICS PAGE 291)

110G/4OZ (⅓ CUP) RAW HONEY

2 TABLESPOONS RAW APPLE CIDER VINEGAR

1CM/½ INCH PIECE GINGER, PEELED AND GRATED

¾ TEASPOON RED CHILLI FLAKES

½ TEASPOON CHAAT MASALA (SEE BASICS PAGE 285)

SEA SALT, OR TO TASTE

### VEGETABLE MAKI ROLLS

4 TOASTED SEAWEED SHEETS (YAKI NORI)

½ RIPE MANGO, PEELED AND CUT JULIENNE

1 TELEGRAPH CUCUMBER, SEEDED AND CUT JULIENNE

½ AVOCADO, PEELED AND SLICED 8MM/⅓ INCH THICK

100G/3½OZ (1 CUP) SUNFLOWER SEED SPROUTS

12 SNOW PEA (MANGETOUT) TENDRILS

12 FLOWERING GARLIC CHIVES

12 CORIANDER (CILANTRO) STEMS

10G/⅓OZ (½ CUP) MINT LEAVES

### TO SERVE

BAMBOO LEAF OR BANANA LEAF SQUARES

8 SPRIGS MINT

To make the spiced nut filling, place the walnuts, almonds, pumpkin and sunflower seeds in a bowl, cover with water and soak for 2 hours before draining and rinsing. Transfer to a blender, add the remaining ingredients and mix until coarsely chopped.

For the tamarind dipping sauce, put all of the ingredients in a blender, add a pinch of salt and blend until combined. Check the seasoning and adjust as necessary.

To make the vegetable maki rolls, place a nori sheet lengthwise, shiny-side down, across a sushi mat. Spread 4 tablespoons (¼ cup) of the nut mix over two-thirds of the sheet, leaving the final third at the far end. Layer one-quarter of the mango, cucumber, avocado, sprouts and herbs (3 stems of coriander per roll) to form an even cylinder shape on the first third of the nut mix. Starting with the edge closest to you, roll the mat away from you, pressing gently but tightly around to form a cylinder.

To serve, cut the vegetable maki rolls into 6 pieces and arrange on a serving plate lined with a banana leaf square. Serve the tamarind dipping sauce in a small bowl on the side and garnish with a mint sprig.

*These crackers are full of goodness. The flaxseeds are loaded with essential fatty acids, calcium and potassium to help eliminate toxic waste in the bowel (you must balance this by drinking plenty of water). Use gluten-free liquid aminos or tamari soy if you are avoiding gluten in your diet.*

Vitamin-Rich | Mineral-Rich | Antioxidant-Rich | High-Protein | Immune-Boosting | Digestive Support
Smart Carbohydrate | Cleansing | Rejuvenating | Energising | Raw | Gluten-Free | Vegan

# FLAXSEED CRACKER 'CLUB' WITH AVOCADO CRUSH, DRIED TOMATOES AND SPROUTS

**SERVES 4**

### FLAXSEED CRACKERS

150G/5OZ (1 CUP) FLAXSEEDS
140G/5OZ (1 CUP) PUMPKIN SEEDS
140G/5OZ (1 CUP) SUNFLOWER SEEDS
2 TABLESPOONS SESAME SEEDS
60ML (¼ CUP) LIQUID AMINOS OR TAMARI SOY (G)
4 CLOVES GARLIC, CHOPPED
1 RED BELL PEPPER (CAPSICUM), FINELY DICED
1 GREEN BELL PEPPER (CAPSICUM), FINELY DICED
1 LEEK, WHITE PART ONLY, FINELY DICED
4G/⅛OZ (¼ CUP) CORIANDER (CILANTRO) LEAVES, CHOPPED
4G/⅛OZ (¼ CUP) FLAT-LEAF PARSLEY LEAVES, CHOPPED
2 TEASPOONS GROUND CUMIN
1 TEASPOON CHILLI POWDER
2 TEASPOONS CURRY POWDER
SEA SALT, TO TASTE

### TO SERVE

250ML (1 CUP) AVOCADO CRUSH (SEE BASICS PAGE 270)
24 SUN-DRIED TOMATOES, SOAKED IN WARM WATER FOR 20 MINUTES, THEN DRAINED
8G/½OZ (¼ CUP) ALFALFA SPROUTS
1 LEBANESE OR ENGLISH CUCUMBER, CUT INTO SPAGHETTI USING A TURNING SLICER OR CUT JULIENNE
17G/⅔OZ (½ CUP) WATERCRESS LEAVES
½ RECIPE RAINBOW SLAW (SEE BASICS PAGE 276)

To make the flaxseed crackers, combine the flaxseeds, pumpkin, sunflower and sesame seeds in a bowl, cover with water and soak for 2 hours. Drain and rinse the seeds, and transfer them to a bowl. Add the remaining ingredients, season with sea salt and mix well. Transfer half of the mixture to a food processor and combine until smooth. Add the processed mixture to the whole seed mixture and stir well. Check the seasoning and adjust as necessary.

Spread the mixture 5mm/¼ inch thick on Teflex or non-stick sheet on dehydrator trays. Using a sharp knife or pizza cutter, cut the mixture into 7x15cm rectangles (2¾x6 inch) – this makes it easier to break into crackers after drying. Dehydrate on 48°C/118°F for 6 to 8 hours. Turn the cracker sheets over and dry for a further 60 minutes, or until crisp. Remove from the dehydrator and cool slightly. Alternatively, dry in an oven heated on its lowest setting. Break the cracker sheets into individual crackers. Crackers can be stored in an airtight container for up to 10 days.

To serve, place 8 flaxseed crackers on a work surface and spread 1 heaped tablespoon of avocado crush evenly over each cracker. Top each cracker with 3 sun-dried tomatoes, followed by alfalfa sprouts and cucumber and watercress. Stack the crackers on top of each other, laying a plain cracker on top to create a 'club sandwich'. Serve the dressed rainbow slaw on the side.

*This is another great raw food recipe – and a healthy alternative to the regular fat-laden pizza. Close your eyes and you'll think you're eating the real thing. The flavours are spot-on. Use gluten-free Tamari soy or liquid aminos if you are avoiding gluten in your diet.*

Vitamin-Rich | Mineral-Rich | Antioxidant-Rich | High-Protein | Immune-Boosting
Digestive Support | Rejuvenating | Energising | Raw | Gluten-Free | Vegan

# BUTTERNUT PUMPKIN AND MACADAMIA NUT PIZZA WITH TOMATO, AVOCADO, MANGO AND BASIL

**SERVES 4**

### PIZZA BASE

135G/4¾OZ (1 CUP) RAW MACADAMIA NUTS
130G/4½OZ (¾ CUP) SUNFLOWER SEEDS
25G/1OZ (¼ CUP) FLAXSEED MEAL
130G/4½OZ (¾ CUP) ALMOND MEAL (FLOUR)
240G/8½OZ (2¼ CUP) BUTTERNUT PUMPKIN, PEELED AND GRATED
7.5G/¼OZ (½ CUP) FLAT-LEAF PARSLEY, CHOPPED
10G/⅓OZ (½ CUPS) BASIL LEAVES, CHOPPED
2 TABLESPOONS CHOPPED OREGANO
2 TABLESPOONS COCONUT NECTAR OR AGAVE NECTAR (G)
SEA SALT, TO TASTE
1 TABLESPOON LIQUID AMINOS OR TAMARI SOY (G)

### PINE NUT 'CHEESE'

310G/11OZ (2 CUPS) PINE NUTS
60ML (¼ CUP) LEMON JUICE
SEA SALT, TO TASTE

### TO SERVE

500ML (2 CUPS) RAW TOMATO SAUCE (SEE BASICS PAGE 276)
4 CARROTS, GRATED
1 RIPE TOMATO, CUT IN HALF LENGTHWISE, THEN THINLY SLICED CROSSWISE
¼ PEELED PINEAPPLE, CORE REMOVED, AND THINLY SLICED CROSSWISE
½ AVOCADO, PEELED AND SLICED CROSSWISE
½ RIPE MANGO, PEELED AND THINLY SLICED LENGTHWISE
12 LARGE BASIL LEAVES, TORN
30G/1½OZ (1 CUP) ALFALFA SPROUTS
70G/2½OZ (2 CUPS) WATERCRESS LEAVES
2 TABLESPOONS LEMON DRESSING (SEE BASICS PAGE 278)

For the pizza base, place the macadamias, sunflower seeds and flaxseed meal in a bowl, cover with water and soak for 2 hours, then drain and rinse. Transfer to a food processor with the almond meal and the chopped pumpkin and mix until smooth. Transfer the mixture to a bowl and stir in the herbs, nectar, sea salt and liquid aminos. Place an 18cm/7 inch ring mould on a Teflex or non-stick sheet on a dehydrator shelf, put 180g (¾ cup) of the nut mixture into the mould and smooth over the surface (it should be 3mm/⅛ inch thick). Remove the ring mould and repeat with the remaining mixture to make 4 bases. Place in the dehydrator at 48°C/118°F for 6 hours, then turn over and dehydrate for another 6 hours. Remove and cool, then store in an airtight container for up to a week.

To make the pine nut 'cheese', place the pine nuts in a bowl, cover with water and soak for 1 hour. Drain and rinse the pine nuts before blending with the lemon juice and sea salt until smooth. With the motor running, gradually add approximately 125ml (½ cup) water until the texture is fluffy. Transfer to a squeeze bottle ready for use.

To serve, spread 125ml (½ cup) raw tomato sauce over each pizza base and scatter the carrot evenly over the sauce. Cut each pizza base into 6 equal wedges. Starting from the outer edge of each pizza wedge, place a piece of tomato, slightly overlap with a piece of pineapple and then overlap this with a piece of avocado. Place a curled piece of mango on the pointy end of the wedge, scatter with basil and drizzle with the pine nut 'cheese'. Top with a little of the alfalfa sprouts. Dress the watercress with the lemon dressing and place on the pizza.

# ZUCCHINI AND CHIA SEED CRISPBREAD WITH CASHEW HUMMUS AND CAULIFLOWER SALAD

SERVES 4

*You'll never want to eat a store-bought crispbread again after tasting these. They include chia seeds, a relative newcomer to the superfood list and more easily digestible than flaxseeds. They also have a longer shelf life. Chia seeds are high in fibre and one of the richest plant-based sources of omega-3.*

Vitamin-Rich | Mineral-Rich | Antioxidant-Rich | High-Protein | Immune-Boosting | Digestive Support | Smart Carbohydrate | Cleansing

### ZUCCHINI AND CHIA SEED CRISPBREAD

125G/4½OZ (1¼ CUPS) WALNUTS

190G/6¾OZ (1¼ CUPS) RAW CASHEWS

3 LARGE ZUCCHINI (COURGETTE), QUARTERED LENGTHWISE AND SLICED

50G/2OZ (½ CUP) FLAXSEED MEAL

1½ TABLESPOONS CHIA SEEDS

1 CLOVE GARLIC, FINELY CHOPPED

8G/⅛OZ (½ CUP) FLAT-LEAF PARSLEY, ROUGHLY CHOPPED

1 TABLESPOON GROUND CUMIN

SEA SALT, TO TASTE

### CASHEW HUMMUS

300G/10½OZ (2 CUPS) RAW CASHEWS

1½ TABLESPOONS LEMON JUICE

1 SMALL CLOVE GARLIC, FINELY CHOPPED

1½ TABLESPOONS RAW TAHINI

### CAULIFLOWER SALAD

125ML (½ CUP) LEMON DRESSING (SEE BASICS PAGE 278)

¼ TEASPOON SUMAC (OR LEMON ZEST)

½ TEASPOON GROUND CUMIN

8 CHERRY TOMATOES, SLICED

1 SMALL CUCUMBER, SLICED INTO ROUNDS

16G/½OZ (1 CUP) FLAT-LEAF PARSLEY, ROUGHLY CHOPPED

1½ TABLESPOONS CHOPPED MINT

1½ TABLESPOONS CHOPPED DILL

2 SPRING ONIONS (SCALLIONS), CUT INTO ROUNDS

¼ SMALL RED ONION, THINLY SLICED

90G/3OZ (1 CUP) CAULIFLOWER FLORETS

### TO SERVE

25G/1OZ (1 CUP) WILD ROCKET (ARUGULA) LEAVES

1 TABLESPOON LEMON DRESSING (SEE BASICS PAGE 278)

To make the crispbread, place the walnuts and cashews in a bowl and cover with water for 1 hour. Drain and rinse the nuts, then transfer them to a food processor with an 'S' blade. Using the pulse button, blitz until the nuts are the consistency of coarse breadcrumbs then transfer to a large bowl. Use the food processor to blitz the zucchini, using the pulse button until the zucchini is the same consistency as the nuts. Add the zucchini to the nuts before stirring in the remaining ingredients. Season with sea salt and mix well to combine.

Take 55g (⅓ cup) of the mixture and shape it into an 8mm thick, 6x12cm rectangle (2½x4¾ inch, ⅓ inch thick). Place the rectangle on a Teflex or non-stick sheet on a dehydrator tray. Repeat with the remaining mixture and dry at 48°C/118°F for 6 hours. Turn over and dry for a further 6 hours. Alternatively, dry in an oven heated on its lowest setting. Cool and store in an airtight container for up to a week.

For the cashew hummus, place the cashews in a bowl and cover with water for 2 hours. Drain and rinse, then transfer to a blender. Add the remaining ingredients and 100ml (scant ½ cup) water, season with sea salt and blend until smooth.

To make the cauliflower salad, whisk together the lemon dressing, sumac and cumin. Toss the remaining ingredients in a bowl to combine and dress just before serving.

To serve, place the crispbreads on a work surface and spread a heaped tablespoon of cashew hummus onto each one. Use a spoon to make a trough in the centre of the hummus. Spoon the cauliflower salad into the trough and place 2 crispbreads on each plate. Dress the rocket with the lemon dressing and divide evenly among the plates.

**Note:** If you end up making extra, the cashew hummus works well with vegetable crudités, while the cauliflower salad works well with grilled fish or chicken, or as a salad on its own.

# CRISPY SWEETCORN AND PUMPKIN TACOS WITH TOMATO AND PAPAYA SALSA, AVOCADO, YOUNG COCONUT CREAM AND 'SPICY BEANS'

**SERVES 6**

This recipe was developed for a yoga retreat at COMO Parrot Cay. It was originally plated similar to nachos (the taco shell recipe dehydrated in sheets and cut into triangles, and then layered with the salad components). It became an instant hit on our menus when one of our chefs decided to play around and make taco shells. So here you have it, with the spicy seeds and raw tomato sauce resembling chilli or pinto beans.

Vitamin-Rich | Mineral-Rich | Antioxidant-Rich | High-Protein | Immune-Boosting
Digestive Support | Rejuvenating | Energising | Raw | Gluten-Free | Vegan

### TACO SHELLS
2 CORN COBS, KERNELS REMOVED
150G/5OZ PUMPKIN, PEELED AND CHOPPED
1 LARGE YELLOW BELL PEPPER (CAPSICUM), SEEDED AND FINELY DICED
75G/3OZ (¾ CUP) FLAXSEED MEAL
7.5G/¼OZ (½ CUP) CORIANDER (CILANTRO) LEAVES, CHOPPED
1 TABLESPOON FRESHLY SQUEEZED LIME JUICE
1 TABLESPOON CHILLI POWDER
2 TEASPOONS GROUND CUMIN
SEA SALT, TO TASTE
18 WOODEN CYLINDRICAL MOULDS, 1½X10CM (¾X4 INCH)

### TOMATO AND PAPAYA SALSA
2 TOMATOES
170G/6OZ (1 CUP) RIPE RED PAPAYA, DICED
50ML (SCANT ¼ CUP OR 2 FL OZ) FRESHLY SQUEEZED LIME JUICE
2 TEASPOONS RAW APPLE CIDER VINEGAR
1 CLOVE GARLIC, FINELY CHOPPED
3 SPRING ONIONS (SCALLIONS), SLICED
¼ TEASPOON RED CHILLI FLAKES
4G/⅛OZ (¼ CUP) CORIANDER (CILANTRO) LEAVES, CHOPPED

### YOUNG COCONUT CREAM
75G/3OZ (½ CUP) CASHEWS
150G/5OZ (1 CUP) YOUNG COCONUT MEAT
60ML (¼ CUP) LEMON JUICE
2 TABLESPOONS RAW APPLE CIDER VINEGAR
1 TABLESPOON WHITE MISO PASTE

### TO SERVE
1 RECIPE SPICY SEED MIX (SEE BASICS PAGE 292)
250ML (1 CUP) RAW TOMATO SAUCE (SEE BASICS PAGE 276)
1 RECIPE AVOCADO CRUSH (SEE BASICS PAGE 270)
2 BABY GEM LETTUCE, CUT INTO 3CM/1¼ INCH LENGTHS AND BASES REMOVED
12 8CM/3 INCH SPRIGS CORIANDER (CILANTRO)

To make the taco shells, place the corn kernels, pumpkin and peppers in a food processor and mix until they are coarsely chopped. Transfer the mixture to a bowl. Add the remaining ingredients and mix well to combine. Place a 10cm/4 inch ring mould on a Teflex or non-stick sheet on a dehydrator tray. Spoon 1½ tablespoons of the mixture into the ring and spread evenly. Repeat with remaining mixture to make 18 tacos. Dehydrate on 48°C/118°F for 3½ hours then turn. At this stage, wrap each shell over the cylinder moulds to form the shape of a taco shell and return to the dehydrator, still on the moulds, for another 3½ hours, or until crisp. Remove each shell from the moulds, leave to cool and store in an airtight container for up to a week.

For the tomato and papaya salsa, cut the tomatoes into quarters and use a small knife to remove the seeds. Place the tomatoes in a sieve over a bowl. Using the back of a ladle, push the juice through a sieve and set it aside. Dice the flesh and place in another bowl. Add the remaining ingredients to this bowl, then mix in the tomato juice. Check the seasoning and adjust as necessary. Spoon into a serving bowl.

To make the young coconut cream, place the cashews in a bowl, cover with purified water and soak for 1 hour, then drain and rinse. Transfer the cashews to the blender, add the remaining ingredients and blend to a smooth purée. With the motor running, gradually add approximately 250ml (1 cup) purified water until the consistency is that of thick sour cream. Spoon into a serving bowl.

To serve, mix the spicy seed mix with the raw tomato sauce to make 'spicy beans' and place in a serving bowl. Spoon the avocado crush, cabbage and coriander sprigs into separate bowls. Place all the components in separate bowls or on a platter and place on the table.

*This nourishing and satisfying hotpot is simple to prepare. The soy seasoning keeps indefinitely, so make a batch and store in a cool, dark place.*

Vitamin-Rich | Mineral-Rich | Antioxidant-Rich | High-Protein | Digestive Support | Calming | Energising | Vegan

# HOTPOT OF VEGETABLES, SILKEN TOFU AND SOBA NOODLES WITH DULSE FLAKES

**SERVES 4**

### HOTPOT

100G/3½OZ SOBA NOODLES (ABOUT ½ PACKET)

¼ TEASPOON CANOLA (RAPESEED) OIL

1 LITRE (4 CUPS) DASHI STOCK (SEE BASICS PAGE 268)

8 SHIITAKE OR SHIMEJI MUSHROOMS, STEMS REMOVED AND CUT IN HALF ON AN ANGLE

100G/3½OZ (1 CUP) SHIMEJI MUSHROOMS, BASES TRIMMED AND BROKEN INTO PIECES

2 CHINESE CABBAGE LEAVES, DICED

50G/2OZ (½ CUP) PEELED BUTTERNUT PUMPKIN, CUT INTO SPAGHETTI ON THE TURNING SLICER OR CUT JULIENNE

45G/1⅔OZ (¼ CUP) SOAKED HIJIKI SEAWEED OR SEA SPAGHETTI (SEE BASICS PAGE 292)

45G/1⅔OZ (¼ CUP) SOAKED WAKAME SEAWEED (SEE BASICS PAGE 292)

4 STEMS BROCCOLI RABE, BROCCOLINI OR MUSTARD GREENS, BASE TRIMMED AND CUT INTO SMALL PIECES

1 BOK CHOY, BASE REMOVED, LEAVES SEPARATED AND CUT IN HALF LENGTHWISE

240G/8½OZ (2 CUPS) SILKEN TOFU, CUT INTO 2CM/¾ INCH CUBES

40G/1½OZ (⅔ CUP) ENOKI MUSHROOMS, BASES REMOVED AND BROKEN INTO BRANCHES (OR OYSTER MUSHROOMS CUT INTO STRIPS)

### SOY SEASONING

2 TABLESPOONS MIRIN

160ML (⅔ CUP) TAMARI SOY

1½ TABLESPOONS RAW BROWN SUGAR

### TO SERVE

1½CM/¾ INCH PIECE GINGER, PEELED AND CUT JULIENNE

1 TABLESPOON SLICED SPRING ONION (SCALLION)

2 TEASPOONS DULSE FLAKES (G)

4G/⅛OZ (¼ CUP) CORIANDER (CILANTRO) LEAVES

To make the soy seasoning, pour the mirin and tamari into a saucepan. Very slowly bring this to the boil. When boiled, add the sugar and cook, stirring until dissolved, bringing almost back to the boil. Remove from the stove, cool and store in a bottle in a dark place.

For the hotpot, cook the soba noodles in boiling salted water for 3 to 4 minutes, or until tender, then drain and toss with a little canola oil. Meanwhile, heat the dashi stock in a saucepan over a medium to high heat. When the stock comes to the boil, reduce the heat to a simmer. Add the shiitake and shimeji mushrooms and cook for 3 minutes. Add soy seasoning to taste, then add the cabbage, pumpkin and seaweeds and cook for 2 minutes, or until the stock returns to the boil. Taste again, adding more soy seasoning if needed. Blanch the broccoli and bok choy separately in boiling salted water for 1 to 2 minutes; remove with a slotted spoon, then drain. Divide the warm noodles among 4 bowls, add the tofu, top with the broccolini and bok choy, then ladle the dashi stock and its mushrooms over the noodles. Place the enoki mushrooms in the middle of each bowl.

To serve, scatter ginger julienne, spring onions, dulse flakes and coriander leaves over the soup. Serve immediately.

# PAD THAI
## WITH BROWN RICE NOODLES, TOFU, CASHEWS, SPROUTS, CHILLI AND TAMARIND

**SERVES 4**

*The challenge was to create a healthy Pad Thai for COMO Metropolitan in Bangkok. The pickled daikon keeps well when refrigerated. Use gluten-free Tamari soy if you are avoiding gluten.*

Vitamin-Rich | Mineral-Rich | Antioxidant-Rich | High-Protein | Digestive Support
Smart Carbohydrate | Rejuvenating | Calming | Energising | Gluten-Free

## PICKLED DAIKON

½ MEDIUM DAIKON

½ TABLESPOON SEA SALT OR ROCK SALT

15G/½OZ (3½ TEASPOONS) ORGANIC BROWN SUGAR

45ML (3 TABLESPOONS) RAW APPLE CIDER VINEGAR

## PAD THAI PASTE

6 CLOVES GARLIC, SLICED

6 SHALLOTS, SLICED

6 CORIANDER (CILANTRO) ROOTS, WASHED, SCRAPED AND SLICED (OR 12 STEMS)

½ TEASPOON WHITE PEPPERCORNS

½ TEASPOON BLACK PEPPERCORNS

1 PINCH SEA SALT, OR TO TASTE

## PAD THAI SAUCE

75G/3OZ (¼ CUP) ORGANIC THAI PALM SUGAR (G)

50G/2OZ (¼ CUP) BROWN SUGAR

60ML (¼ CUP) TAMARIND WATER (SEE BASICS PAGE 291)

2½ TABLESPOONS TAMARI SOY

SEA SALT, TO TASTE

## PAD THAI NOODLES

25G/1OZ (½ CUP) GARLIC CHIVES, CUT INTO 3CM/1¼ INCH LENGTHS

4 SHALLOTS, CUT LENGTHWISE INTO 1CM/½ INCH WEDGES

40G/1½OZ (½ CUP) SUGAR SNAP PEAS, TRIMMED

1 BOK CHOY, BASE REMOVED, LEAVES SEPARATED AND CUT IN HALF LENGTHWISE

4 CHINESE CABBAGE LEAVES, CUT CROSSWISE 1CM/½ INCH THICK

80G/3OZ (1 CUP) BEAN SPROUTS

350G/12OZ BROWN RICE PAD THAI NOODLES, SOAKED IN WARM WATER FOR 15 MINUTES TO SOFTEN

250G/9OZ FIRM TOFU, CUT INTO 1CM/½ INCH CUBES

SEA SALT, TO TASTE

1 LIME, HALVED

½ TEASPOON RED CHILLI FLAKES, PLUS EXTRA TO SERVE

40G/1½OZ (¼ CUP) ROASTED CASHEWS, COARSELY GROUND

1½ TABLESPOONS CANOLA (SUNFLOWER) OIL

## TO SERVE

2 EGG CRÊPES, CUT JULIENNE (SEE BASICS PAGE 290)

40G/1½OZ (½ CUP) BEAN SPROUTS

7.5G/¼OZ (½ CUP) CORIANDER (CILANTRO) LEAVES

8 GARLIC CHIVES

2 LIMES, HALVED

To make the pickled daikon, peel the daikon and cut it into 1x5cm (½x2 inch) batons. Place the batons in a large bowl, add the salt and toss to combine. Transfer the daikon to a perforated tray or colander. Place another tray on top and weigh down with something heavy, such as cans. Leave to stand overnight in the fridge.

Combine the sugar and vinegar in a saucepan, cooking over a low heat to dissolve the sugar. Leave the mixture to cool. Rinse the daikon, then soak in water to leach the salt out for 10 minutes before draining. Transfer to a bowl, pour the vinegar mixture over the daikon and toss. Leave to stand for a minimum of an hour, or preferably overnight.

To make the Pad Thai paste, place all the ingredients in a mortar, add a pinch of sea salt and pound to a paste using the pestle.

For the Pad Thai sauce, place both sugars in a small saucepan and cover with 60ml (¼ cup) water. Cook over a low heat to dissolve. Increase the heat and simmer until the sugar is a light caramel colour. Add the tamarind water, tamari and ¼ teaspoon of sea salt and stir to combine.

To make the Pad Thai noodles, wok-fry a maximum of 2 portions at a time. Divide the garlic chives, shallots and Pad Thai paste between 2 bowls. Divide the sugar snap peas, pickled daikon, bok choy, cabbage and bean sprouts between 2 more bowls. Finally, divide the noodles and tofu between 2 more bowls. Set one bowl of each mixture aside. Have the Pad Thai sauce, sea salt, lime, red chilli flakes and ground cashews next to the stove.

Heat a wok, then add the canola oil. When the oil is almost smoking, add a bowl of the garlic chive mixture and stir-fry for a minute to release the flavours. Next, add a bowl of the vegetable mixture and ¼ teaspoon of the chilli flakes, frying for 2 to 3 minutes. Then add one bowl of noodle mix and half of the Pad Thai sauce, stirring until the sauce has reduced by three quarters. Season with the juice of half a lime and add 1½ tablespoons of the ground cashews. Check the seasoning and remove from the stove. Repeat with the remaining ingredients.

To serve, divide the noodles between bowls, top with the egg crêpes, sprouts, coriander leaves and chilli flakes. Place the garlic chives and lime halves on the side.

*This recipe is an easy-to-prepare light 'pasta' dish, with the quinoa noodles a great gluten-free alternative. They are high in protein and iron, and have a low glycaemic index (31), keeping you satiated for longer. At COMO Uma in Ubud, we also add diced raw yellowfin tuna at the end, tossing it through gently to keep it rare.*

Vitamin-Rich | Antioxidant-Rich | Digestive Support | Calming | Gluten-Free | Vegan

# QUINOA NOODLES WITH MARINATED HEIRLOOM TOMATOES, GARLIC, BLACK OLIVES AND ROCKET

### SERVES 4

**MARINATED HEIRLOOM TOMATOES**

4 HEIRLOOM TOMATOES

2 TEASPOONS COCONUT NECTAR
OR AGAVE NECTAR (G)

1 TABLESPOON LEMON JUICE

½ TABLESPOON RAW APPLE CIDER VINEGAR

4 CLOVES GARLIC, CHOPPED

SEA SALT AND GROUND WHITE PEPPER, TO TASTE

**QUINOA NOODLES**

200G/7OZ QUINOA NOODLES
(OR BROWN RICE PASTA)

2 TABLESPOONS EXTRA-VIRGIN OLIVE OIL

1 TABLESPOON SALTED CAPERS,
RINSED AND DRIED

1 TEASPOON RED CHILLI FLAKES

20 LIGURIAN OR OTHER BRINE-CURED
BLACK OLIVES, PITTED

5G/¼OZ (¼ CUP) BASIL LEAVES, TORN

1 RECIPE SEMI-DRIED CHERRY TOMATOES
(SEE BASICS PAGE 272)

12G/½OZ (½ CUP) WILD ROCKET
(ARUGULA) LEAVES

**TO SERVE**

5G/¼OZ (¼ CUP) BABY OR REGULAR BASIL LEAVES

5G/¼OZ (¼ CUP) WILD ROCKET
(ARUGULA) LEAVES

To make the marinated heirloom tomatoes, cut the tomatoes into quarters and remove the seeds with a paring knife, setting them aside. Dice the flesh into 2cm/¾ inch pieces. Push the seeds through a sieve and catch the juices in a bowl before discarding the seeds. Combine the tomato juice with the diced tomato, nectar, lemon juice, vinegar and the chopped garlic. Season to taste with a pinch of sea salt and a grind of white pepper. Stand for 30 minutes to allow the flavours to infuse.

To make the quinoa noodles, bring a saucepan of lightly salted water to the boil. Add the quinoa noodles and cook 'al dente' before draining.

Meanwhile, heat the extra-virgin olive oil in a frying pan, add the capers and cook until crisp. Add the chilli flakes and cook for 10 seconds. Next, add the marinated tomatoes, olives, basil, semi-dried tomatoes and noodles. Bring to the boil, check the seasoning and stir in the rocket.

To serve, divide the noodles among 4 warmed serving bowls, scatter with the basil and wild rocket and serve immediately.

This veggie burger appeared on the first COMO Shambhala menu at COMO Parrot Cay in 2000. If you wish to omit the burger buns, try iceberg lettuce cups to hold the filling instead.

Vitamin-Rich | Mineral-Rich | Antioxidant-Rich | High-Protein | Digestive Support | Smart Carbohydrate | Rejuvenating | Calming | Energising | Vegan

# 7-GRAIN VEGGIE BURGERS WITH AVOCADO, TOMATO SALSA AND SPROUTS

**SERVES 4**

### VEGGIE PATTIES

50G/2OZ (¼ CUP) PUY LENTILS

50G/2OZ (¼ CUP) RED RICE

50G/2OZ (¼ CUP) MOONG DHAL

50G/2OZ (¼ CUP) CHANNA DHAL

50G/2OZ (¼ CUP) WILD RICE

50G/2OZ (¼ CUP) QUINOA

50G/2OZ (¼ CUP) BARLEY

3 TABLESPOONS OLIVE OIL

2 ONIONS, FINELY DICED

2 CARROTS, DICED

4 STALKS CELERY, DICED

4 CLOVES GARLIC, CHOPPED

2 TEASPOONS FENNEL SEEDS

SEA SALT, TO TASTE

2 TABLESPOONS DIJON MUSTARD

2 TABLESPOONS MISO

2 TABLESPOONS LIQUID AMINOS OR TAMARI SOY (G)

2 TABLESPOONS CHOPPED OREGANO

40G/1½OZ (¾ CUP) 7-GRAIN OR WHOLEMEAL BREADCRUMBS

35G/1½OZ (⅓ CUP) FLAXSEED MEAL, PLUS EXTRA FOR DUSTING

### TOMATO SALSA

3 TOMATOES, SEEDED AND DICED (5MM/¼ INCH)

¼ RED PEPPER, SEEDED AND DICED (5MM/¼ INCH)

4 SPRING ONIONS (SCALLIONS), CUT INTO ROUNDS

1 TABLESPOON CORIANDER (CILANTRO) LEAVES, CHOPPED

1 TABLESPOON CHOPPED FLAT-LEAF PARSLEY LEAVES

1 CLOVE GARLIC, CHOPPED

¼ TEASPOON GROUND CUMIN

¼ TEASPOON TABASCO SAUCE

2 LIMES, JUICED

2 TABLESPOONS EXTRA-VIRGIN OLIVE OIL

### TO SERVE

4 BURGER BUNS, SPLIT IN HALF

125ML (½ CUP) AVOCADO CRUSH (SEE BASICS PAGE 270)

60G/2½OZ (2 CUPS) ALFALFA SPROUTS

½ RECIPE RAINBOW SLAW (SEE BASICS PAGE 276)

For the veggie patties, cook the Puy lentils, red rice, moong dhal, channa dhal, wild rice, quinoa and barley separately. Place each in a saucepan and cover with cold water. Bring to the boil then reduce the heat and simmer until tender. Drain and rinse (cooking time will vary for each grain – follow instructions on the packets).

Preheat the oven to 180°C/350°F. Heat 2 tablespoons of olive oil in a frying pan. When hot, add the onions, carrots, celery and garlic and cook over a low to medium heat for 5 minutes. Add the fennel seeds and sea salt to taste and cook for a further 3 to 5 minutes, or until the onions are soft. Add the mustard, miso and liquid aminos, followed by the cooked grains. Stir over a low heat for about 5 minutes, or until the mixture is dry.

Transfer the mixture to a bowl, add the oregano, breadcrumbs and flaxseed meal and mix to combine. Put 250g/9oz (1 cup) of the mixture into a blender, blending until a paste forms. Return the mixture to a bowl and mix well. Take 150g/5oz (½ cup) of the mixture and form it into a patty. Repeat for the rest of the mix, making 8 patties.

Dust 4 patties lightly with flaxseed meal. Heat a large non-stick frying pan, add 1 tablespoon of olive oil and cook the patties over a low to medium heat for 2 to 3 minutes on each side, or until both sides are golden brown. Transfer to a baking tray and heat in the oven for 5 to 8 minutes, or until warmed through. Remove and keep warm.

To make the tomato salsa, combine all of the ingredients in a bowl and allow to macerate for 20 minutes before serving.

To serve, lay the bun bases out on a work surface. Place a patty on each base and top with 1 heaped tablespoon of avocado crush and 1 heaped tablespoon of salsa, finishing with alfalfa sprouts. Replace the burger bun lid and serve with the dressed slaw on the side.

**Note:** Instead of cooking seven separate grains, you can use a 7-grain mix, using 320g/11oz (1¾ cups) and following packet instructions for cooking. The lentil patty recipe makes 8 patties; the extra patties freeze well for up to a month in an airtight container.

"At COMO Shambhala Estate, we use spices for their flavour and healing properties. When making curries, we temper the whole spices rather than using premixed powders. This requires just a little extra time, but produces a significant difference in taste." CHRISTINA ONG

# SOUR LENTIL, SWEET POTATO AND SPINACH CURRY WITH CHAPATI

**SERVES 4**

## WHOLEMEAL CHAPATI

475G/1LB 3OZ (3 CUPS) UNBLEACHED PLAIN (ALL-PURPOSE) FLOUR

30G/1OZ (¼ CUP) WHOLEMEAL FLOUR

15G/½OZ (3 TEASPOONS) SEA SALT

50G/2OZ (¼ CUP) SUGAR

15G/½OZ (1½ TABLESPOONS) DRIED YEAST

50G/2OZ (¼ CUP) MELTED GHEE (OR CLARIFIED BUTTER)

300ML (1¼ CUPS) SKIMMED MILK

## LENTIL CURRY

150G/5½OZ (¾ CUP) CHANNA DHAL

150G/5½OZ (¾ CUP) MOONG DHAL

1½ TABLESPOONS CANOLA (RAPESEED) OIL

1 TABLESPOON YELLOW MUSTARD SEEDS

85G/3OZ (¼ CUP) FRESH CURRY LEAVES

2 TEASPOONS CUMIN SEEDS

2 TEASPOONS CORIANDER SEEDS

1 SMALL BROWN ONION, THINLY SLICED

4 CLOVES GARLIC, CHOPPED

4CM/1½ INCH PIECE GINGER, PEELED AND CHOPPED

2 TEASPOONS GROUND TURMERIC

2 TEASPOONS GROUND CUMIN

1 TEASPOON GROUND CORIANDER

2 SMALL RED CHILLIES, SLICED

2 LONG GREEN CHILLIES, SLICED

2 VINE-RIPENED TOMATOES, CORE REMOVED, CUT IN HALF AND FINELY SLICED

1 SMALL ORANGE SWEET POTATO, PEELED AND CUT INTO 1CM/½ INCH ROUNDS

8 SMALL BABY CARROTS

125ML (½ CUP) FRESH COCONUT MILK (SEE BASICS PAGE 266)

60ML (¼ CUP) TAMARIND WATER (SEE BASICS PAGE 291)

4 SNAKE BEANS OR LONG GREEN BEANS, CUT INTO 6CM/2½ INCH LENGTHS

12 LARGE CHERRY TOMATOES, CUT IN HALF

12 LARGE ENGLISH SPINACH LEAVES, STEMS REMOVED

## TEMPERED SPICE OIL

60ML (¼ CUP) CANOLA (RAPESEED) OIL

2 SMALL DRIED CHILLIES

1 TEASPOON BLACK MUSTARD SEEDS

8 FRESH CURRY LEAVES

## SALAD

120G/4½OZ PEELED BUTTERNUT PUMPKIN, CUT INTO 7CM/2¾ INCH JULIENNE STRIPS

120G/4½OZ PEELED DAIKON, CUT INTO 7CM/2¾ INCH JULIENNE STRIPS

2 RED RADISHES, SLICED ON A MANDOLIN

1 LONG GREEN CHILLI, SLICED

1 SHALLOT, CUT IN HALF THEN SLICED

2 LIMES, JUICED

½ TEASPOON CHAAT MASALA (SEE BASICS PAGE 285)

## TO SERVE

2 CM/¾ INCH PIECE GINGER, PEELED AND CUT JULIENNE

1 LONG GREEN CHILLI, SLICED

2 TABLESPOONS CORIANDER (CILANTRO) LEAVES

To make the wholemeal chapati, mix the flours, salt, sugar and yeast together in a bowl and make a well in the centre. Pour the ghee and milk into the well. Using your hands, gradually mix the dry ingredients into the wet ingredients to form a soft dough. Turn the dough out onto a lightly floured work surface and knead for 15 minutes until smooth. Cover the dough with a damp cloth and rest for 1 hour. Portion the dough into 10 balls, each 85g/3oz. On a lightly floured surface, use a rolling pin to roll each ball into a 20cm/8 inch circle. Place the dough between sheets of floured baking paper and set aside. Just before serving, heat a heavy-based non-stick frying pan over a medium heat and brush with a little oil. Cook each chapati one at a time for 1 to 2 minutes on each side, or until light golden. Keep warm.

To make the lentil curry, wash the channa dhal and moong dhal separately until the water runs clear, then place in separate saucepans and cover with water. Bring each to the boil, then reduce the heat and simmer for 10 to 15 minutes, or until soft. When cooked, drain each dhal.

Heat the canola oil in a heavy-based saucepan over a medium heat. When hot, add the mustard seeds and cook until they stop popping. Add the curry leaves and whole spices and cook for 2 to 3 minutes, or until the curry leaves are transparent. Next, add the onion, garlic and ginger and cook, stirring occasionally for 8 to 10 minutes until soft. Add the ground spices and cook for a further minute. Add the chillies and tomatoes and cook until the tomatoes have softened, about 6 to 8 minutes. Add the dhals, sweet potato and carrot along with 1 litre (4 cups) water. Bring to a simmer and cook for 6 to 8 minutes, or until the sweet potato and carrot are almost tender. Add the coconut milk, tamarind water and snake beans and cook for 5 more minutes. Stir in the cherry tomatoes and spinach, warming through for up to 2 minutes. Check the seasoning and adjust as necessary.

For the tempered spice oil, heat the oil over a low heat. Add the dried chillies and cook until they start to blister but are not yet blackened. Add the mustard seeds and curry leaves and cook for 2 minutes, or until fragrant and the curry leaves are crisp and chillies darkened. Strain to stop the cooking process, reserving the strained spices. Let the oil cool for 10 to 15 minutes then add the strained spice mixture back into the oil. Stand for 10 minutes to allow the flavours to infuse.

For the salad, combine the pumpkin, daikon, radishes, chilli and shallot in a bowl. Whisk the juice of 2 limes and 3 tablespoons of the tempered spice oil with the chaat masala. Just before serving, pour the dressing over the salad and toss.

To serve, divide the curry among 4 warmed bowls. Scatter with the ginger julienne, chilli and coriander. Serve immediately with warm chapatis and salad on the side.

**Note:** Chapatis can abe bought ready-made to save you time.

# MOROCCAN-SPICED VEGETABLE AND TEMPEH CURRY WITH QUINOA, PRESERVED LEMON AND ALMONDS

**SERVES 4**

*This vegetarian curry works really well as a dinner party dish when paired with the Blood Orange, Artichoke and Broad Bean Salad on page 84. The curry base is deliciously fragrant from the dry spice mix, ginger and preserved lemon; it is also a light base because of the roast tomatoes and vegetable stock.*

Vitamin-Rich | Mineral-Rich | Antioxidant-Rich | High-Protein | Immune-Boosting
Digestive Support | Rejuvenating | Calming | Energising | Gluten-Free

## VEGETABLE AND TEMPEH CURRY

½ SMALL PUMPKIN, CUT INTO 8 WEDGES, 2CM/¾ INCH THICK

2 PARSNIPS, PEELED AND CUT INTO QUARTERS LENGTHWISE, CORE REMOVED

4 BABY CARROTS, PEELED

12 BABY BEANS, CUT IN HALF

15 VINE-RIPENED TOMATOES

5CM/2 INCH PIECE FRESH TURMERIC ROOT, PEELED AND SLICED (OR 1 TEASPOON GROUND TURMERIC)

4 CLOVES GARLIC, SLICED

3 LONG GREEN CHILLIES, SEEDED AND CHOPPED

3 SMALL RED CHILLIES, SLICED

2½ TABLESPOONS OLIVE OIL

2 BROWN ONIONS, FINELY DICED

4CM/1½ INCH PIECE GINGER, PEELED AND FINELY CHOPPED

SEA SALT, TO TASTE

1½ TABLESPOONS MOROCCAN SPICE MIX (SEE BASICS PAGE 280)

85G/3OZ (¼ CUP) RAW HONEY

½ PIECE PRESERVED LEMON, WASHED, PULP REMOVED AND CHOPPED (SEE BASICS PAGE 294)

300ML (1¼ CUPS) VEGETABLE STOCK (SEE BASICS PAGE 269)

240G/8½OZ TEMPEH, CUT INTO 12 CUBES (OR USE FIRM TOFU)

1 LARGE ROASTED RED BELL PEPPER (CAPSICUM), CUT INTO 1½CM/¾ INCH STRIPS (SEE BASICS PAGE 276)

2 TABLESPOONS ORANGE JUICE

1 TABLESPOON LEMON JUICE

## QUINOA WITH PRESERVED LEMONS AND ALMONDS

40G/1½OZ (¼ CUP) RAISINS, SOAKED IN A CUP OF EARL GREY TEA

1 TEASPOON OLIVE OIL

1 TEASPOON MOROCCAN SPICE MIX (SEE BASICS PAGE 280)

640G/1LB 7OZ (4 CUPS) COOKED QUINOA (SEE BASICS PAGE 286)

40G/1½OZ (¼ CUP) DRIED FIGS, DICED

8 SPRING ONIONS (SCALLIONS), THINLY SLICED

35G/1½OZ (¼ CUP) HAZELNUTS, ROASTED, PEELED AND ROUGHLY CHOPPED

20G/¾OZ (¼ CUP) FLAKED ALMONDS, ROASTED

40G/1½OZ (¼ CUP) PINE NUTS, ROASTED

2 TABLESPOONS CHOPPED PRESERVED LEMON (SEE BASICS PAGE 294)

## TO SERVE

40G/1½OZ (¼ CUP) GORDAL GREEN OLIVES, PITTED AND CUT JULIENNE (ALTERNATIVELY, OTHER FIRM, MEATY GREEN OLIVES CAN BE USED)

4G/⅛OZ (¼ CUP) CORIANDER (CILANTRO) LEAVES

20G/¾OZ (¼ CUP) FLAT-LEAF PARSLEY

For the vegetable and tempeh curry, preheat the oven to 160°C/320°F. Cook the pumpkin, parsnips, carrots and beans separately in boiling salted water until just tender. Drain, refresh and set aside. Core the tomatoes and place them in a roasting pan. Roast in the oven for about 45 minutes, or until very soft. Cool slightly, then peel.

Put the turmeric, sliced garlic and chopped chillies in a blender with 1 tablespoon of olive oil and mix into a smooth paste.

Heat the remaining olive oil in a large saucepan over a low to medium heat. When hot, add the onions, ginger and turmeric paste and season to taste with salt. Cook, stirring frequently, over a low heat for about 20 to 30 minutes, or until golden brown. Add the spice mix and cook, stirring, for 3 minutes, or until fragrant. Stir in the honey, preserved lemon and roast tomatoes and simmer over a low to medium heat for 15 to 20 minutes, or until the sauce has reduced and thickened. Pass the sauce through a mouli grater and return to a clean saucepan.

Add a little vegetable stock to the curry sauce if it is too thick. Bring to a simmer and add the tempeh. Cook for 5 minutes to allow the flavours to absorb. Next, add the blanched vegetables and roasted pepper, simmering for 3 to 4 minutes. Season with the orange and lemon juice, adjusting as necessary.

For the quinoa with preserved lemons and almonds, drain the soaked raisins. Heat the olive oil in a nonstick frying pan. When hot, add the spice mix and cook, stirring, for 10 seconds, then add the quinoa and remaining ingredients and sauté, stirring frequently over a medium heat until warmed through and the mixture is dry. Season to taste with salt. Cover and keep warm.

To serve, spoon the vegetable and tempeh curry into 4 bowls. Garnish with green olives, coriander leaves and parsley and serve the sautéed quinoa with preserved lemons and almonds separately in rice bowls.

In this Indonesian curry, the paste gets cooked for a long time, which gives it depth of flavour. Candlenuts are used to thicken the curry (you can use macadamia nuts as a substitute). Cassava leaves, which are widely used in Indonesian cooking, have a wonderful texture and retain a firmness after cooking. Serve with red rice.

Vitamin-Rich | Mineral-Rich | Antioxidant-Rich | High-Protein | Immune-Boosting | Digestive Support | Calming | Energising | Vegan

# FRAGRANT
# INDONESIAN CURRY
# WITH PUMPKIN, TEMPEH
# AND CASSAVA LEAF

**SERVES 4**

## CURRY PASTE

400G/14OZ (3½ CUPS) CANDLENUTS (G)

25G/1OZ CORIANDER SEEDS, TOASTED AND GROUND

2 TEASPOONS WHITE PEPPERCORNS, TOASTED AND GROUND

250G/9OZ (2½ CUPS) SHALLOTS, SLICED

150G/5OZ (1 CUP) GARLIC, SLICED, ABOUT 30 CLOVES

250G/9OZ (2 CUPS) LONG RED CHILLIES, SPLIT LENGTHWISE, SEEDED AND SLICED, ABOUT 20 CHILLIES

8 SMALL RED CHILLIES, SLICED

4CM/1½ INCH PIECE FRESH TURMERIC ROOT, PEELED AND SLICED

75G/3OZ PIECE KENCUR OR YOUNG GINGER, PEELED AND SLICED

4CM/1½ INCH PIECE GINGER, PEELED AND SLICED

100G/3½OZ PIECE GALANGAL, PEELED AND SLICED

SEA SALT, TO TASTE

## PUMPKIN, TEMPEH AND CASSAVA LEAF CURRY

100ML (SCANT ½ CUP) CANOLA (SUNFLOWER) OIL

40 (145G/5OZ) CASSAVA LEAVES (OR USE KALE OR COLLARD GREENS)

3 SALAM LEAVES (OR FRESH CURRY LEAVES)

8 KAFFIR LIME LEAVES, CUT JULIENNE

1.2 LITRES (5 CUPS) FRESH COCONUT MILK (SEE BASICS PAGE 266)

160G/5½OZ PEELED PUMPKIN, CUT INTO 8 WEDGES

2 APPLE EGGPLANTS (SMALL AUBERGINES), CUT INTO QUARTERS

240G/8½OZ BLOCK TEMPEH, CUT INTO BITE-SIZED PIECES

8 CHERRY TOMATOES, CUT IN HALF

1 TABLESPOON LIME JUICE

1 TABLESPOON ORGANIC SWEET SOY

SEA SALT, TO TASTE

## TO SERVE

35G/1½OZ (¼ CUP) YOUNG COCONUT MEAT, CUT JULIENNE

30G/1OZ (¼ CUP) PEELED PUMPKIN, CUT JULIENNE

1 LONG RED CHILLI SPLIT, SEEDED AND CUT JULIENNE

4G/⅛OZ (¼ CUP) CORIANDER (CILANTRO) LEAVES

To make the curry paste, preheat oven to 170°C/330°C. Place the candlenuts on a baking tray and roast for 3 to 5 minutes. Cool, then pound with a pestle and mortar. Transfer to a blender with the remaining ingredients and season to taste with the sea salt. Blend to a smooth paste, adding a little water if the mixture is too dry.

To make the pumpkin, tempeh and cassava leaf curry, cook the cassava leaves in boiling salted water for about 5 minutes, or until tender. Drain and refresh under cold running water.

Heat the oil in a large heavy-based saucepan. Add the curry paste, lime leaves and salam leaves and cook, stirring frequently, over a low heat for 45 minutes to an hour. Stir in the coconut milk and bring to a simmer. Add the pumpkin, eggplant and tempeh and simmer for 10 to 12 minutes, or until the vegetables are tender. Next, add the cassava leaves and cherry tomatoes and season with the lime juice and sweet soy. Bring to the boil then remove from the heat.

To serve, spoon the curry into a large serving bowl. Scatter with the ginger, coconut, pumpkin julienne, chilli and coriander leaves. Serve immediately.

# WOK-FRIED
## BRAISED TEMPEH WITH
## MUSHROOMS, ASPARAGUS AND
## THAI SWEET BASIL

**SERVES 4**

*It is important to impart flavour into Tempeh when it is used in a 'dry' dish without a sauce. Here, we braise the Tempeh first, softening and moistening it to reduce its chalkiness. The Thai sweet basil really makes this dish come alive. Use gluten-free liquid aminos or Tamari soy if you are avoiding gluten in your diet.*

Vitamin-Rich | Mineral-Rich | Antioxidant-Rich | High-Protein | Digestive Support | Calming | Energy | Gluten-Free | Vegan

### BRAISED TEMPEH

1 VINE-RIPENED TOMATO, CUT IN HALF AND SLICED

1 SHALLOT, SLICED

1 CLOVE GARLIC, SLICED

1CM/½ INCH PIECE GINGER, PEELED AND SLICED

500ML (2 CUPS) VEGETABLE STOCK (SEE BASICS PAGE 269)

480G/1LB 1OZ TEMPEH, CUT INTO BITE-SIZED TRIANGLES (OR FIRM TOFU)

### MUSHROOMS, ASPARAGUS AND THAI SWEET BASIL

3 CLOVES GARLIC, SLICED

1½CM/¾ INCH PIECE GINGER, PEELED AND SLICED

SEA SALT, TO TASTE

40ML (2½ TABLESPOONS) SUNFLOWER OIL

½ RED ONION, CUT INTO WEDGES

8 SHIITAKE MUSHROOMS, STEMS REMOVED AND CUT IN HALF ON THE ANGLE

8 OYSTER MUSHROOMS, STEMS TRIMMED AND BROKEN IN HALF

4 GREEN ASPARAGUS SPEARS, WOODY BASES TRIMMED, THEN CUT IN HALF ON THE ANGLE

2 LONG RED CHILLIES, SPLIT LENGTHWISE, SEEDED AND CUT IN HALF ON THE ANGLE

8 SPRING ONIONS (SCALLIONS), GREEN TOPS REMOVED AND CUT INTO 4CM/1½ INCH BATONS

1 BOK CHOY, BASE TRIMMED AND LEAVES SEPARATED

4 SMALL CHINESE CABBAGE LEAVES, CUT IN HALF LENGTHWISE AND EDGES TRIMMED TO POINTS

2 TABLESPOONS EVAPORATED COCONUT PALM SUGAR (OR ORGANIC BROWN SUGAR) (G)

2 TABLESPOONS LIQUID AMINOS OR TAMARI SOY (G)

125ML (½ CUP) VEGETABLE STOCK (SEE BASICS PAGE 269)

5G/¼OZ (¼ CUP) THAI SWEET BASIL LEAVES

4 DROPS (ABOUT ¼ TEASPOON) ORGANIC SESAME OIL

### TO SERVE

8 SPRING ONIONS (SCALLIONS), CUT JULIENNE

8 SPRIGS THAI BASIL

20G/¾OZ (¼ CUP) BEAN SPROUTS

GROUND WHITE PEPPER

To make the braised tempeh, combine the tomato, shallot, garlic, ginger and vegetable stock in a saucepan. Bring to the boil and add the tempeh. Reduce the heat to simmer and cook for 15 to 20 minutes, or until the liquid has reduced by three quarters. Remove the braised tempeh, discarding the tomato liquid and aromatics.

For the mushrooms, asparagus and Thai sweet basil, place the garlic, ginger and a pinch of salt in a mortar and pound to a paste using the pestle. Heat a wok over a medium heat and add the sunflower oil. When hot, add the garlic paste and onion and stir-fry for 1 minute, or until just turning golden. Add the mushrooms, asparagus and chillies and stir-fry for a further 2 minutes. Add the tempeh, spring onions, bok choy and cabbage, and stir-fry gently for 2 minutes, ensuring not to break the tempeh. Add the palm sugar and cook for a further 20 seconds to lightly caramelise. Add the liquid aminos and stock, gently frying until the liquid is reduced by half. Add the basil and sesame oil, then remove from the heat and serve.

To serve, divide the braised tempeh and mushroom mixture among 4 warmed bowls. Scatter with the spring onions, basil and bean sprouts, finishing with a grind of white pepper.

# Fish and Seafood

CHAPTER 5

COMO Shambhala Cuisine without fish and seafood would be like a house without foundations, with the role of the ocean in our kitchens much inspired by our locations. COMO's island properties – in the Caribbean, Thailand, Maldives and Indonesia – each bring a host of local flavours and techniques, while we also draw upon Middle Eastern and Japanese influences.

With fish and seafood, our chefs are militant about freshness. We buy live crayfish, crab and lobster, and just-caught for anything else. We always try to cook fish on the day of purchase, and rarely letting it go beyond 24 hours. For any raw seafood dishes, we use sashimi-grade quality, and with tuna, only the top end of the fish where there's less sinew. Indeed, if there's a tip on how to buy fish, then it's about trusting in your sense of smell (the naturally-occurring oils in fish tend to oxidise with time, giving off a whiff). You should also be able to see a glistening rainbow in the flesh when held to the light.

As to the fish available to you locally – use it confidently (while respecting the sustainability issues wherever you are in the world), replacing the specified fish in these recipes by choosing something similar in texture.

For anything raw, you can substitute whatever you like, being aware that oily fish has the most flavour due to its fat content.

Careful preparation pays off. A good fishmonger can clean, gut and scale a whole fish for you. Once home, be careful not to soak your seafood in water, or run it under a tap for long. The flesh can become waterlogged, like a sponge. And when it comes to the cooking, there's a trick to caramelising just the 'presentation side'. This is chef-speak, but it makes the dish so much more visually appealing, while also adding flavour. By keeping the other side underdone, you won't overcook the flesh, be it a scallop or fillet of salmon.

# SALMON TARTARE WITH POMEGRANATE DRESSING AND CUMIN-SCENTED YOGHURT

**SERVES 4**

*This Middle Eastern-flavoured tartare makes an elegant appetiser that's easy to prepare and assemble. Its inspiration is raw Kibbeh, a mezze dish that normally consists of spiced and seasoned hand-chopped lamb.*

Vitamin-Rich | Mineral-Rich | Antioxidant-Rich | High-Protein | Rejuvenating | Gluten-Free

## POMEGRANATE DRESSING

2 VERY RIPE VINE-RIPENED TOMATOES, DICED

1 TEASPOON POMEGRANATE MOLASSES

2 TABLESPOONS RAW RED WINE VINEGAR

1 TEASPOON LEMON JUICE

1 TABLESPOON AGAVE NECTAR (G)

SEA SALT AND GROUND WHITE PEPPER, TO TASTE

2 CLOVES GARLIC, SLICED

½ TEASPOON SUMAC (OR LEMON ZEST)

1 SMALL RED CHILLI, CHOPPED

2 SPRIGS THYME

60ML (¼ CUP) EXTRA-VIRGIN OLIVE OIL

## CUMIN-SCENTED YOGHURT

1 TEASPOON CUMIN SEEDS

2 CLOVES GARLIC, SLICED

SEA SALT, TO TASTE

125ML (½ CUP) LOW-FAT GREEK-STYLE YOGHURT

2 TEASPOONS FRESHLY SQUEEZED LEMON JUICE

## TARTARE FILLING

240G/8½OZ SASHIMI-GRADE SALMON, FINELY DICED

40G/1½OZ (¼ CUP) COOKED QUINOA (SEE BASICS PAGE 286)

4 SPRING ONIONS (SCALLIONS), SLICED

2 SHALLOTS, FINELY DICED

½ LEBANESE OR ENGLISH CUCUMBER, PEELED, CUT LENGTHWISE INTO QUARTERS, SEEDED AND VERY FINELY DICED

14G/½OZ (½ CUP) MIXED HERBS SUCH AS DILL, MINT AND PARSLEY LEAVES, ROUGHLY CHOPPED

## TO SERVE

4 RED CHERRY TOMATOES, CUT INTO QUARTERS AND SEEDED

1 RED RADISH, THINLY SLICED AND PLACED IN ICE WATER

9G/⅓OZ (¼ CUP) WATERCRESS LEAVES

5G/¼OZ (¼ CUP) BABY ROCKET (ARUGULA) LEAVES (OR REGULAR ROCKET)

1 TABLESPOON SUNFLOWER SEEDS

1 TABLESPOON POMEGRANATE SEEDS

For the pomegranate dressing, combine the diced tomatoes, pomegranate molasses, vinegar, lemon juice and agave nectar in a bowl. Season with sea salt, cover and marinate for 30 minutes to allow the flavours to develop. Using a sieve, strain into a bowl, pushing down on the solids with a ladle to extract all the liquid. Place the garlic, sumac, chilli and thyme in a mortar and pound with the pestle, then transfer to a bowl. Whisk in the tomato liquid and extra-virgin olive oil before seasoning with a grind of white pepper.

To make the cumin-scented yoghurt, dry-roast the cumin seeds in a frying pan over a medium heat for 2 to 3 minutes, or until fragrant. Transfer to a mortar and use the pestle to grind the seeds to a powder before transferring them to a bowl. Place the garlic with a little sea salt in the mortar and pound with the pestle before adding it to the cumin powder. Stir in the yoghurt and lemon juice, then cover and stand for 30 minutes in the fridge to allow the flavours to infuse. Push through a sieve and transfer to a container ready for use.

To make the tartare filling, combine all of the ingredients in a bowl, add 125ml (½ cup) of the pomegranate dressing and toss well. Keep it chilled (preferably over a bowl of ice) in order to retain all the healthy oils.

To serve, place a rectangular mould or an 8cm/3 inch ring mould in the centre of 4 plates. Spoon a quarter of the tartare mixture into each mould and press down gently with the back of a spoon. Lightly dress the tomatoes, radish, watercress and rocket with the pomegranate dressing and toss to combine. Arrange a quarter of the salad around each tartare and scatter over the sunflower and pomegranate seeds. Make a quenelle with a teaspoon of cumin yoghurt and place on each tartare. Remove the mould and serve immediately.

*While easy to prepare, ceviche relies heavily on the quality of ingredients. The fish needs to be firm and fresh, tomatoes ripe, and all the ingredients chilled before serving. For the home cook, ceviche is a good recipe to prepare well in advance, as it improves as it marinates.*

Vitamin-Rich | Mineral-Rich | Antioxidant-Rich | High-Protein | Rejuvenating | Raw | Gluten-Free

# CEVICHE OF SEA BASS WITH HEIRLOOM TOMATOES, PALM HEART AND SPICY TOMATO DRESSING

**SERVES 4**

### SPICY TOMATO DRESSING

3 VERY RIPE VINE-RIPENED TOMATOES, ROUGHLY CHOPPED

60ML (¼ CUP) LIME JUICE, STRAINED

1 TABLESPOON AGAVE NECTAR (G)

2 CORIANDER (CILANTRO) ROOTS, CLEANED, SCRAPED AND BRUISED (OR 4 STEMS)

2 CLOVES GARLIC, BRUISED

6 SHAKES OF TABASCO SAUCE

2 TABLESPOONS PASSIONFRUIT JUICE

60ML (¼ CUP) EXTRA-VIRGIN OLIVE OIL

SEA SALT, TO TASTE

### CEVICHE SALAD

240G/8½OZ SASHIMI-GRADE SEA BASS FILLET, DICED INTO 1½CM/¾ INCH PIECES

1 SMALL RED CHILLI, SLICED

1 HEIRLOOM RED OXHEART TOMATO, CUT INTO WEDGES

1 HEIRLOOM RED ZEBRA-STRIPED TOMATO, SLICED 1CM/½ INCH THICK

1 HEIRLOOM GREEN ZEBRA TOMATO, SLICED 1CM/½ INCH THICK

¼ RED ONION, THINLY SLICED

4 SPRING ONIONS (SCALLIONS), SLICED

½ RED BELL PEPPER (CAPSICUM), CUT JULIENNE

½ GREEN BELL PEPPER (CAPSICUM), CUT JULIENNE

### TO SERVE

1 BABY ROMAINE, LEAVES SEPARATED

4G/⅛OZ (¼ CUP) CORIANDER (CILANTRO) LEAVES

To make the spicy tomato dressing, combine all the ingredients, except the olive oil. Season with sea salt and leave to marinate for 30 minutes. Push the ingredients through a sieve, catching the liquid in a bowl (you need to collect about 300ml, or just over 1 cup, of juice). Gradually whisk in the olive oil.

For the ceviche salad, combine the diced fish, chilli and 125ml (½ cup) of the spicy tomato dressing in a bowl. Leave to marinate for 2 minutes. In a separate bowl, combine the tomatoes with the remaining ingredients and 125ml (½ cup) of the dressing. Drain the marinated sea bass lightly. Add the fish mixture to the tomato salad and toss gently.

To serve, place 2 lettuce leaves in each bowl, spoon half the ceviche among the bowls and top with the remaining lettuce and ceviche. Scatter with coriander leaves. Serve immediately.

"In Bangkok, where we have a COMO Metropolitan hotel in the buzzing South Sathorn neighbourhood, I like nothing more than getting lost in the markets, picking out herbs, spices and the local produce sold by the kilo." CHRISTINA ONG

The blue crab in Thailand is of exceptional quality. Hence there is almost always a crab salad on the menu at COMO Metropolitan in Bangkok. This version consists of sweet, sour and tropical fruits with a good amount of Asian herbs and fresh spice. The chilli-lime dressing is a very typical Thai dipping sauce generally served with boiled or steamed seafood and fish. Use gluten-free fish sauce if you are avoiding gluten in your diet.

Vitamin-Rich | Mineral-Rich | Antioxidant-Rich | High-Protein | Immune-Boosting | Rejuvenating | Gluten-Free

# CRAB, LONGAN AND GREEN MANGO SALAD WITH CASHEWS AND CHILLI-LIME DRESSING

**SERVES 4**

## CRAB SALAD

240G/8½OZ HAND-PICKED COOKED CRAB MEAT

2 GREEN MANGOES, PEELED, CHEEKS REMOVED AND CUT JULIENNE

2 SHALLOTS, THINLY SLICED

4 KAFFIR LIME LEAVES, VERY THINLY SLICED

¼ POMELO, BROKEN INTO SMALL SEGMENTS (OR 45G/1½OZ/¾ CUP NAVEL ORANGE OR GRAPEFRUIT SEGMENTS)

½ RIPE STARFRUIT (CARAMBOLA), CUT LENGTHWISE INTO LONG SLICES (OR 2.5CM/1 INCH SLICE GREEN MELON, SLICED LENGTHWISE)

1 GREEN GUAVA OR GREEN APPLE, PEELED AND CUT JULIENNE

½ ROSE APPLE, CORE REMOVED, CUT INTO SMALL WEDGES, IF AVAILABLE

12 LONGANS OR LYCHEES, PEELED, SEEDED AND CUT IN HALF

28G/1OZ (1 CUP) MIXED HERBS SUCH AS CORIANDER (CILANTRO), THAI BASIL AND MINT LEAVES

2 STALKS LEMONGRASS, TOPS AND OUTER LAYERS REMOVED, THINLY SLICED

## CHILLI-LIME DRESSING

2 CLOVES GARLIC, SLICED

2 CORIANDER (CILANTRO) ROOTS, CLEANED, SCRAPED AND SLICED (OR 4 STEMS)

SEA SALT, TO TASTE

2 SMALL HOT GREEN CHILLIES

2 SHALLOTS, SLICED

125ML (½ CUP) LIME JUICE, STRAINED

1 TABLESPOON ORGANIC THAI PALM SUGAR (G)

2 TABLESPOONS GOOD QUALITY FISH SAUCE

## TO SERVE

40G/1½OZ (¼ CUP) ROASTED CASHEWS, COARSELY CRUSHED

1 LONG RED CHILLI, SEEDED AND CUT JULIENNE

To make the chilli-lime dressing, place the garlic, coriander root and pinch of sea salt in a mortar and pound with the pestle to a paste. Add the shallots and bruise with the pestle, then stir in the lime juice and sugar until the sugar dissolves. Add the fish sauce and adjust the seasoning as necessary.

For the crab salad, place the crab meat in a bowl, dress with 2 tablespoons of the chilli-lime dressing and toss. Combine the remaining salad ingredients in another bowl and mix with the remaining dressing.

To serve, arrange the dressed salad down the centre of the plate and top with the crab. Scatter with crushed cashews and chilli then serve.

With sashimi, always try to use the top end of the fish, which slices more evenly. Serve extra dressing on the side – and revel in the freshness. Use gluten-free tamari soy if you are avoiding gluten in your diet.

Vitamin-Rich | Mineral-Rich | Antioxidant-Rich | High-Protein | Digestive Support | Smart Carbohydrate | Rejuvenating | Raw | Gluten-Free

# HIRAMASA KINGFISH SASHIMI WITH ORANGE, AVOCADO AND GINGER-TAMARI DRESSING

### SERVES 4

### GINGER-TAMARI DRESSING

2½ TABLESPOONS FRESHLY SQUEEZED ORANGE JUICE, STRAINED

2½ TABLESPOONS FRESHLY SQUEEZED LIME JUICE, STRAINED

125ML (½ CUP) RAW APPLE CIDER VINEGAR

60ML (¼ CUP) TAMARI SOY

¼ TEASPOON FINELY GRATED GINGER

¼ TEASPOON FINELY GRATED ORANGE ZEST

### SASHIMI

240G/8½OZ SASHIMI-GRADE HIRAMASA KINGFISH OR OTHER SASHIMI-GRADE FISH FILLET

### TO SERVE

1 BABY ROMAINE LETTUCE, LEAVES SEPARATED AND TRIMMED INTO POINTS

½ RIPE AVOCADO, CUT INTO QUARTERS, SLICED VERY FINE AND CURLED

1 ORANGE, PEELED AND SEGMENTED

1 SMALL GREEN CHILLI, SLICED

2 CM/¾ INCH PIECE YOUNG GINGER, PEELED AND CUT JULIENNE

12 FLOWERING GARLIC CHIVES, IF AVAILABLE

3 SPRIGS DILL LEAVES

1 RED RADISH, THINLY SLICED AND PLACED IN ICED WATER TO CRISP

2 TABLESPOONS SOAKED HIJIKI SEAWEED OR SEA SPAGHETTI (SEE BASICS PAGE 292)

1 TEASPOON TOASTED SESAME SEEDS

To make the ginger-tamari dressing, combine all the ingredients in a bowl, add 2½ tablespoons of water and stir to combine.

To make sashimi, cut the kingfish into 16 slices.

To serve, lay 4 slices of kingfish flat onto each plate. Place a lettuce leaf to the side of the fish and place an avocado curl on top. Place an orange segment inside each avocado curl followed by a chilli slice. Spoon over some of the dressing and garnish with the ginger, chives, if using, dill, radish and seaweed and finish with a sprinkle of sesame seeds.

*This salad was popular from the moment we put it on the menu at COMO Parrot Cay. Dulse is a 'sea superfood', with the iodine vital to maintain a healthy thyroid. Use gluten-free Tamari soy if you are avoiding gluten.*

Vitamin-Rich | Antioxidant-Rich | High-Protein | Gluten-Free

# RAW TUNA, RADISH AND SOYBEAN SALAD WITH JAPANESE-INSPIRED DRESSING

## SERVES 4

### JAPANESE-INSPIRED DRESSING

½ SMALL ONION, FINELY CHOPPED
SEA SALT, TO TASTE
60ML (¼ CUP) RAW APPLE CIDER VINEGAR
60ML (¼ CUP) TAMARI SOY
1 TEASPOON RED CHILLI FLAKES
1 TEASPOON DRY JAPANESE MUSTARD POWDER
OR HOT ENGLISH MUSTARD POWDER
2 TABLESPOONS AGAVE NECTAR (G)
60ML (¼ CUP) SUNFLOWER OIL
1 TABLESPOON SESAME OIL
½ TEASPOON FRESHLY GROUND BLACK PEPPER

### RAW TUNA, RADISH AND SOYBEAN SALAD

½ PEELED DAIKON
30G/1OZ (¼ CUP) FRESH OR
FROZEN EDAMAME BEANS
240G/8½OZ SASHIMI-GRADE TUNA, DICED
45G/1⅔OZ (½ CUP) SOAKED WAKAME SEAWEED
(SEE BASICS PAGE 292)
4 SPRING ONIONS (SCALLIONS), SLICED
1 LEBANESE OR ENGLISH CUCUMBER, CUT IN HALF
LENGTHWISE, SEEDED AND SLICED
6 SMALL CHINESE CABBAGE LEAVES, CUT IN HALF
LENGTHWISE AND TRIMMED INTO POINTS
1½CM/½ INCH PIECE YOUNG GINGER,
PEELED AND CUT JULIENNE
½ AVOCADO, CUT INTO QUARTERS,
PEELED THEN CUT INTO EIGHTHS

### TO SERVE

7G/¼OZ (¼ CUP) MICRO SHISO SPROUTS
(OR OTHER MICRO GREENS)
1 TEASPOON DULSE FLAKES (OPTIONAL) (G)
2 TEASPOONS BLACK SESAME SEEDS

For the Japanese-inspired dressing, place the onion in a bowl and season with sea salt. Leave to stand for 30 minutes, then rinse and drain. In another bowl, combine the drained onion, vinegar, tamari, chilli flakes and mustard. Whisk in the agave nectar, followed by the oils and black pepper. Set aside.

To make the tuna, radish and soybean salad, using a turning slicer, cut the daikon into spaghetti. Alternatively, julienne the daikon. Blanch the edamame in boiling water for 1 minute then drain and refresh in iced water. Pod and peel the beans.

Combine the diced tuna, drained seaweed, spring onions, cucumber, cabbage, edamame beans and ginger in a bowl. Add 2 tablespoons of the Japanese-inspired dressing and toss to combine.

To serve, place 2 pieces of cabbage in the centre of each plate and place a piece of avocado on top. Spoon over half of the raw tuna salad mixture then top with another piece of cabbage. Repeat with the avocado and remaining raw tuna salad. Garnish with the daikon, sprouts, dulse flakes, if using, and sesame seeds and finish with a drizzle of dressing.

**Note:** If you want a more substantial dish, this salad can also work well with chilled soba noodles; ensure that they are 100% buckwheat and certified gluten-free if you are following a gluten-free diet.

# GRILLED SEA SCALLOPS, PINEAPPLE AND WING BEAN SALAD WITH COCONUT-CHILLI DRESSING

**SERVES 4**

'Yum Tua Pu' or Wing Bean Salad, is a well-known salad from central Thailand. It has great depth of flavour from the roasted chilli paste, which we lighten by grilling the ingredients whole instead of shallow-frying them in a wok. The pineapple, Asian herbs and lime leaf really freshen this salad. Use gluten-free fish sauce if you are avoiding gluten in your diet.

Vitamin-Rich | High-Protein | Heart Healthy | Gluten-Free

### COCONUT-CHILLI DRESSING
10 LARGE SHALLOTS
150G/5OZ LARGE CLOVES GARLIC
(ABOUT 3 BULBS)
2 TABLESPOONS CANOLA (RAPESEED) OIL
135G/4¾OZ (½ CUP) ORGANIC THAI PALM SUGAR (G)
2 TEASPOONS CHILLI POWDER
1½ TABLESPOONS FISH SAUCE
85ML (⅓ CUP) TAMARIND WATER
(SEE BASICS PAGE 291)
125ML (½ CUP) FRESH COCONUT MILK
(SEE BASICS PAGE 266)

### PINEAPPLE AND WING BEAN SALAD
½ SMALL PINEAPPLE
2 WING BEANS, STRING REMOVED, TRIMMED AND
CUT INTO 6CM/2½ INCH LENGTHS
(OR 4 FRENCH/GREEN BEANS)
1 BELGIAN ENDIVE (CHICORY), BASE TRIMMED,
LEAVES SEPARATED AND CUT IN HALF
LENGTHWISE, TRIMMED INTO POINTS
75G/3OZ (½ CUP) YOUNG COCONUT
MEAT, CUT JULIENNE
28G/1OZ (1 CUP) MIXED HERBS
SUCH AS CORIANDER (CILANTRO),
THAI BASIL AND MINT LEAVES
40G/1½OZ (½ CUP) BEAN SPROUTS
2 SMALL SHALLOTS, THINLY SLICED
4 KAFFIR LIME LEAVES, VERY THINLY SLICED

### TO SERVE
1 TABLESPOON CANOLA (RAPESEED) OIL
12 FRESH JUMBO SEA SCALLOPS,
WITHOUT THE ROE
SEA SALT, TO TASTE
½ LIME

To make the coconut-chilli dressing, soak 10 to 12 bamboo skewers in water for 30 minutes. Wash the shallots and garlic with the skin on, then thread onto soaked bamboo skewers. Heat a chargrill over a low heat and cook the shallot and garlic skewers for 45 minutes, turning occasionally, or until the centre of each ingredient is soft and outside lightly charred. Cool, then cut the shallots and garlic in half and squeeze the flesh out of the skins into a bowl.

Heat the canola oil in a saucepan, add the grilled shallot and garlic flesh and cook over a medium heat, stirring occasionally, for 10 minutes. Continue stirring then add the palm sugar and cook for 2 to 3 minutes until lightly caramelised. Stir in the chilli powder and fish sauce to stop the sugar from over-caramelising and cook for a further minute. Add the tamarind water and coconut milk, bring to the boil, then reduce the heat and simmer for 2 minutes. Transfer to a blender and mix until smooth. Check the seasoning and adjust as necessary.

To make the pineapple and wing bean salad, peel the pineapple, cut it in half lengthwise, remove the core and cut each half on the angle into 6 pieces. Blanch the wing beans in boiling salted water for 30 seconds, then drain and refresh in iced water. Combine the pineapple, Belgian endive and wing beans with the remaining ingredients in a bowl and toss gently with some of the coconut-chilli dressing.

To serve, heat the canola oil in a heavy-based frying pan over a medium to high heat. Season the scallops with sea salt and cook them in the hot pan for 1 to 2 minutes until golden brown on one side. Turn over and cook for 1 minute. Transfer to a warmed plate and squeeze over the lime juice. Spoon some of the coconut-chilli dressing onto each plate. Divide and arrange the salad, top with the scallops and serve immediately.

**Note:** If you don't have a barbecue or chargrill, you can place the ingredients on a rack in the oven and roast on a medium to high heat.

This dish was created for COMO Metropolitan in Bangkok, where we source live freshwater crayfish from the Royal Project Foundation in northern Thailand. This organisation was set up as a cooperative-style farm to provide locals with an alternative to opium production. Freshwater crayfish are best bought live and should be cooked just before eating. Use gluten-free fish sauce if you are avoiding gluten in your diet.

Vitamin-Rich | Mineral-Rich | Antioxidant-Rich | High-Protein | Rejuvenating | Gluten-Free

# FRESHWATER CRAYFISH, POMELO AND PALM HEART SALAD WITH SPICY LIME DRESSING

### SERVES 4

### SPICY LIME DRESSING

2 CLOVES GARLIC, SLICED

2 CORIANDER (CILANTRO) ROOTS, CLEANED, SCRAPED AND SLICED (OR 4 STEMS)

2 LONG RED CHILLIES, SPLIT, SEEDED AND SLICED

SEA SALT, TO TASTE

1 SMALL HOT RED CHILLI

100G/3½OZ (⅓ CUP) ORGANIC THAI PALM SUGAR (G)

2 TABLESPOONS GOOD QUALITY FISH SAUCE

180ML (¾ CUP) FRESHLY SQUEEZED LIME JUICE, STRAINED

¼ TEASPOON FINELY GRATED LIME ZEST

### FRESHWATER CRAYFISH, POMELO AND PALM HEART SALAD

12 LIVE FRESHWATER CRAYFISH, ABOUT 85G/3OZ EACH

2 SMALL PALM HEARTS, CUT INTO BATONS

75G/3OZ (½ CUP) YOUNG COCONUT MEAT, CUT JULIENNE

4 LARGE POMELO SEGMENTS, BROKEN INTO CHUNKS (OR 180G/6OZ/1 CUP NAVEL ORANGE OR GRAPEFRUIT SEGMENTS)

¼ FENNEL BULB, THINLY SHAVED ON A MANDOLIN

4 KAFFIR LIME LEAVES, VERY FINELY SLICED

2 STALKS LEMONGRASS, TOPS AND TOUGH OUTER LAYER REMOVED, THINLY SLICED

1 LONG RED CHILLI, SPLIT LENGTHWISE, SEEDED AND CUT JULIENNE

7.5G/¼OZ (½ CUP) CUP CORIANDER (CILANTRO) LEAVES

2 SMALL SHALLOTS, THINLY SLICED

### TO SERVE

1 BABY ROMAINE LETTUCE, BASE REMOVED, LEAVES SEPARATED AND TRIMMED

For the spicy lime dressing, place the garlic, coriander root and long red chillies with a pinch of sea salt in a mortar and pound with the pestle to a coarse consistency. Add the small red chilli and bruise with the pestle. Stir in the palm sugar, fish sauce, lime juice and lime zest. Check the seasoning – this dressing should be a balance of hot, sour, salty and sweet.

To make the crayfish, pomelo and palm heart salad, place the crayfish in the freezer for 30 minutes to put them to sleep. Bring a large pot of boiling salted water to the boil and cook for 3 minutes. Drain, refresh in iced water and drain again. Peel the tail, and crack the claws with the back of a knife. Place the crayfish in a bowl and drizzle with 2 tablespoons of spicy lime dressing. Combine the remaining ingredients in a bowl, add 60ml (¼ cup) of the spicy lime dressing and toss gently to combine.

To serve, divide the dressed salad, 1 large spoonful at a time, among the plates, building the lettuce and crayfish into the salad as you go.

**Note:** If crayfish is not available, substitute with cooked prawns, lobster or crab.

# CUMIN-SPICED PRAWNS
## WITH BABY CARROTS, OLIVES
## AND CHICKPEAS
## AND ORANGE BLOSSOM
## DRESSING

**SERVES 4**

*This Mediterranean-inspired salad marries the orange and cumin with the olives, creamy carrot and chickpea purée. To simplify this dish, poach the prawns instead of grilling them.*

Vitamin-Rich | Mineral-Rich | Antioxidant-Rich | High-Protein | Digestive Support | Rejuvenating | Calming | Gluten-Free

## CARROT AND CHICKPEA PURÉE

2 TABLESPOONS OLIVE OIL

½ SMALL ONION, CHOPPED

1 CLOVE GARLIC, SLICED

1 CARROT, CHOPPED

250G/9OZ (1¼ CUPS) COOKED CHICKPEAS (SEE BASICS PAGE 286)

500ML (2 CUPS) VEGETABLE STOCK (SEE BASICS PAGE 269)

1 TABLESPOON RAW TAHINI

1¼ TABLESPOONS GROUND CUMIN

2 TABLESPOONS FRESHLY SQUEEZED LEMON JUICE

1½ TABLESPOONS EXTRA-VIRGIN OLIVE OIL

SEA SALT AND GROUND WHITE PEPPER, TO TASTE

## BABY CARROTS, OLIVES AND CHICKPEA SALAD

12 BABY GREEN BEANS, TAILED AND CUT IN HALF ON THE ANGLE

4 SMALL BABY CARROTS, PEELED

50G/2OZ (¼ CUP) COOKED CHICKPEAS, PEELED (SEE BASICS PAGE 286)

¼ RED ONION, THINLY SLICED

125ML (½ CUP) ORANGE BLOSSOM DRESSING (SEE BASICS PAGE 279)

¼ CARROT, CUT INTO SPAGHETTI ON A TURNING SLICER

16 SMALL BLACK LIGURIAN, NIÇOISE OR OTHER BRINE-CURED BLACK OLIVES, PITTED

¼ BULB FENNEL, SHAVED ON A MANDOLIN

14G/½OZ (½ CUP) MIX OF FLAT-LEAF PARSLEY AND DILL LEAVES

## CUMIN-SPICED PRAWNS

½ TABLESPOON GROUND CUMIN

SEA SALT, TO TASTE

8 LARGE KING PRAWNS (SHRIMP), PEELED AND DEVEINED WITH TAILS LEFT INTACT

1 TABLESPOON OLIVE OIL

½ LEMON

## TO SERVE

40G/1½OZ (¼ CUP) FLAKED ALMONDS, TOASTED

To make the carrot and chickpea purée, heat the olive oil in a saucepan over a low to medium heat. When hot, add the onion, garlic and carrot and cook, stirring occasionally, for about 20 minutes, or until softened. Add the chickpeas and vegetable stock, bring to the boil and cover with a cartouche (see Glossary, page 296). Reduce the heat to a simmer and cook for about 30 to 40 minutes, or until the liquid is reduced to a quarter and the chickpeas and carrots are very soft. Cool slightly, then transfer to a blender. Add the tahini, cumin, lemon juice and oil and blend to a smooth purée, adding water if necessary. Check the seasoning and adjust as necessary.

For the baby carrot, olive and chickpea salad, bring a saucepan of lightly salted water to the boil and blanch the beans for a minute. Remove with a slotted spoon and refresh in iced water. Blanch the carrots in boiling water for 1 to 2 minutes, drain and refresh in iced water, drain again and cut into thirds lengthwise. Combine the beans, baby carrots, chickpeas and onion in a bowl and dress with 1½ tablespoons of the orange blossom dressing. In another bowl, combine the carrot spaghetti, olives, fennel and herbs. Dress with 1 tablespoon of the orange blossom dressing and toss gently.

For the cumin-spiced prawns, place the cumin seeds and sea salt in a mortar and pound with the pestle until you have a coarse consistency. Toss the prawns in the cumin salt, ensuring an even coat. Heat a heavy-based frying pan or flat grill over a medium heat, add the olive oil and cook the prawns for about 2 minutes on each side, or until golden brown. Transfer to a warmed plate and squeeze the lemon juice over.

To serve, spoon 1 tablespoon of the chickpea and carrot purée in the centre of each plate. Using the back of a spoon, smooth over to form a circle, making a well in the middle. Arrange the dressed beans, baby carrots, chickpeas and onions in the well, then arrange the carrot salad, prawns and herbs on top, finishing with the almonds. Spoon the remaining dressing over and around the plate.

*The most important element of this dish is the quality of the crab, which is why we use live crabs, steamed and hand-picked. This dish also celebrates zucchini in its raw state, combined with refreshing mint and lemon to make the perfect summer dish.*

Vitamin-Rich | Mineral-Rich | Antioxidant-Rich | High-Protein | Immune-Boosting | Rejuvenating | Gluten-Free

# ZUCCHINI CARPACCIO WITH CRAB, PRESERVED LEMON, PINE NUTS AND MINT

**SERVES 4**

### ZUCCHINI CARPACCIO

2 ZUCCHINI (COURGETTES), CUT INTO 12CM/ 4¾ INCH LENGTHS THEN SLICED LENGTHWISE ON A MANDOLIN

2 TABLESPOONS LEMON DRESSING (SEE BASICS PAGE 278)

### CRAB, ZUCCHINI AND PRESERVED LEMON SALAD

240G/8½OZ (¾ CUP) HAND-PICKED COOKED CRAB MEAT

3 BABY ZUCCHINI (COURGETTES), THINLY SLICED ON A MANDOLIN

4 SPRING ONIONS (SCALLIONS), THINLY SLICED

2 TEASPOONS PRESERVED LEMON, CHOPPED

7G/¼OZ (¼ CUP) MIXED BABY MINT AND DILL LEAVES (OR REGULAR MINT)

### TO SERVE

2 TABLESPOONS LEMON DRESSING (SEE BASICS PAGE 278)

1 LONG RED CHILLI, SPLIT LENGTHWISE, SEEDED AND CUT JULIENNE

12G/½OZ (½ CUP) ROCKET (ARUGULA) LEAVES

1 TABLESPOON PINE NUTS, TOASTED

To make the zucchini carpaccio, layer 6 thin ribbons to form an overlapping rectangle on the plate. Repeat with the remaining zucchini for each portion.

For the crab, zucchini and preserved lemon salad, combine the crab, zucchini, spring onions, preserved lemon and herbs in a bowl. Add the lemon dressing and toss to combine.

To serve, drizzle the lemon dressing over the zucchini carpaccio. Place the dressed crab, zucchini and preserved lemon salad in a line down the centre of each zucchini carpaccio. Garnish with chilli, rocket and pine nuts before serving immediately.

*We serve this island classic at Kudus House – the Indonesian restaurant at COMO Shambhala Estate in Bali. The tuna needs to be done to a medium rare in order to 'flake'. The fresh lemongrass and torch ginger sambal traditionally accompanies grilled items, especially seafood.*

Vitamin-Rich | Mineral-Rich | Antioxidant-Rich | High-Protein | Rejuvenating | Gluten-Free

# SPICED FLAKED YELLOWFIN TUNA AND SNAKE BEAN SALAD WITH SHALLOT AND TORCH GINGER SAMBAL

### SERVES 4

### SHALLOT AND TORCH GINGER SAMBAL

20G/¾OZ TORCH GINGER FLOWER BUD, OUTER LAYERS REMOVED, BUD FINELY SLICED

4 STALKS LEMONGRASS, TOPS AND TOUGH OUTER LEAVES REMOVED, FINELY SLICED

4 KAFFIR LIME LEAVES, VERY FINELY SLICED

8 SHALLOTS, THINLY SLICED

6 BIRD'S EYE CHILLIES, SPLIT LENGTHWISE, SEEDED AND SLICED

2 CLOVES GARLIC, FINELY CHOPPED

5 TEASPOONS FRESHLY SQUEEZED LIME JUICE

100ML (SCANT ½ CUP) VIRGIN COCONUT OIL

SEA SALT AND GROUND WHITE PEPPER, TO TASTE

### SPICED TUNA

80ML (⅓ CUP) VEGETARIAN BALI SPICE PASTE (SEE BASICS PAGE 280)

400G/14OZ BLOCK SASHIMI-GRADE YELLOWFIN TUNA

SEA SALT, TO TASTE

1 LIME

### SNAKE BEAN AND COCONUT SALAD

4 SNAKE BEANS OR LONG GREEN BEANS, BLANCHED, REFRESHED AND CUT INTO 2CM/¾ INCH PIECES

8 SPRING ONIONS (SCALLIONS), THINLY SLICED

4 APPLE EGGPLANTS (SMALL AUBERGINES), TOPS REMOVED, CUT IN HALF AND THINLY SLICED

30G/1OZ (⅓ CUP) FRESHLY GRATED COCONUT

3 SMALL RED HOT CHILLIES, SLICED

20G/¾OZ (1 CUP) LEMON BASIL LEAVES

4 PETALS OF TORCH GINGER FLOWER, FINELY SLICED

4 KAFFIR LIME LEAVES, VERY FINELY SLICED

### TO SERVE

80ML (⅓ CUP/2 LIMES) LIME JUICE, FOR SEASONING

4 TRIMMED PIECES OF BANANA LEAF TO LINE THE PLATES (OPTIONAL)

1 LONG RED CHILLI, SPLIT LENGTHWISE, SEEDED AND CUT JULIENNE

1 LIME, QUARTERED

To make the shallot and torch ginger sambal, combine the ginger flower, lemongrass, lime leaves, shallots, chillies, garlic and lime juice in a heatproof bowl. Heat the coconut oil in a small saucepan until very hot, then carefully pour over the fresh ingredients. Season with sea salt and a grind of white pepper.

For the snake bean and coconut salad, combine all of the ingredients in a bowl.

To make the spiced tuna, rub the Bali spice evenly over the fish and marinate for 30 minutes. Heat a flat grill or heavy-based frying pan, season the tuna with sea salt and cook for 3 to 4 minutes, or until golden brown. Turn and cook the other side for a further 3 to 4 minutes for medium rare. Transfer to a warmed plate, squeeze the lime juice over and rest for 4 minutes before flaking the tuna into large shards.

To serve, add the flaked tuna to the snake bean and coconut salad along with the shallot and torch ginger sambal and season with the lime juice. Place the banana leaf squares, if using, on serving plates, spoon the salad evenly among them and garnish with the chilli, placing a lime quarter on the side.

**Note:** If torch ginger is unavailable, omit and use a little extra lemongrass. In place of apple eggplant, use extra-long beans.

*If you don't have the equipment to cook sous vide, then poach the fish in a bowl over a steamer or covered in the oven. For both methods, use water seasoned with sliced shallots, basil, salt, pepper, basil oil and lemon zest. Cover the fish with the liquid and cook as you would poached or steamed fish. If you are short of time, buy the artichokes and roasted peppers.*

Vitamin-Rich | Mineral-Rich | Antioxidant-Rich | High-Protein | Digestive Support | Smart Carbohydrate | Rejuvenating | Calming | Energising | Gluten-Free

# OLIVE OIL-POACHED JOHN DORY WITH BEAN AND SEAWEED SALSA AND JERUSALEM ARTICHOKE PURÉE

## SERVES 4

### OLIVE OIL-POACHED JOHN DORY
4 PORTIONS JOHN DORY FILLETS OR OTHER FIRM-TEXTURED WHITE FISH FILLETS (140G/5OZ)

8 LARGE ITALIAN BASIL LEAVES

125ML (½ CUP) FRUITY EXTRA-VIRGIN OLIVE OIL

SEA SALT, TO TASTE

### BEAN AND SEAWEED SALSA
12 BABY GREEN BEANS

30G/1OZ (¼ CUP) FRESH OR FROZEN EDAMAME BEANS

1 LEMON

16G/½OZ (1 CUP) FLAT-LEAF PARSLEY, SLICED

180G/6OZ (1 CUP) SOAKED HIJIKI SEAWEED OR SEA SPAGHETTI CHOPPED (SEE BASICS PAGE 292)

2 TABLESPOONS SALTED CAPERS, RINSED, DRAINED AND CHOPPED

3 TABLESPOONS LEMON DRESSING (SEE BASICS PAGE 278)

SEA SALT AND GROUND WHITE PEPPER, TO TASTE

### TO SERVE
4 BABY GLOBE ARTICHOKES, CUT IN HALF AND COOKED À LA GRECQUE (SEE BASICS PAGE 270)

1 ROASTED RED BELL PEPPER (CAPSICUM), CUT INTO 2CM/¾ INCH STRIPS (SEE BASICS PAGE 276)

200G/7OZ (1 CUP) JERUSALEM ARTICHOKE PURÉE, (SEE BASICS PAGE 274)

12 MIZUNA LEAVES, STEMS TRIMMED (OR ROCKET/ARUGULA)

For the olive oil-poached John Dory, season the fish with sea salt and place a basil leaf on both sides of each fillet. Place the fillets in separate vacuum bags and add 30ml (2 tablespoons) of extra-virgin olive oil to each. Expel all the air from the bags and seal well. Place the bags in an immersion water circulator, set on 62°C/144°F, and cook sous-vide for 9 to 10 minutes. Allow the fish to rest for 5 minutes then remove from the bags and place on a warmed plate.

To make the bean and seaweed salsa, blanch the green beans and edamame beans in boiling salted water for 1 minute. Drain and refresh in iced water. Slice the green beans into rounds. Roughly chop the edamame beans. Cut all rind and pith from the lemon, then carefully cut down either side of the segment membrane to remove the segment. Slice the segments and place them in a bowl. Once finished squeeze any juice from the core and membrane over the segments.

Just before serving, combine the sliced beans, edamame and lemon segments with parsley, seaweed and capers. Season to taste and add enough lemon dressing to moisten. Mix gently to combine.

To serve, preheat an oven to 160°C/320°F. Place the artichokes and peppers on an oven tray and heat for 5 minutes, or until warmed through. Heat the Jerusalem artichoke purée in a small pot and when hot, spoon 1 tablespoon of artichoke purée off-centre at the top of a plate and drag the spoon down to form a line. Spoon the warmed artichokes and peppers onto the purée. Place the John Dory alongside the purée and spoon over the salsa. Scatter the mizuna leaves around the plate and serve immediately.

*This recipe was created for our first yoga retreat at COMO Parrot Cay – and has remained on the menu ever since. It is the perfect light dish in hot weather. Without the fish, the gazpacho works well as a delicious soup.*

Vitamin-Rich | Mineral-Rich | Antioxidant-Rich | High-Protein | Rejuvenating | Gluten-Free

# HIRAMASA KINGFISH WITH CUCUMBER AND HONEY MELON GAZPACHO, HEIRLOOM TOMATOES AND OLIVES

## SERVES 6

### GAZPACHO

4 GREEN APPLES

½ HONEYDEW MELON

3 LONG GREEN CHILLIES, SPLIT LENGTHWISE AND SEEDED

3 LEBANESE OR ENGLISH CUCUMBER, CUT IN HALF LENGTHWISE AND SEEDED

1 GREEN BELL PEPPER (CAPSICUM), CUT INTO QUARTERS AND SEEDED

4 CLOVES GARLIC

½ SMALL RED ONION, CHOPPED

SEA SALT AND GROUND WHITE PEPPER, TO TASTE

### SEARED HIRAMASA KINGFISH

1 TABLESPOON OLIVE OIL

6 PIECES OF HIRAMASA KINGFISH (EACH 140G/5OZ), SKINNED

½ LEMON

### TO SERVE

1 TABLESPOON RAW APPLE CIDER VINEGAR

1 YELLOW HEIRLOOM TOMATO, CUT INTO 6 WEDGES

1 SMALL RED HEIRLOOM TOMATO, CUT INTO 6 SLICES

1 SMALL GREEN ZEBRA-STRIPED HEIRLOOM TOMATO, CUT INTO 6 WEDGES

¼ HONEYDEW MELON, SKIN REMOVED, SEEDED AND CUT INTO 6 THIN SLICES

½ LEBANESE OR ENGLISH CUCUMBER, CUT IN HALF, SEEDED AND SLICED

¼ RED ONION, SLICED LENGTHWISE

5G/¼OZ (¼ CUP) DILL LEAVES AND BASIL LEAVES

18 LIGURIAN OR OTHER BRINE-CURED BLACK OLIVES, PITTED

1 TABLESPOON SALTED CAPERS, RINSED AND DRAINED

To make the gazpacho, put the apples through a juice extractor, catching the liquid in a jug (you will need 500ml/ 2 cups juice). Next, juice the melon (to produce 375ml/1½ cups) and follow this by juicing the chillies. Put all the juices in a blender and add the remaining ingredients. Season and blend until smooth.

To make the seared hiramasa kingfish, heat a large heavy-based frying pan over a medium heat. Heat the olive oil and cook the kingfish, skin-side up, for 3 to 4 minutes, or until golden. Turn over and cook for a further 2 minutes, then transfer the fish to a warmed plate, caramelised side up. Squeeze lemon juice over the fish and rest for 2 minutes before serving.

To serve, pour 125ml (½ cup) of the gazpacho into each bowl and season each with half a teaspoon of apple cider vinegar. Divide the tomatoes, melon and cucumber among the bowls. Combine the onion, herbs, olives and capers in a separate bowl and dress with 2 teaspoons of the apple cider vinegar. Season to taste and divide the salad between the serving bowls, then top with the fish and serve immediately.

**Note:** It is vital to keep the gazpacho and garnish well chilled until serving.

# FLAKED SALMON WITH CAULIFLOWER, POMEGRANATE AND QUINOA TABBOULEH AND SMOKY EGGPLANT PURÉE

**SERVES 4**

This is an all-time COMO Shambhala classic — a perfect lunchtime meal as it's light but oh so flavourful. The zing from the pomegranate molasses and sumac really cut through the oily flavours of the salmon and the smoky eggplant purée adds another great dimension to the dish.

Vitamin-Rich | Mineral-Rich | Antioxidant-Rich | High-Protein | Digestive Support | Rejuvenating | Calming | Energising | Gluten-Free

## TABBOULEH DRESSING
1 CLOVE GARLIC
½ TEASPOON SUMAC (OR LEMON ZEST)
SEA SALT, TO TASTE
2 TOMATOES
2½ TABLESPOONS FRESHLY SQUEEZED LEMON JUICE
1 TEASPOON POMEGRANATE MOLASSES
2 TABLESPOONS RAW APPLE CIDER VINEGAR
1 TABLESPOON AGAVE NECTAR (G)
125ML (½ CUP) EXTRA-VIRGIN OLIVE OIL

## TABBOULEH
150G/5OZ (1 CUP) CAULIFLOWER, FINELY CHOPPED
30G/1OZ (⅓ CUP) POMEGRANATE SEEDS
4 SPRING ONIONS (SCALLIONS), SLICED
4 CHERRY TOMATOES, SLICED
80G/3OZ (½ CUP) COOKED QUINOA
(SEE BASICS PAGE 286)
¼ LEBANESE OR ENGLISH CUCUMBER,
CUT IN HALF, SEEDED AND SLICED
10G/⅓OZ (⅓ CUP) MIXED HERBS SUCH AS MINT,
FLAT-LEAF PARSLEY AND DILL, CHOPPED
SEA SALT AND GROUND
WHITE PEPPER, TO TASTE

## SMOKY EGGPLANT PURÉE
1KG/2¼LB EGGPLANTS (AUBERGINES)
1 CLOVE GARLIC, SLICED
2 TABLESPOONS FRESHLY SQUEEZED LEMON JUICE
2 TEASPOONS GROUND CUMIN
60ML (¼ CUP) EXTRA-VIRGIN OLIVE OIL
2 TABLESPOONS RAW TAHINI

## SPICED FLAKED SALMON
4 PIECES SKINLESS SALMON FILLET (EACH 140G/5OZ)
1¼ TEASPOONS GROUND CUMIN
1¼ TEASPOONS GROUND FENNEL
1¼ TEASPOONS GROUND CORIANDER
SEA SALT, TO TASTE
1 TABLESPOON OLIVE OIL
½ LEMON

## TO SERVE
25G/1OZ (1 CUP) WILD ROCKET (ARUGULA)
1 SMALL BULB FENNEL, CORE REMOVED AND
SHAVED ON A MANDOLIN
1–2 TABLESPOONS LEMON DRESSING
(SEE BASICS PAGE 278)

For the tabbouleh dressing, place the garlic, sumac and a pinch of salt in a mortar and pound with the pestle to a paste, then transfer to a bowl. Put the tomatoes through a juice extractor and catch the juice in a jug (you will need 125ml/½ cup). Whisk the tomato juice and lemon juice into the garlic paste, then do the same with the pomegranate molasses, vinegar and agave nectar. Gradually whisk in the extra-virgin olive oil and season to taste.

To make the tabbouleh, combine all the ingredients, adding enough tabbouleh dressing to moisten. Season to taste and set aside to allow the flavours to develop.

To make the smoky eggplant purée, heat a chargrill over a medium heat. Prick the eggplants with a fork then cook, turning regularly, until the skin is blackened and charred and the flesh is soft. Place the eggplant in a sieve to cool and drain away any excess water. When cool, peel the eggplant and squeeze some of the excess water from the flesh. Place the eggplant, garlic, lemon, cumin, oil and tahini in a blender and mix to a smooth purée.

For the spiced flaked salmon, preheat the oven to 180°C/350°F. Combine the spices with the sea salt. Sprinkle the spice mix over 1 side of each fish fillet. Heat a large ovenproof frying pan over a medium heat and warm the olive oil. When hot, cook the salmon, skin-side up, for 3 to 4 minutes, or until golden. Turn the fish over, then place the pan in the hot oven and cook for a further 2 to 3 minutes for medium rare, turning once. Transfer the fish to a plate and season with a squeeze of lemon juice. Rest for 3 minutes.

To serve, spoon the tabbouleh mix down the centre of 4 plates. Flake the spiced salmon into large pieces and place on top of the tabbouleh. Arrange an eggplant purée quenelle to the side. Toss the rocket and fennel with lemon dressing, season to taste and arrange on top of the fish. Serve immediately.

**Note:** The spice stores well so any extra can be used to season any seafood, chicken or lamb. The cauliflower tabbouleh works well as a side salad on its own without the salmon. For finely chopped cauliflower, remove the stem and core first, before chopping until the cauliflower resembles resemble a quinoa grain.

*A whole fish works well for sharing. If you're not comfortable with serving a whole fish, the recipe lends itself to portioned skin-on fish fillets, which can be plated the same way. At COMO Cocoa Island in the Maldives, we use rosy jobfish for this dish; it is wonderful when cooked on the bone. Use gluten-free Tamari soy if you are avoiding gluten.*

Vitamin-Rich | Mineral-Rich | Antioxidant-Rich | High-Protein | Digestive Support | Rejuvenating | Energising | Gluten-Free

# WHOLE STEAMED SNAPPER IN FRAGRANT GINGER AND SHIITAKE MUSHROOM BROTH WITH SESAME OIL

**SERVES 4**

### GINGER AND TAMARI BROTH
4 STAR ANISE

2 CINNAMON QUILLS

8CM/3 INCH PIECE GINGER, BRUISED

4 CLOVES GARLIC, BRUISED

½ BUNCH SPRING ONIONS (SCALLIONS), TRIMMED

100G/3½OZ YELLOW ROCK SUGAR (OR REGULAR SUGAR)

250ML (1 CUP) TAMARI SOY

250ML (1 CUP) SHAOXING WINE

### STEAMED SNAPPER
2KG/4½LB WHOLE SNAPPER, CLEANED AND SCALED

8CM/3 INCH PIECE (½ CUP) GINGER, PEELED AND CUT JULIENNE

### TO SERVE
2 BOK CHOY, BASE REMOVED AND LEAVES SEPARATED

8 LARGE SHIITAKE MUSHROOMS, CUT IN HALF ON THE ANGLE WITH STEMS REMOVED

12 SPRING ONIONS (SCALLIONS), CUT JULIENNE

GROUND WHITE PEPPER

80ML (⅓ CUP) PURE SESAME OIL

7.5G/¼OZ (½ CUP) CORIANDER (CILANTRO) LEAVES

1 LONG RED CHILLI, SPLIT LENGTHWISE, SEEDED AND CUT JULIENNE

300G/10½OZ (2 CUPS) COOKED BROWN JASMINE RICE (SEE BASICS PAGE 286)

To make the ginger and tamari broth, combine all the ingredients with 500ml (2 cups) water in a saucepan and bring to the boil. Reduce the heat to a simmer and cook for 8 minutes. Remove from the heat and leave to stand for 30 minutes to allow the flavours to infuse. Strain, cool and store in an airtight container in the fridge.

For the steamed snapper, bring a steamer filled with water to the boil. Place the snapper in a large shallow bowl and ladle in enough tamari and ginger broth to cover the fish. Scatter with half of the ginger. Place the bowl in the steamer, cover and steam for 15 to 20 minutes, or until the fish is cooked (exact cooking time depends on the thickness of the fish). Remove the bowl from the steamer and rest for 5 minutes.

To serve, place the bok choy on a plate, place in the steamer, cover then cook for 1 to 2 minutes until tender but still crunchy and green.

Bring 500ml (2 cups) of the tamari and ginger broth to the boil in a saucepan. Add the mushrooms and half of the remaining julienned ginger. Return to the boil, then reduce the heat to low. Arrange the bok choy leaves over a large platter and carefully place the fish on top. Spoon the broth, mushrooms and ginger over the fish and scatter with spring onions, the remaining ginger and 5 grinds of white pepper.

Meanwhile, bring the sesame oil to smoking point in a small saucepan and carefully spoon over the fish (the mixture will spit). Scatter with the coriander and chilli and serve with rice.

**Note:** The ginger tamari broth keeps indefinitely if refrigerated; it can also be used for tofu, chicken and vegetables such as pumpkin, dried shiitakes, white radish and cabbage.

# BRAISED BASS GROUPER IN SPICY TOMATO AND LEMONGRASS CURRY WITH GREEN PAPAYA NOODLES

### SERVES 4

This Thai-inspired curry dish was created for COMO Metropolitan in Bangkok. Traditionally served with rice or fresh rice noodles, known as 'khanom jin', we pair this tomato-based curry with green papaya 'noodles' instead. If pak chi farang or long leaf coriander is unavailable, use coriander stems. Use gluten-free fish sauce if you are avoiding gluten in your diet.

Vitamin-Rich | Mineral-Rich | Antioxidant-Rich | Heart Healthy | Digestive Support | Rejuvenating | Calming | Gluten-Free

### TOMATO AND LEMONGRASS CURRY

3 SMALL HOT RED CHILLIES, SLICED

25G/1OZ (¼ CUP) GALANGAL, PEELED AND FINELY SLICED

65G/2½OZ (½ CUP OR 9 SMALL STALKS) LEMONGRASS, TOPS AND OUTER LAYERS REMOVED AND SLICED

½ TEASPOON KAFFIR LIME ZEST, FINELY GRATED WITH NO WHITE PITH

3 CORIANDER (CILANTRO) ROOTS, CLEANED, SCRAPED AND CHOPPED (OR 6 STEMS)

75G/3OZ (¾ CUP) SHALLOTS, SLICED

65G/2½OZ (½ CUP OR 15 CLOVES) GARLIC, SLICED

5CM/2 INCH PIECE FRESH TURMERIC ROOT, PEELED AND FINELY SLICED (OR 1 TEASPOON GROUND TURMERIC)

2 TABLESPOONS CANOLA (RAPESEED) OIL

4 KAFFIR LIME LEAVES, VERY FINELY SLICED

SEA SALT, TO TASTE

8 LARGE VINE-RIPENED TOMATOES, FINELY DICED

2 STALKS LEMONGRASS, BRUISED

### BRAISED BASS GROUPER

560G/1LB 4OZ BASS GROUPER FILLET, TAKEN FROM THE TOP END OF THE FILLET

1 SMALL GREEN PAPAYA, PEELED, QUARTERED AND SEEDED

800ML (3⅓ CUPS) THAI FISH STOCK (SEE BASICS PAGE 268)

2 LONG RED CHILLIES, SPLIT LENGTHWISE, SEEDED AND CUT INTO QUARTERS

4 KAFFIR LIME LEAVES, VERY FINELY SLICED

4 TEASPOONS FISH SAUCE

2 TEASPOONS ORGANIC THAI PALM SUGAR (G)

4 SNAKE BEANS OR LONG GREEN BEANS, CUT INTO 8CM/3 INCH LENGTHS

4 APPLE EGGPLANTS (SMALL AUBERGINES), CUT INTO QUARTERS

2 TEASPOONS FRESHLY SQUEEZED LIME JUICE

### TO SERVE

8 STEMS PAK CHI FARANG (LONG LEAF CORIANDER) CLEANED AND CUT INTO POINTS

4 KAFFIR LIME LEAVES, VERY THINLY SLICED

8 SPRIGS LEMON BASIL OR THAI BASIL LEAVES

40G/1½OZ (½ CUP) BEAN SPROUTS

To make the tomato and lemongrass curry, place the chillies, galangal, sliced lemongrass, lime zest, coriander roots, shallots, garlic and turmeric in a mortar and pound with the pestle to a fine paste. Heat the oil in a heavy-based saucepan and add the curry paste and lime leaves, seasoning with sea salt. Cook, stirring constantly with a wooden spoon, for about 15 to 20 minutes, or until fragrant and the rawness has been cooked out. Add the tomatoes and bruised lemongrass and simmer over a low to medium heat for 30 minutes.

For the braised bass grouper, skin the bass grouper fillet, cut into 8 even pieces and set aside. Using a turning slicer, cut the papaya into spaghetti and twirl into 4 bundles. Place a steamer filled with water over a medium heat and bring to the boil.

Combine the tomato and lemongrass curry with the fish stock in a saucepan, bring to the boil over a medium heat and add the chillies and lime leaves. Add the fish sauce and palm sugar, check the seasoning and adjust as necessary.

Add the fish pieces, snake beans and apple eggplant and return to the boil, then reduce the heat to a simmer and cook for 3 minutes. Turn the fish pieces over and cook for a further 3 minutes. Remove from the heat and add lime juice to taste, cover with a lid and rest for 4 minutes.

Meanwhile, place the papaya noodles in the steamer, cover with a lid and steam for 3 to 4 minutes, or until tender.

To serve, spoon the curry sauce into 4 bowls, top with a bundle of papaya noodles then scatter with the coriander, lime leaves, basil leaves and bean sprouts.

# AROMATIC POACHED
# HALIBUT WITH
# SOUTHERN INDIAN-INSPIRED
# TOMATO AND COCONUT CURRY

SERVES 4

*This presentation of this dish is quite a modern take on a traditional curry. The sauce is very full flavoured. Hence only a small amount is served and this balances well with the fish poached in coconut water.*

Vitamin-Rich | Mineral-Rich | Antioxidant-Rich | High-Protein | Immune-Boosting | Digestive Support | Rejuvenating | Energising | Gluten-Free

## TOMATO AND COCONUT CURRY

80ML (⅓ CUP) SUNFLOWER OIL

2 SMALL BROWN ONIONS, SLICED

3 CORIANDER (CILANTRO) ROOTS, CLEANED, SCRAPED AND BRUISED (OR 6 STEMS)

6 CLOVES GARLIC, SLICED

4CM/1½ INCH PIECE GINGER, PEELED AND CUT JULIENNE

SEA SALT, TO TASTE

2 TEASPOONS CUMIN SEEDS

2 TEASPOONS CORIANDER SEEDS

4 LONG RED DRIED CHILLIES

3 TEASPOONS RED CHILLI FLAKES

180G/6OZ (2 CUPS) FRESHLY GRATED COCONUT

2 TEASPOONS GROUND CORIANDER

2 TEASPOONS GROUND CUMIN

1 TABLESPOON JAGGERY (OR ORGANIC THAI PALM SUGAR) (G)

6 VINE-RIPENED TOMATOES, COARSELY CHOPPED

75G/3OZ (⅓ CUP) TOMATO JAM (SEE BASICS PAGE 290)

60ML (¼ CUP) TAMARIND WATER (SEE BASICS PAGE 291)

500ML (2 CUPS) FRESH COCONUT MILK (SEE BASICS PAGE 266)

## AROMATIC POACHED FISH

4 PORTIONS OF HALIBUT, TURBOT OR FLOUNDER (EACH 140G/5OZ)

250ML (1 CUP) YOUNG COCONUT WATER OR VEGETABLE STOCK (SEE BASICS PAGE 269)

2CM/¾ INCH PIECE GINGER, PEELED AND CUT JULIENNE

8 FRESH CURRY LEAVES

1 CORIANDER (CILANTRO) ROOT, CLEANED, SCRAPED AND BRUISED (OR 2 STEMS)

SEA SALT, TO TASTE

1 LIME, CUT IN HALF

## CURRY GARNISH

8 CHERRY TOMATOES

12 OKRA

16 ENGLISH SPINACH LEAVES, CUT INTO 18CM/7 INCH LENGTHS

## TO SERVE

4G/⅛OZ (¼ CUP) CORIANDER (CILANTRO) LEAVES

12 FRESH CURRY LEAVES, SHALLOW-FRIED UNTIL TRANSLUCENT

1 LONG GREEN CHILLI, SLICED

To make the tomato and coconut curry, heat the oil in a large saucepan over a low to medium heat. When hot, add the onions, coriander root, garlic and ginger. Season to taste with sea salt and cook, stirring occasionally for 10 to 15 minutes, or until softened. Add the whole spices and chillies and cook for a further 20 minutes. Next, add the grated coconut and ground spices and cook for a further 5 minutes, or until fragrant. Stir in the coconut milk, the jaggery, tomatoes, tomato jam, and tamarind water, and bring to the boil. Reduce the heat to a simmer and cook for 40 minutes. Transfer to a blender and mix until smooth. Check the seasoning and adjust as necessary.

For the poached fish, place a filled steamer on the stove and bring to the boil. Place the fish pieces in a large shallow bowl and ladle enough coconut water over the fish to cover. Scatter with the ginger, curry leaves and coriander root, seasoning with sea salt. Place the bowl in the steamer, cover and steam for 8 to 10 minutes (depending on the thickness of the fish). Remove the bowl from the steamer and rest for 2 minutes, seasoning with the lime juice.

To make the curry garnish, bring a large saucepan of lightly salted water to the boil just before serving. Cook the cherry tomatoes for 10 seconds, remove with a slotted spoon, refresh in iced water, then peel. Blanch the okra for 2 minutes and remove with a slotted spoon. Blanch the spinach until wilted, then remove and lightly squeeze to remove some of the water.

To serve, spoon the curry sauce among 4 warmed bowls and top with blanched spinach, tomatoes and okra. Remove the fish from the poaching liquid and place over the vegetables. Sprinkle with the coriander, fried curry leaves and sliced chilli.

**Note:** You could use store-bought garam masala in the fish marinade instead of the individual powdered spices. This dish is best served with steamed brown basmati rice.

*This is a quintessential Thai dish of clear, spicy and sour soup. There are many variations of 'Tom yum', but this recipe is our 'go-to' favourite. Use gluten-free fish sauce if you are avoiding gluten in your diet.*

Vitamin-Rich | Mineral-Rich | Antioxidant-Rich | High-Protein | Digestive Support | Rejuvenating | Calming | Energising | Gluten-Free

# STEAMED SEA BASS IN FRAGRANT HOT AND SOUR BROTH WITH MUSHROOMS AND CHERRY TOMATOES

**SERVES 4**

### POACHED SEA BASS

4 PIECES BLACK SEA BASS FILLET, OR WILD BARRAMUNDI (EACH 140G/5OZ), SKIN ON

900ML (3¾ CUPS) THAI FISH STOCK (SEE BASICS PAGE 268)

8 SMALL KAFFIR LIME LEAVES, VERY THINLY SLICED

4 CHINESE CABBAGE LEAVES

2 SMALL SHALLOTS, HALVED AND CUT INTO 5MM/¼ INCH WEDGES

2 SMALL HOT RED CHILLIES, BRUISED AND STEM REMOVED

4 STALKS LEMONGRASS, TOPS AND OUTER LAYERS REMOVED, FINELY SLICED

2 PIECES GALANGAL (EACH 8CM/3 INCHES), PEELED AND FINELY SLICED

8 LARGE SHIITAKE MUSHROOMS, STEMS REMOVED AND CUT IN HALF

2 TABLESPOONS FISH SAUCE

8 CHERRY TOMATOES, CUT IN HALF

2 TABLESPOONS LIME JUICE

### TO SERVE

4G/⅛OZ (¼ CUP) CORIANDER (CILANTRO) LEAVES

2 STEMS PAK CHI FARANG (LONG LEAF CORIANDER), THINLY SLICED

1 LONG RED CHILLI, SPLIT LENGTHWISE, SEEDED AND CUT JULIENNE

2 KAFFIR LIME LEAVES, VERY THINLY SLICED

300G/10½OZ (2 CUPS) COOKED BROWN JASMINE RICE (SEE BASICS PAGE 286)

For the steamed sea bass, fill a double-tiered steamer pot with water and bring to the boil over a medium heat. Place the fish pieces in a shallow bowl that fits the steamer basket, cover the fish with Thai fish stock (about 250ml/1 cup) and a pinch of sliced kaffir lime leaves. Place the cabbage leaves on a steamer shelf on a shallow plate, then place the plate of fish on the other steamer shelf. Cover with the lid and steam for 7 to 8 minutes, depending on the thickness of the fish pieces.

To serve, place the remaining Thai fish stock in a saucepan, add the shallots, chillies, lemongrass, galangal and remaining sliced kaffir lime leaves. Bring to the boil, then reduce the heat to a simmer and add the mushrooms. Season the broth with fish sauce then add the cherry tomatoes and simmer for a further 2 minutes. Remove from the heat and season to taste with lime juice.

Roll the cabbage leaves to form long cylinders, use these to form a base in the bottom of each bowl, then top each with a piece of poached fish. Ladle the broth and its vegetables into the bowls, scatter with coriander leaves, pak chi farang, chilli and sliced lime leaves. Serve immediately with brown jasmine rice.

**Note:** The stock keeps well in the freezer; just add more aromatic herbs such as lemongrass and kaffir lime before serving.

*This popular dish at COMO Shambhala Estate in Bali works well with quinoa noodles on the side. It is a simple dish to assemble after the bases are made. Use gluten-free Tamari soy if you are avoiding gluten.*

Vitamin-Rich | Mineral-Rich | Antioxidant-Rich | High-Protein | Digestive Support | Smart Carbohydrate | Rejuvenating | Energising | Gluten-Free

# PEPPER-CRUSTED YELLOWFIN TUNA WITH WOK-FRIED GREENS, MUSHROOMS AND THAI BASIL

### SERVES 4

### PEPPER-CRUSTED YELLOWFIN TUNA

I TABLESPOON BLACK PEPPERCORNS

I TABLESPOON WHITE PEPPERCORNS

I TABLESPOON CORIANDER SEEDS

4 TRIMMED BLOCKS SASHIMI-GRADE YELLOWFIN TUNA (EACH 140G/5OZ)

SEA SALT, TO TASTE

I TABLESPOON CANOLA (RAPESEED) OIL

½ LEMON

### CHILLI AND LEMON DRESSING

250ML (I CUP) SAKE

I ½ TABLESPOONS LEMON JUICE

I ½ TABLESPOONS TAMARI SOY

3 PINCHES OF CRACKED BLACK PEPPER

2 PINCHES RED CHILLI FLAKES

I TEASPOON GRATED GARLIC

I TEASPOON GRATED FRESH GINGER

### WOK-FRIED GREENS, MUSHROOMS AND THAI BASIL

80ML (⅓ CUP) SAKE

2 TABLESPOONS TAMARI SOY

2 TABLESPOONS CANOLA (RAPESEED) OIL

½ RED ONION, CUT INTO I ½CM/¾ INCH WEDGES

4 LARGE SHIITAKE MUSHROOMS, HALVED AND STEMS REMOVED

4 SNAKE BEANS OR LONG GREEN BEANS, CUT INTO 8CM/3 INCH LENGTHS

2 BRANCHES KALE, LEAVES ONLY, CUT INTO 6CM/2½ INCH LENGTHS

I SMALL HEAD BROCCOLI, BASE TRIMMED AND CUT INTO BRANCHES (ABOUT 8 PIECES)

125ML (½ CUP) VEGETABLE STOCK (SEE BASICS PAGE 269)

5G/¼OZ (¼ CUP) THAI BASIL LEAVES (OR ITALIAN BASIL)

### TO SERVE

30G/IOZ (I CUP) SNOW PEA (MANGETOUT) TENDRILS

To make the pepper-crusted yellowfin tuna, toast each of the spices separately in a frying pan over a medium heat for 2 minutes, or until fragrant. Transfer to a mortar, cool and then crush with the pestle. Mix all the spices together in a bowl. Coat the tuna in the pepper crust on one side and season lightly with sea salt. Heat the oil in a heavy-based frying pan, add the tuna and cook for I to 2 minutes until seared and a 5mm/¼ inch line of cooked tuna is visible. Turn and repeat on the remaining 3 sides but do not sear the ends. Transfer the fish to a plate and rest in a warm place for 4 minutes, seasoning with a squeeze of lemon juice.

For the chilli and lemon dressing, bring the sake to the boil in a saucepan and cook until reduced by half. Cool, then add the remaining ingredients.

To make the wok-fried greens, heat the sake in a small saucepan. Light the sake with a flame and cook until the flame dies out. Pour into a bowl, add the tamari and mix well before setting aside. Heat a wok over a high heat, add the oil and when almost smoking, add the onion and mushrooms and stir-fry for 20 seconds. Add the beans, kale and broccoli and stir-fry for a further 45 to 60 seconds. Add 2 tablespoons of vegetable stock if the mixture looks like it will catch and burn. Add the sake mixture and cook until the sauce is reduced to a quarter. Add the chilli and lemon dressing and stir-fry until reduced by half, then stir in the basil.

To serve, divide the wok-fried greens, mushrooms and Thai basil among 4 warmed bowls. Slice the tuna into Icm/½ inch thick slices and place on top of the stir-fry, scattering with snow pea tendrils.

**Note:** Be careful not to overcook the stir-fried vegetables, as the aim is to retain the vegetables' crunch and colour.

# SOUR ORANGE
## CURRY OF RIVER TROUT WITH BUTTERNUT PUMPKIN, CHERRY TOMATOES AND FRESH BROWN RICE NOODLES

SERVES 4

This is our adaptation of a very popular lunch dish found on the streets of Bangkok. The recipe may seem somewhat odd, boiling and pounding the fish only to return it to the pot of curry. But this step is well worth the effort, as it helps to thicken the curry and produces a very light but flavoursome dish. Use gluten-free fish sauce if you are avoiding gluten in your diet.

Vitamin-Rich | Mineral-Rich | Antioxidant-Rich | High-Protein | Digestive Support | Rejuvenating | Calming | Energising | Gluten-Free

### ORANGE CURRY PASTE

10 DRIED LONG RED CHILLIES
8 SHALLOTS, SLICED
5 CLOVES GARLIC, SLICED
3 STALKS LEMONGRASS, TOPS AND OUTER LAYERS REMOVED, SLICED
3 CM/1¼ INCH PIECE GALANGAL, PEELED AND SLICED
5 ORANGE CHILLIES, SPLIT LENGTHWISE, SEEDED AND STEMS REMOVED

### PICKLED CUCUMBER

1 LEBANESE OR ENGLISH CUCUMBER, THINLY SLICED LENGTHWISE ON A MANDOLIN
1 TEASPOON SEA SALT
60ML (¼ CUP) RAW APPLE CIDER VINEGAR
1½ TABLESPOONS RAW SUGAR

### SOUR ORANGE CURRY OF RIVER TROUT

4 WHOLE RIVER TROUT (300G/10½OZ), CLEANED AND SCALED (OR SALMON OR SEA TROUT)
4 STEMS CHAYOTE SHOOT (OR 4 STEMS OF SPINACH OR WATER SPINACH)
1.2 LITRES (5 CUPS) THAI FISH STOCK (SEE BASICS PAGE 268)
2 SMALL RED CHILLIES, BRUISED
4 KAFFIR LIME LEAVES, BRUISED
¼ BUTTERNUT PUMPKIN, PEELED, SEEDED AND CUT INTO 8MM/⅓ INCH THICK SLICES
60ML (¼ CUP) TAMARIND WATER (SEE BASICS PAGE 291)
1 TABLESPOON ORGANIC THAI PALM SUGAR (G)
2 TABLESPOONS FISH SAUCE
2 LONG RED CHILLIES, SPLIT LENGTHWISE, SEEDED AND CUT IN HALF ON THE ANGLE
4 LARGE CHERRY TOMATOES, CUT IN HALF
5G/¼OZ (¼ CUP) THAI BASIL LEAVES

### TO SERVE

4 BUNDLES FRESH BROWN RICE NOODLES (EACH 100G/3½OZ)
8 SPRIGS THAI BASIL
200G/7OZ WHITE CABBAGE, CUT INTO 4 WEDGES
6 SNAKE BEANS OR LONG GREEN BEANS, CUT INTO 12CM/4¾ INCH LENGTHS
1 LEBANESE OR ENGLISH CUCUMBER, PEELED AND CUT INTO LONG SHARDS

To make the orange curry paste, soak the dried red chillies in just-boiled water for 30 minutes. Drain and place the chillies in a blender with the remaining ingredients. Blend to a smooth paste, adding a little water if the paste is too dry.

For the pickled cucumber, place the sliced cucumber in a bowl, sprinkle with the sea salt and leave to stand for 20 minutes. Rinse the cucumber and pat dry with a paper towel.

Combine the vinegar, sugar and 1½ tablespoons of water in a saucepan. Bring to the boil to dissolve the sugar. Remove from the heat and cool. Pour the cooled vinegar mixture over the cucumber and leave to stand for 30 minutes, then drain.

To make the sour orange curry of river trout, remove the heads and fins from the fish and cut three 6cm/2½ inch thick cutlets from each fish, starting from the head. With the tail pieces, remove the flesh from the fish in a fillet, then remove the skin, and set aside.

Cook the skinned tail fillet in boiling water for 3 to 4 minutes, or until cooked through. Drain and cool, then place in a mortar and pound with the pestle. Cut the chayote shoots into 5cm/2 inch lengths, blanch in boiling salted water for 30 seconds, refresh in iced water, drain and set aside.

Place the orange curry paste and fish stock in a saucepan and stir to combine. Bring to the boil then reduce the heat to a simmer. Add the small red chillies and kaffir lime leaves and cook, stirring occasionally, for 25 minutes. Add the pounded fish, butternut pumpkin, tamarind water, palm sugar and fish sauce, return to a simmer and cook for 5 minutes. Add the long red chillies and fish cutlets, return to the boil, then reduce the heat to a simmer and cook for 4 minutes. Turn the fish pieces over and cook for a further 2 to 3 minutes until almost cooked. Add the cherry tomatoes, basil and chayote shoots and cook until warmed through.

To serve, place a bundle of noodles in each of the bowls. Arrange the basil sprigs, drained pickled cucumber, cabbage, beans and sliced cucumber on a platter. Spoon the curry into a large bowl to share. Serve immediately.

# Meat and Poultry

CHAPTER 6

When cooking and serving meat, we aim for quality and balance on the plate. Unlike many gastronomic traditions in which meat is dominant, we believe that the protein should complement and be equal in proportion to the grain or vegetable.

In Bhutan, yak meat is available to us. Farmed for its milk, yak is a lean meat similar to very dark game, like bison or venison, delivering a fantastic rich red colour on the plate. See Carpaccio of Yak with Grilled Matsutake Mushrooms and Fern Tip Salad (page 198), served simply with some Szechuan pepper for zing. Of course, yak is not readily available in many parts; the recipe works just as well with beef or venison.

We serve both grass-fed beef and wagyu at COMO. Although wagyu is grain-fed, it possesses healthy white fat – as opposed to yellow fat – and contains a good proportion of the desirable monounsaturated fats and essential fatty acids.

With chicken, we only use free-range, organic and hormone-free meat. When raised on grass in a large pen, the chickens get the chlorophyll, worms and insects they need. Such chickens may not be as tender as the battery-farmed alternatives, nor as consistent in size, but there are numerous ways to address this. Sous vide cooking, for instance, tenderises the meat.

*This Thai-inspired chicken salad was first developed for COMO Metropolitan in Bangkok. It has been through a few variations, but this recipe is the best. Pounding the lemongrass for the dressing brings out its fragrance. Use gluten-free tamari soy if you are avoiding gluten in your diet.*

Vitamin-Rich | Mineral-Rich | Antioxidant-Rich | High-Protein | Rejuvenating | Energising | Gluten-Free

# SHREDDED CHICKEN, CHERRY TOMATO AND SNAKE BEAN SALAD WITH A TAMARIND AND LEMONGRASS DRESSING

### SERVES 4

### TAMARIND AND LEMONGRASS DRESSING

4 LEMONGRASS STALKS, TOPS AND OUTER LAYERS REMOVED, FINELY SLICED

2 PINCHES SEA SALT

2 CLOVES GARLIC, SLICED

I SHALLOT, SLICED

2 SMALL RED CHILLIES, SLICED

2 CORIANDER (CILANTRO) ROOTS, CLEANED AND SCRAPED (OR 4 STEMS)

100G/3½OZ (⅓ CUP) ORGANIC THAI PALM SUGAR (G)

2 TABLESPOONS TAMARI SOY

250ML (I CUP) TAMARIND WATER (SEE BASICS PAGE 291)

4 CORIANDER (CILANTRO) SPRIGS, LEAVES AND STEMS FINELY SLICED

### SHREDDED CHICKEN, CHERRY TOMATO AND SNAKE BEAN SALAD

6 SNAKE BEANS OR LONG GREEN BEANS

I WHITE-COOKED CHICKEN, SHREDDED (SEE BASICS PAGE 294)

40G/1½OZ (¼ CUP) ROASTED CASHEWS, ROUGHLY CHOPPED

½ GREEN MANGO, CUT JULIENNE

I SMALL LEBANESE OR ENGLISH CUCUMBER, CUT IN HALF LENGTHWISE, THEN CUT JULIENNE

6 CHERRY TOMATOES, CUT IN HALF

40G/1½OZ (½ CUP) BEAN SPROUTS

60G/2½OZ (½ CUP) BLACK WOOD EAR MUSHROOMS, BASES REMOVED AND TORN, IF AVAILABLE

2 LEMONGRASS STALKS, TOPS AND OUTER LAYERS REMOVED, FINELY SLICED

5G/¼OZ (¼ CUP) CORIANDER (CILANTRO) LEAVES

5G/¼OZ (¼ CUP) MINT LEAVES

5G/¼OZ (¼ CUP) THAI BASIL LEAVES

4 KAFFIR LIME LEAVES, VERY THINLY SLICED

To make the tamarind and lemongrass dressing, place the lemongrass and sea salt in a mortar and pound with the pestle to a coarse paste. Add the garlic, shallot, chillies and coriander roots and pound until coarsely crushed. Then add the palm sugar, tamari and tamarind water and stir well to dissolve. Just before serving, add the coriander stems and leaves.

To make the chicken and snake bean salad, blanch the beans in boiling salted water for 1 minute, then refresh in iced water. Drain and cut into 8cm/3 inch lengths.

To serve, combine the shredded chicken with the remaining salad ingredients in a large bowl and dress well. Toss gently and spoon onto 4 plates.

**Note:** Cooking the chicken the Chinese 'white-cooked' way (see Basics page 294) may seem tedious, but it's well worth it for the resulting texture, which is silky, moist and never dry. This salad also works well without meat.

# POACHED CHICKEN AND MANGO SALAD WITH FRESH COCONUT CHUTNEY AND CURRY LEAVES

**SERVES 4**

*This southern Indian-inspired salad is well worth the preparation effort for its flavour: the tempered spices and chaat masala really lift the dish. You do, however, need to be careful not to overheat the oil when tempering the spices to prevent burning.*

Vitamin-Rich | Mineral-Rich | Antioxidant-Rich | High-Protein | Rejuvenating | Gluten-Free

### COCONUT CHUTNEY

100G/3½OZ (1 CUP) FRESHLY GRATED COCONUT

1 LONG GREEN CHILLI, SEEDED AND SLICED

7.5G/¼OZ (½ CUP) CORIANDER (CILANTRO) LEAVES, ROUGHLY CHOPPED

1 TEASPOON FINELY GRATED GINGER

1 TABLESPOON LIME JUICE

SEA SALT, TO TASTE

### POACHED CHICKEN AND MANGO SALAD

4 SMALL CHICKEN BREASTS FILLETS, SKIN REMOVED

SEA SALT AND GROUND WHITE PEPPER, TO TASTE

4 CURRY LEAVES

80ML (⅓ CUP) SUNFLOWER OIL

2 SMALL VINE-RIPENED TOMATOES

1 RIPE MANGO

1 LONG GREEN CHILLI, SLICED

5G/¼OZ (¼ CUP) CORIANDER (CILANTRO) LEAVES

1 SMALL LEBANESE OR ENGLISH CUCUMBER, CUT IN HALF LENGTHWISE, SEEDED AND SLICED

¼ SMALL RED ONION, SLICED

### TEMPERED OIL

60ML (¼ CUP) CANOLA (RAPESEED) OIL

½ TEASPOON BLACK MUSTARD SEEDS

6 CURRY LEAVES

½ TEASPOON CUMIN SEEDS

½ TEASPOON CHAAT MASALA (SEE BASICS PAGE 285)

2–3 TEASPOONS LIME JUICE, TO TASTE

### TO SERVE

BANANA LEAF, FOR LINING THE PLATE (OPTIONAL)

To make the coconut chutney, place the coconut, chilli, coriander leaves, ginger, lime juice and 125ml (½ cup) water in a blender and blend to a coarse purée. Season with sea salt and transfer to a bowl.

For the tempered oil, heat the canola oil in a saucepan over a low to medium heat. Add the mustard seeds and cook until they pop. Add the curry leaves and cumin seeds and cook for 2 minutes. Remove from the heat before they colour, transfer to a bowl and stir in the chaat masala and lime juice to taste.

To make the poached chicken and mango salad, season each chicken breast with sea salt and pepper. Place each breast in separate vacuum bags with a curry leaf and a tablespoon of sunflower oil. Expel all the air from the bags and seal well. Place the bags in an immersion water circulator set at 64°C/147°F and cook sous vide for 1 hour. Remove from the water and place in a bowl of iced water to cool. When cool, remove the chicken from the bags and drain off the oil. Cut each chicken breast into 5 even wedges.

Cut the tomatoes into quarters and discard the seeds. Cut each quarter in half again, lengthwise. Peel the mango and remove the cheeks from the stone. Cut each cheek in half lengthwise, then into wedges. In a bowl, combine the tomatoes and mango with the remaining salad ingredients.

To serve, add the coconut chutney to the salad and combine well, then add 2 tablespoons of the tempered oil and season to taste with salt. Place a banana leaf, if using, on each plate and spoon a third of the salad ingredients onto the plate. Top with half of the chicken and repeat with the remaining ingredients, layering the chicken through the salad. Serve immediately.

**Note:** If you do not have the equipment to cook sous-vide, the 'white-cooked' chicken recipe (page 294) can also be used for this salad.

*This Japanese-inspired carpaccio is an easy dish you can prepare hours before serving. It relies on good-quality ingredients. We use wagyu, but choose your favourite beef, as long as it is fresh, not frozen. Use gluten-free Tamari soy if you are avoiding gluten in your diet.*

Vitamin-Rich | Antioxidant-Rich | High-Protein | Smart Carbohydrate | Gluten-Free

# CARPACCIO OF WAGYU BEEF WITH MARINATED SHIITAKE MUSHROOMS AND BUTTERNUT PUMPKIN

### SERVES 4

### CARPACCIO

240G/8OZ WAGYU BEEF SIRLOIN OR TENDERLOIN, FINELY SLICED AND SEPARATED INTO 4 60G/2OZ PORTIONS

### PONZU DRESSING

2 TEASPOONS COLD DASHI STOCK (SEE BASICS PAGE 268)

2½ TABLESPOONS LIME JUICE

2½ TABLESPOONS RAW APPLE CIDER VINEGAR

2½ TABLESPOONS TAMARI SOY

2 TEASPOONS MIRIN

### MARINATED MUSHROOM AND BUTTERNUT PUMPKIN SALAD

120G/4½OZ BUTTERNUT PUMPKIN, PEELED

2 TABLESPOONS SOAKED HIJIKI SEAWEED OR SEA SPAGHETTI (SEE BASICS PAGE 292)

4 MARINATED SHIITAKE MUSHROOMS, SLICED (SEE BASICS PAGE 275)

1½CM/¾ INCH PIECE YOUNG GINGER, PEELED AND CUT JULIENNE

### TO SERVE

4 TEASPOONS SESAME OIL

20G/¾OZ (⅓ CUP) ENOKI MUSHROOMS, BASES REMOVED AND BROKEN INTO 3 CM/1¼ INCH PIECES

2 RED RADISHES, THINLY SLICED ON A MANDOLIN THEN PLACED IN ICED WATER TO CRISP

7G/¼OZ (¼ CUP) CHIVES, CUT INTO 4CM/1½ INCH BATONS

½ TEASPOON TOASTED SESAME SEEDS

To make the carpaccio, lay the 60g/2oz portions of sliced beef flat between 2 pieces of lightly oiled baking paper. Using a wooden rolling pin or the smooth edge of a meat mallet, pound the beef until it is 3mm/⅛ inch thick. Trim each portion with a sharp paring knife through the paper. Cover and refrigerate until required.

For the ponzu dressing, combine all the ingredients in a bowl and mix well. Cover and refrigerate until ready to use.

To make the marinated mushroom and butternut pumpkin salad, use a turning slicer to cut the pumpkin into spaghetti and break into 7cm/2¾ inch lengths. Alternatively, cut into 7cm/2¾ inch julienne strips. Combine the pumpkin, drained seaweed, sliced mushrooms and ginger in a bowl.

To serve, remove one side of the paper from the beef carpaccio and place each portion meat-side down on a chilled plate before carefully removing the remaining paper. Divide the salad evenly among the 4 plates and drizzle each with 1½ tablespoons of ponzu dressing. Heat the sesame oil until it is almost smoking then spoon a teaspoon over each carpaccio. Scatter with enoki mushrooms, radishes, chives and sesame seeds, then serve immediately.

"I try to buy organic, but don't fixate on it. I look instead for foods that have been intelligently farmed without hormones and pesticides. If only more places were like Bhutan, where yaks still graze on the Himalayan pastures in the traditional way." CHRISTINA ONG

*A gamey meat like yak works really well for carpaccio. Yak, however, is hard to source outside of the Himalayas, so use venison or beef instead. The matsutake mushrooms from Bhutan work wonderfully well and the Szechuan pepper is wonderfully fragrant, with a unique zing to it.*

Vitamin-Rich | Mineral-Rich | Antioxidant-Rich | High-Protein | Rejuvenating | Gluten-Free

# CARPACCIO OF YAK WITH GRILLED MATSUTAKE MUSHROOMS AND FERN TIP SALAD

### SERVES 4

### CARPACCIO OF YAK

240G/8OZ YAK (OR VENISON OR BEEF) TENDERLOIN OR SIRLOIN, FINELY SLICED AND SEPARATED INTO 4 60G/2OZ PORTIONS

### MUSHROOMS AND FERN TIP SALAD

4 FERN TIPS, WIPED CLEANED WITH A CLOTH (OR GREEN ASPARAGUS)

2 TABLESPOONS EXTRA-VIRGIN OLIVE OIL

6 MATSUTAKE MUSHROOMS, SLICED 8MM/⅓ INCH THICK (OR BROWN BUTTON MUSHROOMS)

SEA SALT AND GROUND WHITE PEPPER, TO TASTE

2 CLOVES GARLIC, FINELY CHOPPED

2 TEASPOONS LEMON JUICE, OR TO TASTE

### TO SERVE

LEMON JUICE, TO TASTE

4 PINCHES SZECHUAN SALT AND PEPPER (SEE BASICS PAGE 285)

4 PINCHES BHUTANESE DRIED CHILLI FLAKES (OR REGULAR RED CHILLI FLAKES)

1 TABLESPOON EXTRA-VIRGIN OLIVE OIL

17G/⅔OZ (½ CUP) WATERCRESS LEAVES

1 TABLESPOON TOASTED PINE NUTS

1 LEMON, CUT INTO 6 WEDGES

To make the carpaccio, lay the 60g/2oz portions of sliced yak flat between 2 pieces of lightly oiled baking paper. Using a wooden rolling pin or the smooth edge of a meat mallet, pound the yak until it is 3mm/⅛ inch thick. Trim each portion with a sharp paring knife through the paper. Cover and refrigerate until required.

For the mushroom and fern tip salad, cook the fern tips in boiling salted water for 15 seconds, or until al dente. Remove the fern tips from the hot water, refresh them in iced water and drain.

Heat the olive oil in a heavy-based frying pan. Add the mushrooms to the pan, season with sea salt and sauté until softened. Add the garlic and sauté until lightly caramelised. Add the lemon juice to stop the caramelisation process and cook for a further 10 seconds. Remove from the stove, season with a grind of pepper then transfer the cooked mushrooms to a bowl.

To serve, remove one side of the paper from the beef carpaccio and place each portion meat-side down on a chilled plate before carefully removing the remaining paper. Season the meat with lemon juice, Szechuan salt and pepper, chilli flakes and a drizzle of extra-virgin olive oil. Divide the grilled matsutake mushroom, fern tips and watercress among the plates and sprinkle over the pine nuts. Serve immediately with a lemon wedge on the side.

# SPICED CHICKEN SKEWERS
## WITH BARLEY,
## DRIED FRUIT AND NUT SALAD
## AND HARISSA YOGHURT
### SERVES 4

*This dish is a real favourite of our regular guests at Bali's COMO Shambhala Estate. The marinade works well with any protein, tenderising and flavouring the chicken beautifully. Harissa is always good to have on hand to add to yoghurt, as in this recipe, or to use in soups. The barley salad also works well on its own. This dish is best plated as a family-style shared meal.*

Vitamin-Rich | Mineral-Rich | Antioxidant-Rich | High-Protein | Immune-Boosting | Digestive Support | Rejuvenating | Energising

## CHICKEN SKEWERS

1 PRESERVED LEMON, RINSED, PULP REMOVED AND CHOPPED (SEE BASICS PAGE 294)

12 CLOVES GARLIC, SLICED

1 SMALL RED ONION, SLICED

3CM/1¼ INCH PIECE GINGER, PEELED AND CHOPPED

1 TEASPOON GROUND CUMIN

1 TEASPOON CAYENNE PEPPER

1 TEASPOON PAPRIKA

125ML (½ CUP) OLIVE OIL

2½ TABLESPOONS LEMON JUICE

SEA SALT AND GROUND WHITE PEPPER, TO TASTE

4G/⅛OZ (¼ CUP) FLAT-LEAF PARSLEY

5G/¼OZ (¼ CUP) CORIANDER (CILANTRO) LEAVES

4 (700G/1LB 8OZ) CHICKEN BREAST FILLETS, CUT INTO 2CM/¾ INCH CHUNKS

½ LEMON

## BARLEY, DRIED FRUIT AND NUT SALAD

360G/12OZ (2 CUPS) COOKED WARM BARLEY (SEE BASICS PAGE 288)

2 STALKS CELERY, DICED

1 BABY FENNEL, CORE REMOVED AND DICED

¼ SMALL RED ONION, DICED

2 MEDJOOL DATES, PITTED AND DICED

2 DRIED APRICOTS, DICED

2 SMALL DRIED FIGS, DICED

2 TABLESPOONS DRIED CRANBERRIES

2 TABLESPOONS TOASTED FLAKED ALMONDS

2 TABLESPOON PINE NUTS, TOASTED

2 TABLESPOONS HAZELNUTS, ROASTED, PEELED AND COARSELY CHOPPED

4 SPRING ONIONS (SCALLIONS), SLICED

5G/¼OZ (¼ CUP) FLAT-LEAF PARSLEY, CHOPPED

5G/¼OZ (¼ CUP) CORIANDER (CILANTRO) LEAVES, ROUGHLY CHOPPED

125ML (½ CUP) ORANGE BLOSSOM DRESSING (SEE BASICS PAGE 279)

## TO SERVE

2 RED RADISHES, SLICED

50G/2OZ (2 CUPS) WILD ROCKET (ARUGULA)

1 ORANGE, PEELED AND SEGMENTED

3 TABLESPOONS ORANGE BLOSSOM DRESSING (SEE BASICS PAGE 279)

2 TABLESPOONS TOASTED SESAME SEEDS

125ML (½ CUP) HARISSA YOGHURT (SEE BASICS PAGE 282)

For the chicken skewers, soak 8 bamboo skewers in water for 1 hour. Put the preserved lemon, garlic, onion, ginger, spices, olive oil and lemon juice in a blender. Season to taste with salt and pepper and blend to a fine paste. Add the herbs, combine and transfer to a bowl. Mix the chicken into the marinade, cover and marinate in the fridge for at least 1 hour.

Heat a grill or barbecue to a medium to high heat. Thread the chicken pieces onto soaked bamboo skewers and season. Grill for about 4 minutes on each side, or until golden and cooked through. Transfer to a plate, squeeze over the lemon juice and allow to rest.

To make the barley, dried fruit and nut salad, combine the warm barley with the remaining ingredients, except the dressing. Dress with the orange blossom dressing and toss gently. Transfer to a bowl.

To serve, place the radishes, rocket and orange segments in a bowl and gently toss through with the orange blossom dressing. Transfer to a serving bowl. Place the skewers on a platter, sprinkle with sesame seeds and serve with barley salad, radish salad and harissa yoghurt.

GRILLED CHICKEN
WITH BRAISED PUY LENTILS,
GREEN APPLE,
CELERY AND MINT SALAD

SERVES 4

*It may seem surprising to serve chicken with lentils, but this preparation is fresh and light because of the salad of apple, celery and fresh herbs. The apple and mustard vinaigrette adds a sharpness to balance the dish, while cooking the breast on the bone helps to keep the chicken moist and juicy.*

Vitamin-Rich | Mineral-Rich | Antioxidant-Rich | High-Protein | Digestive Support | Rejuvenating | Calming | Energising | Gluten-Free

### BRAISED LENTILS

250G/9OZ (1⅓ CUPS) PUY LENTILS
2 TABLESPOONS OLIVE OIL
½ SMALL LEEK, WHITE PART ONLY, DICED
2 CLOVES GARLIC, FINELY CHOPPED
½ BROWN ONION, FINELY DICED
½ STALK CELERY, DICED
½ SMALL CARROT, DICED
SEA SALT, TO TASTE
300ML (1¼ CUPS) CHICKEN STOCK
(SEE BASICS PAGE 268)
4 SPRIGS THYME
2 TEASPOONS THYME LEAVES

### GREEN APPLE VINAIGRETTE

1 GREEN APPLE, PEELED AND CORED
1½ TABLESPOONS DIJON MUSTARD
1½ TABLESPOONS RAW RED WINE VINEGAR
2 TEASPOONS RAW HONEY
60ML (¼ CUP) EXTRA-VIRGIN OLIVE OIL

### GRILLED CHICKEN

2 DOUBLE CHICKEN BREASTS, ON THE BONE WITH
WINGS ATTACHED, ABOUT 640G/1LB 7OZ EACH
1 TABLESPOON RAW HONEY
4 SPRIGS THYME, LEAVES PICKED
2 TABLESPOONS RAW APPLE CIDER VINEGAR
2 TABLESPOONS EXTRA-VIRGIN OLIVE OIL
SEA SALT AND GROUND WHITE PEPPER, TO TASTE
OLIVE OIL, FOR BRUSHING

### GREEN APPLE AND CELERY SALAD

4 SMALL TENDER STALKS CELERY, THINLY SLICED
5G/⅛OZ (¼ CUP) TENDER CELERY LEAVES
½ GREEN APPLE, SLICED INTO HALF-MOONS
8 BELGIAN ENDIVE LEAVES (CHICORY),
CUT IN HALF LENGTHWISE
10G/⅓OZ (¼ CUP) CHERVIL LEAVES
5G/⅛OZ (¼ CUP) FLAT-LEAF PARSLEY LEAVES
2 TABLESPOONS VERJUICE (OR LEMON JUICE)
2 TABLESPOONS EXTRA-VIRGIN OLIVE OIL

### TO SERVE

2 TEASPOONS FRESHLY GRATED HORSERADISH

For the braised lentils, put the lentils in a saucepan and cover with cold water. Bring to the boil, then drain and rinse. Wipe the saucepan clean, then warm the oil over a medium heat. Add the vegetables, season to taste with salt and cook for about 6 minutes, or until tender.

Add the lentils, stock and thyme sprigs, bring to the boil then reduce the heat to a simmer. Cover with a cartouche (see Glossary, page 296) and cook over a low heat slowly for 30 to 40 minutes, or until the lentils are soft but not broken. Remove from the heat and stir in the picked thyme leaves and season with a grind of white pepper.

To make the green apple vinaigrette, put the apple, mustard, red wine vinegar and honey in a blender and blend to a fine purée. With the motor running, gradually add the olive oil, then transfer to a squeeze bottle.

To make the grilled chicken, split the chicken breasts in half but leave them on the bone. Trim the wing off while leaving the base of the wing attached. Remove the skin and wishbone.

In a bowl, combine the honey, thyme, vinegar and oil. Season with sea salt and white pepper. Pour over the chicken and marinate in the fridge for at least 1 hour. Heat an iron skillet or flat grill over a medium to high heat. Brush the chicken with a little olive oil and cook, bone-side down, on the grill for 5 to 6 minutes, or until the outside is lightly caramelised, then turn 90 degrees to create a criss-cross pattern. Cook for a further 5 to 6 minutes, before turning the breasts over and cooking for another 5 minutes. Check the chicken is cooked and when done, transfer to a plate, cover and rest for 3 minutes.

To make the apple and celery salad, mix the celery, celery leaves, apple, endive and herbs in a bowl. Whisk the verjuice with oil and season to taste. Pour the dressing over the salad and toss gently to combine.

To serve, use a knife to remove the bone from the chicken, then cut the breast in half. On 4 plates, draw an oval of green apple vinaigrette. Spoon the lentils into the oval, then top with half of the salad and then the chicken. Layer on the remaining salad and finish with the fresh horseradish.

*This recipe uses lamb fillets, tenderised in the spicy marinade. The skewers work well when cooked on a barbecue griddle plate or chargrill imparting even better flavour. Use metal skewers for drama.*

Vitamin-Rich | Mineral-Rich | Antioxidant-Rich | High-Protein | Immune-Boosting | Digestive Support
Smart Carbohydrate | Rejuvenating | Calming | Energising | Gluten-Free

# SPICED LAMB SKEWERS WITH QUINOA, GRAPE AND WALNUT SALAD WITH TAHINI YOGHURT SAUCE

### SERVES 4

### SPICED LAMB SKEWERS
2 TABLESPOONS RAW RED WINE VINEGAR
2 TEASPOONS CHOPPED THYME LEAVES
2½ TABLESPOONS GROUND CUMIN
2½ TABLESPOONS SWEET PAPRIKA
½ TEASPOON FRESHLY GROUND BLACK PEPPER
SEA SALT AND GROUND WHITE PEPPER, TO TASTE
10 LARGE LAMB FILLETS, ABOUT 140G/5OZ EACH
OLIVE OIL, FOR BRUSHING THE LAMB
½ LEMON

### VERJUICE DRESSING
2 CLOVES GARLIC
SEA SALT TO TASTE
1 TEASPOON GROUND CUMIN
60ML (¼ CUP) VERJUICE (OR LEMON JUICE)
60ML (¼ CUP) EXTRA-VIRGIN OLIVE OIL

### QUINOA, GRAPE AND WALNUT SALAD
320G/11½OZ (2 CUPS) COOKED QUINOA, COOLED TO ROOM TEMPERATURE (SEE BASICS PAGE 286)
12 SEEDLESS GREEN GRAPES, SLICED CROSSWISE
2 STALKS TENDER CELERY, SLICED
¼ SMALL RED ONION, SLICED
4 SPRING ONIONS (SCALLIONS), SLICED
8 WALNUTS, BROKEN INTO PIECES
4G/⅛OZ (¼ CUP) FLAT-LEAF PARSLEY LEAVES
25G/1OZ (¼ CUP) CORIANDER (CILANTRO) LEAVES
1 BABY GEM OR BABY COS LETTUCE, BASE REMOVED AND CUT CROSSWISE INTO 1½CM/¾ INCH SLICES

### TAHINI YOGHURT SAUCE
3 CLOVES GARLIC, SLICED
125ML (½ CUP) RAW TAHINI
1 TABLESPOON LEMON JUICE
SEA SALT, TO TASTE
125ML (½ CUP) GREEK-STYLE LOW-FAT YOGHURT
60ML (¼ CUP) HOT WATER
60ML (¼ CUP) EXTRA-VIRGIN OLIVE OIL

To make the spiced lamb skewers, soak 8 bamboo skewers in water for 2 hours to avoid them burning while cooking. Place the vinegar, thyme, spices, pepper and sea salt in a bowl and mix well. Trim the lamb of sinew and cut into 2cm/¾ inch pieces. Add to the marinade and toss to coat well. Cover and stand in the fridge for at least 1 hour. Skewer the marinated lamb pieces onto the soaked bamboo skewers. Heat an iron skillet or chargrill over a medium to high heat. Brush with a little olive oil and cook the lamb skewers for 2 to 3 minutes on all sides, until golden brown and medium rare. Transfer to a warmed plate. Squeeze lemon juice over the skewers. Cover and rest for 3 minutes.

To make the verjuice dressing, pound the garlic with a little salt using a pestle and mortar until it has turned into a paste. Whisk in the ground cumin, verjuice and extra-virgin olive oil.

To make the quinoa, grape and walnut salad, combine all the ingredients in a bowl and add the verjuice dressing. Toss gently to combine.

For the tahini yoghurt sauce, put the garlic, tahini, lemon juice and salt in the blender and blend to a fine paste. Add the yoghurt, hot water and extra-virgin olive oil and season to taste.

To serve, divide the salad among 4 plates. Arrange 2 skewers on each plate with a quenelle of the tahini yoghurt sauce on the side.

*This is a perfect late-spring dish, with the nuttiness from the Jerusalem artichoke purée giving extra depth. If heirloom tomatoes aren't available then use ripe Campari, baby Roma tomatoes or small red tomatoes on the vine. You want this dish to taste of the sun.*

Vitamin-Rich | Mineral-Rich | Antioxidant-Rich | High-Protein | Immune-Boosting | Rejuvenating | Energising | Gluten-Free

# SEARED LAMB LOIN WITH CONFIT TOMATOES, ZUCCHINI, AND MINT AND GREEN OLIVE TAPENADE

**SERVES 4**

### ROAST LAMB LOIN
1 TABLESPOON OLIVE OIL
2 LARGE LAMB LOINS, TRIMMED OF FAT AND SINEW, ABOUT 140G/5OZ
SEA SALT AND GROUND WHITE PEPPER, TO TASTE
½ LEMON
2 SPRIGS THYME

### MINT AND GREEN OLIVE TAPENADE
2 CLOVES GARLIC, SLICED
1 TABLESPOON SALTED CAPERS, RINSED
SEA SALT, TO TASTE
110G/4OZ (1 CUP) PITTED GREEN QUEEN OLIVES
1 TEASPOON FINELY GRATED LEMON ZEST
¼ TEASPOON RED CHILLI FLAKES
10G/⅓OZ (½ CUP PACKED) MINT LEAVES
1 TEASPOON LEMON JUICE
2½ TABLESPOONS EXTRA-VIRGIN OLIVE OIL

### CONFIT TOMATOES
12 SMALL HEIRLOOM TOMATOES, 6 RED AND 6 YELLOW
2 CLOVES GARLIC, CUT IN HALF AND BRUISED
125ML (½ CUP) EXTRA-VIRGIN OLIVE OIL
3 TABLESPOONS AGAVE NECTAR (G)
1½ TABLESPOONS RAW RED WINE VINEGAR
4 SPRIGS THYME
SEA SALT AND GROUND WHITE PEPPER, TO TASTE

### TO SERVE
1 ZUCCHINI (COURGETTE), SLICED INTO THICK RIBBONS ON A MANDOLIN
1 TABLESPOON LEMON DRESSING (SEE BASICS PAGE 278)
SEA SALT AND GROUND WHITE PEPPER, TO TASTE
200G/7OZ (1 CUP) JERUSALEM ARTICHOKE PURÉE (SEE BASICS PAGE 274)
4 ZUCCHINI (COURGETTE) BLOSSOMS (OPTIONAL)

For the roast lamb loin, preheat the oven to 220°C/425°F. Heat the olive oil in a heavy-based frying pan. Season the lamb with sea salt and pepper then cook for 2 to 3 minutes on each side until lightly caramelised and golden. Place in the hot oven with the thyme sprigs for 6 to 8 minutes, turning once for medium rare. Transfer to a warmed plate, squeeze the lemon juice over the cooked lamb and leave to rest for 2 to 3 minutes, which should result in well-rested medium-rare lamb.

To make the mint and green olive tapenade, place the garlic, capers and a little salt in a mortar and pound with the pestle until coarsely pounded. Add the olives and pound to a rough paste, then add the lemon zest, chilli flakes and mint and pound until combined. Add the lemon juice and olive oil, mixing well. Check the seasoning and adjust as necessary.

To make the confit tomatoes, preheat the oven to 100°C/212°F. Place 2 sheets of baking paper on 2 sheets of foil and set aside. Blanch the tomatoes in boiling water for 15 seconds, drain and plunge into iced water. Drain and peel the tomatoes.

Place the yellow tomatoes in one bowl and the red tomatoes in another. Combine the garlic, olive oil, agave nectar, vinegar and thyme sprigs to make a dressing, and divide between the 2 bowls of tomatoes. Season to taste and combine. Place each tomato mixture on a separate prepared foil parcel. Enclose the tomatoes securely to form a sealed package. Roast in the oven for 30 to 40 minutes, or until the tomatoes are soft but still holding their shape.

To serve, blanch the zucchini in boiling salted water for 30 seconds before draining and seasoning with lemon dressing, salt and pepper. Heat the artichoke purée over a low to medium heat. Spoon 2 tablespoons of artichoke purée into the centre of each plate. Arrange the confit tomatoes and zucchini on top of the purée. Slice the lamb in half lengthways and place on the vegetables. Garnish with torn zucchini flowers, if using, and a quenelle of tapenade on the side.

*Flank steak has great flavour and wagyu flank is even better, best cooked medium-rare.*

Vitamin-Rich | Mineral-Rich | Antioxidant-Rich | High-Protein | Immune-Boosting | Rejuvenating | Energising | Gluten-Free

# GRILLED WAGYU BEEF FLANK STEAK WITH ROASTED PEPPER, BROCCOLINI AND DRIED TOMATO TAPENADE

**SERVES 4**

### TOMATO TAPENADE

2 CLOVES GARLIC, SLICED

SEA SALT AND GROUND WHITE PEPPER, TO TASTE

1½ TABLESPOONS SALTED BABY CAPERS, RINSED

12 SUN-DRIED TOMATOES, SOAKED IN WARM WATER FOR 20 MINUTES, THEN DRAINED

80G/3OZ (½ CUP) PITTED LIGURIAN, NIÇOISE OR OTHER BRINE-CURED BLACK OLIVES

2 TEASPOONS LEMON JUICE

2 TABLESPOONS EXTRA-VIRGIN OLIVE OIL

### ROASTED PEPPER, BROCCOLINI AND TOMATO SALAD

60ML (¼ CUP) RAW RED WINE VINEGAR

60ML (¼ CUP) EXTRA-VIRGIN OLIVE OIL

1½ TABLESPOONS COCONUT NECTAR OR AGAVE NECTAR (G)

SEA SALT AND GROUND WHITE PEPPER, TO TASTE

4 CAMPARI OR LARGE CHERRY TOMATOES, CUT IN HALF

8 STEMS BROCCOLINI, BASES TRIMMED AND PEELED

1 LARGE ROASTED RED BELL PEPPER (CAPSICUM), GRILLED AND CUT INTO 8 STRIPS (SEE BASICS PAGE 276)

2 SPRIGS THYME

5G/¼OZ (¼ CUP) BABY BASIL LEAVES (OR REGULAR BASIL)

5G/¼OZ (¼ CUP) FLAT-LEAF PARSLEY LEAVES

### WAGYU FLANK STEAK

4 WAGYU FLANK STEAKS, ABOUT 160G/5½OZ EACH

1 CLOVE GARLIC, CHOPPED

4 SPRIGS THYME

SEA SALT AND GROUND WHITE PEPPER, TO TASTE

1 TABLESPOON RAW RED WINE VINEGAR

1 TABLESPOON EXTRA-VIRGIN OLIVE OIL

For the tomato tapenade, place the garlic and a pinch of sea salt in a mortar and pound with the pestle to a paste. Add the capers and pound into the paste. Next, add the tomatoes, olives, lemon and extra-virgin olive oil. Pound well to combine and season to taste.

To make the roasted pepper, broccolini and tomato salad, combine 2 tablespoons of the red wine vinegar, 2 tablespoons of the olive oil and 1 tablespoon of the nectar in a bowl. Season with sea salt and a grind of white pepper, add the halved tomatoes and toss to combine. Place on a foil-lined oven tray and grill under a medium heat for 20 to 30 minutes until the tomatoes soften but still hold their shape and look slightly dried. Set aside and keep warm until serving.

With the remaining vinegar, oil and nectar, toss through the grilled peppers and season to taste. Blanch the broccolini in boiling salted water for 30 to 40 seconds, remove with a slotted spoon and mix with the peppers and herbs in a bowl. Check the seasoning and adjust as necessary.

With the wagyu flank steak, rub the garlic and thyme into the meat. Season with sea salt and a grind of white pepper. Cover and leave to stand for 15 minutes to allow the flavours to infuse. Heat a chargrill over a medium to high heat and cook the beef for 4 to 5 minutes on each side (this is for medium rare). Transfer to a plate and season with the vinegar and extra-virgin olive oil, cover loosely with foil and rest for 4 minutes.

To serve, slice the beef in half lengthwise. Arrange the peppers, broccolini and tomatoes on the plate, place the beef on top and finish with a quenelle of tapenade. Pour over the meat's resting juices and serve immediately.

This is another light beef option. The grilled mushroom and red onion salad works well on its own. You may be surprised at how good the grilled onions can taste, while the fresh horseradish delivers a delicious kick.

Vitamin-Rich | Mineral-Rich | Antioxidant-Rich | High-Protein | Immune-Boosting
Digestive Support | Smart Carbohydrate | Rejuvenating | Energising | Gluten-Free

# GRILLED WAGYU BEEF SIRLOIN WITH GRILLED MUSHROOMS, BABY BEETS AND FRESH HORSERADISH

**SERVES 4**

### ROAST BABY BEETROOT

8 BABY BEETROOT, TOPS REMOVED, WASHED AND SCRUBBED

1 TABLESPOON RAW APPLE CIDER VINEGAR

1 TABLESPOON ORGANIC BROWN SUGAR

1 TABLESPOON OLIVE OIL

### GRILLED MUSHROOM AND RED ONION SALAD

1 RED ONION, CUT INTO 1CM/½ INCH SLICES

2 TEASPOONS LEMON JUICE

70ML (⅓ CUP) EXTRA-VIRGIN OLIVE OIL

SEA SALT AND GROUND WHITE PEPPER, TO TASTE

4 BROWN BUTTON MUSHROOMS, PEELED WITH STEMS REMOVED

2½ TABLESPOONS BALSAMIC VINEGAR

14G/½OZ (½ CUP) MIXED HERBS SUCH AS MINT, PARSLEY, DILL

12G/½OZ (½ CUP) WILD ROCKET (ARUGULA)

### GRILLED WAGYU SIRLOIN

4 160G/5½OZ WAGYU BEEF SIRLOIN STEAKS

SEA SALT AND GROUND WHITE PEPPER, TO TASTE

1 TABLESPOON BALSAMIC VINEGAR

1 TABLESPOON EXTRA-VIRGIN OLIVE OIL

### TO SERVE

1 BABY BEETROOT, PEELED AND THINLY SLICED ON A MANDOLIN

2 TEASPOONS FRESHLY GRATED HORSERADISH

For the roast beetroot, preheat the oven to 180°C/350°F. Place a large sheet of foil on a work surface and top this with a sheet of baking paper, placing the beetroot in the centre. Drizzle the beetroot with the vinegar, sugar and olive oil. Bring the sides of the foil together to form a parcel, then place on an oven tray and roast in the hot oven for 1 to 1½ hours, or until tender when tested with a skewer. Remove from the oven and when the beetroot is cool enough to handle, peel and cut each in half.

To make the grilled mushroom and red onion salad, heat a chargrill to a medium to high heat. Toss the onion slices with the lemon juice and 1 tablespoon of extra-virgin olive oil. Season to taste with sea salt. Cover and stand for 20 minutes to allow the flavours to develop. Then, chargrill the onions for about 3 to 4 minutes each side, or until soft.

Season the mushrooms with sea salt and a grind of white pepper, then chargrill for about 2 minutes on each side, or until soft, then transfer to a bowl. Whisk 2 tablespoons of the balsamic vinegar with 2 tablespoons of the extra-virgin olive oil and pour over the mushrooms, tossing gently to combine. Mix the mushrooms with the onions and adjust the seasoning as necessary.

Combine the herbs and rocket in another bowl. Whisk in the remaining balsamic vinegar and remaining extra-virgin olive oil. Pour over the salad, season to taste and toss through.

For the wagyu sirloin, season the beef with sea salt and white pepper. Chargrill each side for 4 to 5 minutes (for medium rare). Transfer to a plate, drizzle with the balsamic vinegar and extra-virgin olive oil and rest in a warm place for 4 minutes.

To serve, arrange the mushroom salad and roasted beetroot in the centre of the plates and top with half the rocket salad. Trim the edges of the steak then place the beef on top of the salad. Place the remaining salad on the meat. Scatter the plate with beetroot slices and a grating of fresh horseradish. Pour the resting juices from the beef over and serve with a good grind of pepper.

# Sweet Treats

CHAPTER 7

COMO Shambhala's dessert recipes are built on clean, pure flavours. For that reason, it's essential to shop wisely, using seasonal, fresh ingredients. Get the selection right, and you can't get much simpler than a perfect mango carpaccio, featured on page 236.

This chapter features a lot of raw dessert preparation techniques. This lengthens the prep time, but once you're past the first steps of soaking and blitzing, you're almost there – aside from the time it takes for the raw dessert to set. Use a freezer to get to the desired core temperature. Some ingredients can help set a filling, such as cacao butter, coconut oil and nuts, which you will see in a number of recipes. You will also notice some natural liquid sweeteners, including agave, honey or maple syrup. I try to moderate these sugary notes, while also ensuring exceptional flavours.

Taste in the end is what binds these recipes together, be they shared, plated desserts, cakes, jellies, mousses, raw tarts or simple but elegant fruit-based puddings. A number of recipes have no dairy or gluten. All are best consumed within 24 hours, but the desserts that keep the longest are the coconut jelly (page 234), the three raw tarts (pages 224, 238 and 240) and the cookies (page 242). If you're entertaining, the tart bases can be prepared in advance with the fillings made closer to the time you require them.

This is a refreshing summery dessert to serve when watermelons are at their peak in colour and sweetness. Hibiscus flowers (also known as rosella) contain even more vitamin C than oranges. They help to improve circulation and balance blood pressure by reducing blood viscosity.

Heart Healthy | Raw | Gluten-Free | Vegan

# WATERMELON, STRAWBERRY AND POMEGRANATE SALAD WITH HIBISCUS FLOWER SORBET

### SERVES 6

### HIBISCUS FLOWER SORBET
50G/2OZ (1¼ CUPS) DRIED HIBISCUS FLOWERS
500G/1LB1OZ (1¼ CUPS) STRAWBERRIES, HULLED
280G/10OZ (SCANT 1 CUP) AGAVE NECTAR (G)

### POMEGRANATE JELLY
1 LARGE POMEGRANATE
(OR, 220ML/SCANT 1 CUP BOTTLED
FRESH PURE POMEGRANATE JUICE)
1½ TABLESPOONS AGAVE NECTAR (G)
1 TEASPOON AGAR AGAR POWDER

### HIBISCUS FLOWER SYRUP
10G (¼ CUP) DRIED HIBISCUS FLOWERS
8 FRESH ORGANIC RED HIBISCUS FLOWERS
100G/3½OZ (⅓ CUP) AGAVE NECTAR (G)
1 TABLESPOON FRESHLY SQUEEZED LIME JUICE

### TO SERVE
500G/1LB1OZ WATERMELON, RIND REMOVED
250G/9OZ STRAWBERRIES, HULLED AND HALVED
1 POMEGRANATE, SEEDS REMOVED
FRESH RED HIBISCUS FLOWERS (OPTIONAL)

To make the hibiscus flower sorbet, bring 500ml (2 cups) water to the boil and add the dried flowers. Remove from the heat and leave to stand for 30 minutes to allow the flavours and colour to infuse. Strain through a sieve into a jug and discard the flowers.

Meanwhile, purée the hulled strawberries in a blender (you should have 500ml/2 cups of strawberry purée). Combine the strawberry purée, the hibiscus water and agave nectar in a bowl and mix well. Transfer the sieved strawberry purée to an ice-cream machine and churn until frozen. Spoon into an airtight container and freeze to firm up.

To make the pomegranate jelly, push the seeds of the pomegranate through a juice extractor and catch the juice in a jug (you will need 220ml/scant 1 cup). Combine the pomegranate juice, agave nectar and agar agar in a saucepan. Bring to the boil, then strain through a sieve into a 10x15cm (4x6 inch) plastic container. Cool slightly, then cover and refrigerate for at least 1 hour. Once set, tip the jelly out onto a clean board and cut into irregular wedges.

For the hibiscus flower syrup, bring 400ml/1⅔ cups water to the boil and add the dried flowers. Remove from the heat and stand for 10 minutes to allow the flavours to infuse. Strain and place in a blender with the fresh hibiscus flowers and process until puréed. Add the agave nectar and lime juice and blend to combine. Strain through a fine sieve into a glass container.

To serve, cut the watermelon into triangular wedges and place 5 pieces on each of the 6 plates. Scatter the strawberries and pomegranate jelly over and around the watermelon. Sprinkle with the pomegranate seeds and top with a scoop of strawberry hibiscus sorbet. Pour the hibiscus syrup over the fruit and finish with a fresh hibiscus flower.

**Note:** The fresh flowers lend colour and body to the syrup. If not available, add a puréed strawberry or two instead.

*This is a great alternative to the traditional carrot and walnut cake. The yoghurt for the frosting needs to be thick, resembling the consistency of double cream. Hang the yoghurt in a cheesecloth to drain off some of the liquid. The zucchini used to cover the cake should be young and firm, without too many seeds.*

Vitamin-Rich | Mineral-Rich | High Protein

# ZUCCHINI, WALNUT AND APPLE CAKE WITH LEMON-SCENTED YOGHURT

### SERVES 8

### ZUCCHINI CAKE

2 EGGS

220G/8OZ (1 CUP) BROWN SUGAR

110G/4OZ (½ CUP) OLIVE OIL

180G/6½OZ (1½ CUPS) GRATED ZUCCHINI (COURGETTE)

7CM/3 INCH PIECE GINGER, PEELED AND FINELY GRATED

1 GRANNY SMITH APPLE, PEELED, CORE REMOVED AND GRATED

170G/6OZ (1¼ CUPS) FINELY GROUND WALNUTS

150G/5OZ (1 CUP) UNBLEACHED PLAIN (ALL-PURPOSE) FLOUR

1 PINCH SEA SALT

3 TEASPOONS BAKING POWDER

2 ZUCCHINI (COURGETTES), FOR SLICING AND LAYERING OVER THE CAKE

### LEMON-SCENTED YOGHURT

480ML (2 CUPS) LOW-FAT GREEK STYLE YOGHURT

100G/3½OZ (SCANT ⅓ CUP) RAW HONEY

1 TEASPOON FINELY GRATED LEMON ZEST

### LEMON-HONEY GLAZE

2 TABLESPOONS FRESHLY SQUEEZED LEMON JUICE

2 TABLESPOONS RAW HONEY

### SPICED WALNUTS

100G/3½OZ WALNUTS

2 TABLESPOONS PURE MAPLE SYRUP

¼ TEASPOON GROUND CINNAMON

1 PINCH SEA SALT

### TO SERVE

2 TABLESPOONS MINT LEAVES

To make the zucchini cake, preheat the oven to 160°C/320°F. Lightly oil and line the base of a 10x22cm (4x8½ inch) loaf tin. Whisk the eggs and brown sugar in a bowl until light and fluffy. Gradually add the olive oil, whisking until combined.

In a separate bowl, combine the grated zucchini, ginger and apple before stirring into the egg mixture. Combine the ground walnuts, flour, salt and baking powder in a bowl then fold into the mixture.

Pour the mixture into the prepared tin and bake in the hot oven for about 50 minutes, or until cooked. It is best to test this with a skewer (when inserted in to the cake, the skewer should come out clean). Cool in the tin for 10 minutes, then transfer to a wire rack to cool. When cool, slice crosswise into a pair of even layers.

Meanwhile, bring a pot of water to the boil. Using a mandolin, slice the zucchini lengthwise into 3mm/⅛ inch thick strips. Blanch the zucchini in boiling water for 10 seconds, then refresh in iced water. Once cool, drain the zucchini and pat dry on paper towels before setting aside.

To make the lemon-scented yoghurt cream, place the yoghurt in a bowl, add the honey and lemon zest and mix well. Cover and refrigerate until ready to use.

To make the lemon-honey glaze, combine the lemon juice and honey in a small bowl and mix until combined.

To make the spiced walnuts, preheat the oven to 110°C/230°F. Place the walnuts in a bowl. Add the maple syrup, cinnamon and sea salt. Place the nuts on a baking tray and dry in the oven for 2 hours. Store in an airtight jar for up to a week.

To serve, use a palette knife to spread half of the lemon-scented yoghurt onto the base layer of the cake and top with the second layer. Spread the remaining yoghurt over the whole cake to cover. Lay the zucchini slices crosswise over the cake, slightly overlapping and draping down each side. Brush with the glaze and decorate with spiced walnuts and mint leaves.

*This is the perfect vegan chocolate mousse. It could also be deemed raw if the cacao butter were softened in the sun or very gently in the kitchen below 66°C/151°F.*

Vitamin-Rich | Mineral-Rich | Digestive Support | Raw | Gluten-Free

# CACAO MOUSSE
# WITH
# FRESH RASPBERRIES
# AND PISTACHIOS

**SERVES 4**

**CACAO MOUSSE**

35G/1½OZ (¼ CUP) RAW CACAO POWDER
1 LARGE BANANA, PEELED AND SLICED
200G/7OZ AVOCADO FLESH
85G/3OZ (¼ CUP) RAW HONEY
35G/1½OZ (¼ CUP) YOUNG COCONUT MEAT
90G/3OZ (¼ CUP) MAPLE SYRUP
1 TABLESPOON FRESHLY SQUEEZED LIME JUICE
80G/3OZ (¼ CUP) CACAO BUTTER, ROOM TEMPERATURE (G)
1 PINCH SEA SALT

**TO SERVE**

175G/6OZ (1½ CUPS) RASPBERRIES
35G/1½OZ (¼ CUP) SHELLED PISTACHIOS, CHOPPED

To make the cacao mousse, place all the ingredients, except the cacao butter and salt, in a blender until well combined. Add the cacao butter and salt and blend until smooth and emulsified. Spoon into serving glasses, cover and refrigerate for at least a couple of hours, or until set.

To serve, scatter the fresh raspberries on top of the mousse and sprinkle with the pistachios.

*The exceptional butternut pumpkins of Bhutan were the inspiration for this wholesome cake. They impart a uniquely rich flavour and vibrant colour.*

Vitamin-Rich | Antioxidant-Rich

# WHOLEMEAL BUTTERNUT PUMPKIN AND ORANGE CAKE WITH BUTTERNUT PUMPKIN CREAM

**SERVES 16**

### BUTTERNUT PUMPKIN CAKE

4 EGGS

310G/11OZ (1⅓ CUPS) BROWN SUGAR

300ML (1¼ CUPS) OLIVE OIL

240G/8½OZ (1 CUP) ROASTED BUTTERNUT PUMPKIN PURÉE (SEE BASICS PAGE 272)

320G/11OZ (2 CUPS) WHOLEMEAL FLOUR

2 TEASPOONS BAKING POWDER

1 PINCH SEA SALT

2 ORANGES, SKIN AND WHITE PITH REMOVED, SEGMENTED

### BUTTERNUT PUMPKIN CREAM

240ML (1 CUP) LOW-FAT GREEK-STYLE YOGHURT

180G/6OZ (½ CUP) RAW HONEY

480G/1LB 1OZ (2 CUPS) ROASTED BUTTERNUT PUMPKIN PURÉE (SEE BASICS PAGE 272)

1 VANILLA BEAN (POD), SPLIT LENGTHWISE AND SEEDS SCRAPED OUT

### CANDIED PUMPKIN SEEDS

50G/2OZ (¼ CUP) PUMPKIN SEEDS

1 TEASPOON RAW HONEY

½ TEASPOON SEA SALT

### TO SERVE

PUMPKIN BLOSSOMS, PETALS PLUCKED (OPTIONAL)

To make the butternut pumpkin cake, preheat the oven to 160°C/320°F. Lightly oil and line the base of 3 cake tins (each 18cm/7 inches). Using an electric beater, whisk the eggs and brown sugar in a bowl until light and fluffy. Gradually whisk in the olive oil then add the butternut pumpkin. Incorporate the flour, baking powder and sea salt into the mixture. Pour the batter evenly between the prepared cake tins. Bake for 35 minutes, or until a skewer inserted into the middle of the cake comes out clean. Leave the cake to stand in the tin for 5 minutes, then turn out on a wire rack to cool.

To make the butternut pumpkin cream, place the yoghurt, honey, butternut pumpkin purée and scraped seeds of the vanilla bean into a bowl and whisk to combine. Cover and refrigerate until ready to use.

For the candied pumpkin seeds, place the pumpkin seeds in a bowl, cover with water and soak for 1 hour. Rinse, drain and pat dry with a paper towel. Combine the seeds, honey and sea salt in a bowl. Spread the seeds over a Teflex or non-stick sheet on a dehydrator tray and dry on 48°C/118°F for 12 hours, until crisp and dry. Alternatively, dry in an oven heated on its lowest settting. Store in an airtight glass jar for a week.

To serve, place one cake on a serving plate and top with a third of the butternut pumpkin cream and then a third of the orange segments. Place a second cake on top and spread with another third of the pumpkin cream and orange segments. Place the third cake on top and spread the remaining pumpkin cream on top and sides to cover, smoothing with a spatula. Finish with the candied pumpkin seeds and pumpkin blossoms.

*Rose apples add a crisp texture and delicate scent to this dish, contrasting against the smooth cashew and strawberry filling.*

High Protein | Digestive Support | Raw | Gluten-Free | Vegan

# STRAWBERRY, VANILLA AND CASHEW TART WITH ROSE APPLE

**SERVES 6**

### COCONUT ALMOND BASE

40G/1½OZ (½ CUP) FLAKED ALMONDS

125G/4½OZ (1¼ CUPS) DRIED STRAWBERRIES

30G/1OZ (1 TABLESPOON PLUS 1 TEASPOON) AGAVE NECTAR (G)

40G/1½OZ (½ CUP) UNSWEETENED DESICCATED (DRY) COCONUT

2½ TABLESPOONS VIRGIN COCONUT OIL

50G/2OZ CACAO BUTTER (G)

¼ TEASPOON SEA SALT

### STRAWBERRY, VANILLA AND CASHEW FILLING

225G/8OZ (1½ CUPS) CASHEWS

60ML (¼ CUP) YOUNG COCONUT WATER

65G/2½OZ (½ CUP) STRAWBERRIES, HULLED

75G/3OZ (½ CUP) YOUNG COCONUT MEAT

60ML (¼ CUP) COCONUT OIL

1 TABLESPOON FRESHLY SQUEEZED LEMON JUICE

½ VANILLA BEAN (POD), SPLIT LENGTHWISE

90G/3OZ (⅓ CUP) AGAVE NECTAR (G)

½ TEASPOON SEA SALT

### TO SERVE

250G/9OZ STRAWBERRIES, HULLED AND CUT INTO QUARTERS

2 ROSE APPLES, QUARTERED, CORED AND SLICED LENGTHWISE

PESTICIDE-FREE BABY PINK ROSE PETALS (OPTIONAL)

STORE-BOUGHT DEHYDRATED STRAWBERRIES (OPTIONAL)

For the coconut almond base, line the base and sides of 8 fluted tart tins with removable bases (each 8cm/3 inch) with clingfilm. Place all the ingredients in a food processor. Using the pulse button, process until the mixture resembles coarse breadcrumbs. Transfer the mixture to a bowl, cover and refrigerate for 30 minutes until firm. Divide the mixture evenly into each prepared tart tin and press the mixture over the base and sides until 3mm/⅛ inch thick. Place the tart cases in the dehydrator for 3 hours at 48°C/118°F. Alternatively, dry in an oven heated on its lowest setting. Remove and cool before use.

To make the strawberry, vanilla and cashew filling, place the cashews in a bowl, cover with water and soak for 3 hours before draining and rinsing. Place the cashews and the remaining ingredients in a blender and process until the mixture is smooth and emulsified. Refrigerate the mixture until it is set, about 6 hours.

To serve, place the tart cases on 8 plates. Spoon the mixture into the cases, then top each with sliced strawberries and rose apples. Sprinkle with baby pink roses and dehydrated strawberries.

**Note:** If rose apples are not available, use stone fruits such as peaches, plums or nectarines.

"In the tropical Caribbean, sweetness is in the air: the fruits, the pineapples, the pretty delicacies that our chefs at COMO Parrot Cay prepare to lighten an already light-as-cloud day." CHRISTINA ONG

*This dessert has been known to convert the most avid cheesecake connoisseur away from the dairy-based version. It was first showcased at COMO Parrot Cay and is full of the flavours of the Caribbean.*

# MANGO AND PASSIONFRUIT 'CHEESECAKE' WITH BANANA AND MACADAMIA NUT CRUST

## SERVES 12

### CHEESECAKE CRUST

210G/7½OZ (1½ CUPS) MACADAMIA NUTS
90G/3OZ (1 CUP) FRESHLY GRATED COCONUT
2 TABLESPOONS AGAVE NECTAR (G)
1 TABLESPOON FINELY GRATED LIME ZEST
60ML (¼ CUP) VIRGIN COCONUT OIL
1 PINCH SEA SALT

### MANGO CHEESECAKE FILLING

225G/8OZ (1½ CUPS) RAW CASHEWS
125ML (½ CUP) PASSIONFRUIT JUICE
5 TEASPOONS AGAR AGAR
1 VANILLA BEAN (POD), SPLIT LENGTHWISE AND SEEDS SCRAPED OUT
2 LARGE MANGOES, PEELED AND DICED
125ML (½ CUP) ALMOND NUT MILK (SEE BASICS PAGE 267)
90G/3OZ (⅓ CUP) AGAVE NECTAR (G)
2 TABLESPOONS FRESHLY SQUEEZED LIME JUICE
250ML (1 CUP) VIRGIN COCONUT OIL

### PASSIONFRUIT SYRUP

2 TABLESPOONS PASSIONFRUIT PULP
120G/4½OZ (⅓ CUP) AGAVE NECTAR (G)

### TO SERVE

5 MANGOES
3 BABY BANANAS, PEELED AND QUARTERED LENGTHWISE
CHEMPAKA FLOWERS (OPTIONAL)

To make the cheesecake crust, line the base of a 20cm/8 inch springform pan with baking paper. Place the macadamias in a bowl, cover with water and soak for 2 hours. Drain and rinse the nuts and pat them dry with a paper towel. Transfer the macadamias to a food processor and, using the pulse button, pulse until the mixture resembles coarse breadcrumbs, then place in a bowl. Add the remaining ingredients and mix to combine. Cover and refrigerate for 30 minutes to set. Press the mixture over the base of the prepared pan (it should be 5mm/¼ inch thick). Cover and refrigerate until ready to use.

To make the mango cheesecake filling, place the cashews in a bowl, cover with water and soak for 4 hours, drain and rinse. Combine the passionfruit juice and agar agar in a small saucepan, whisk over a medium to high heat and bring to the boil. Transfer the juice to a blender. Scrape the vanilla seeds into the mixture, add the remaining ingredients and blend to a smooth purée, then pour over the prepared crust. Cover and refrigerate for at least 4 hours, or until set.

To make the passionfruit syrup, mix the passionfruit with agave nectar and store in a glass jar.

To serve, carefully release the collar from the cake, slide the cake off the base and onto a serving plate. Peel the mangoes, then using a sharp knife, remove the base so the mango sits flat on the board and slice the cheeks into 1mm/1/16 inch thick slices. Place the mango slices so they are slightly overlapping each other all over the cake and draping down the side, ensuring the whole cake is covered. Top with baby bananas, scatter with Chempaka flowers, if using, and drizzle with the passionfruit syrup.

**Note:** Soak the cashews for as long as possible in order to obtain a really smooth texture for the filling. Baby bananas are intensely sweet and creamy. If unavailable, use a regular banana instead, sliced crosswise.

*This lively dessert is a great alternative to rice pudding and is jam-packed with nutrients. The flavours of the beetroot, cardamom, orange and goat-milk yoghurt marry beautifully.*

Heart Healthy | Gluten-Free

# BEETROOT AND QUINOA PUDDING WITH CARDAMOM-SCENTED GOAT MILK YOGHURT SORBET

**SERVES 8**

### BEETROOT PUDDING

250G/9OZ BEETROOT, ABOUT 4 PIECES

150G/5OZ (SCANT ½ CUP) RAW HONEY

325ML (1⅓ CUPS) ALMOND NUT MILK
(SEE BASICS PAGE 267)

150ML (⅔ CUP) FRESHLY SQUEEZED ORANGE JUICE

35G/1½OZ (¼ CUP) CORNFLOUR (CORNSTARCH)

120G/4½OZ (¾ CUP) COOKED QUINOA
(SEE BASICS PAGE 286)

### GOAT MILK YOGHURT SORBET

6 CARDAMOM PODS, CRUSHED

480ML (2 CUPS) LOW-FAT GREEK-STYLE
GOAT MILK YOGHURT

300G/10½OZ (SCANT 1 CUP) RAW HONEY

2½ TABLESPOONS FRESHLY
SQUEEZED LEMON JUICE

### TO SERVE

3 BLOOD ORANGES, PEELED, ALL PITH REMOVED
THEN CUT INTO SEGMENTS

2 TABLESPOONS RAW HONEY

1 BABY BEETROOT, PEELED AND
THINLY SLICED ON A MANDOLIN

2 TABLESPOONS STORE-BOUGHT PUFFED QUINOA
OR PUFFED SPELT (OPTIONAL)

To make the beetroot pudding, lightly oil a 10x22cm (4x8½ inch) loaf tin. Peel the beetroot and use a mandolin to cut it julienne. Cook the beetroot in boiling, lightly-salted water for 3 to 4 minutes, or until al dente. Drain in a colander.

Combine the honey, almond nut milk and orange juice in a saucepan and bring to the boil over a medium heat. Combine the cornflour with 1½ tablespoons water and add to the almond nut milk mixture. Continue cooking, whisking until the mixture returns to the boil, then reduce the heat and simmer for 3 minutes. Add the beetroot and quinoa and cook, stirring regularly, over a low heat for 20 minutes. Pour the mixture into an oiled tin, cool for 30 minutes on a rack, then refrigerate for 3 to 4 hours, or until set.

To make the goat milk yoghurt sorbet, bring 300ml (1¼ cups) water to the boil. Add the cardamom pods, remove from the heat and allow the flavours to infuse for 10 minutes. Add the remaining ingredients to the saucepan and whisk well to combine. Strain through a sieve and discard the pods. Churn the mixture in an ice-cream machine until almost frozen (do not over-churn or the mixture will split). Transfer to a plastic container and freeze to firm up.

To serve, place a slice of beetroot quinoa pudding on a plate, top with blood orange segments, drizzle with honey and scatter with sliced raw beetroot and puffed quinoa.

*Soursops are highly flavourful, and the velvety texture of this sorbet is amazing. Aloe vera in its fresh form after peeling is extremely bitter. Our processing method removes that taste. Give it a go, because the final combination of cooling flavours is well worth the effort that goes into this slightly more complicated recipe.*

Heart Healthy | Digestive Support | Gluten-Free | Vegan

# CHILLED CUCUMBER SOUP WITH ALOE VERA AND SOURSOP SORBET

**SERVES 8**

### POACHED ALOE VERA
500G/1LB 1OZ PEELED ALOE VERA (2 LARGE STEMS)
500G/1LB 1OZ (SCANT 1½ CUPS) AGAVE NECTAR (G)

### SOURSOP SORBET
2 VERY RIPE SOURSOPS OR CUSTARD APPLES
250G/9OZ (¾ CUP) AGAVE NECTAR (G)

### CHILLED CUCUMBER SOUP
2–3 LEBANESE OR ENGLISH CUCUMBERS
2 TABLESPOONS AGAVE NECTAR (G)

### TO SERVE
1 LEBANESE CUCUMBER, PEELED, CUT INTO QUARTERS LENGTHWISE AND SEEDED
1 AVOCADO, PEELED, CUT INTO EIGHTHS, THEN INTO SMALL WEDGES
15G/½OZ DRIED BASIL SEEDS, SOAKED IN WATER FOR 1 HOUR
1 GREEN MANGO CHEEK, CUT JULIENNE
1 TEASPOON GINGER JULIENNE
2 TABLESPOONS LEMON BASIL LEAVES

To make the poached aloe vera, bring 2 litres (8 cups) salted water to the boil. Meanwhile, wash the peeled aloe vera under running water to remove the slimy outer membrane. Cut the stems into 3cm/1¼ inch triangular wedges and place in a stainless steel bowl. Carefully pour 500ml (2 cups) boiling salted water over the aloe vera and stir well to agitate, then drain. Repeat this process 3 more times, then place the drained aloe vera in a clean bowl. Pour 350g/12oz (1 cup) of agave nectar over the aloe vera, or enough to cover. Cover with clingfilm and refrigerate overnight. The next day, drain the aloe vera and discard the nectar. Place the aloe vera in an airtight container and cover with the remaining agave nectar.

To make the soursop sorbet, peel the outer skins from the soursops and use a small sharp knife to remove the seeds. Juice the flesh through a juice extractor then place in a bowl, add the agave nectar to the strained purée and churn in an ice-cream machine until frozen. Transfer to an airtight container and freeze to firm up.

To make the chilled cucumber soup, push the whole cucumbers through a juice extractor and catch the juice in a jug. Add the agave nectar and stir to combine, then strain through a sieve. Cover and refrigerate until ready to serve.

To serve, cut each quarter of Lebanese cucumber into 10 wedges. Place a 10cm/4 inch ring mould on each serving plate, spoon 60ml (¼ cup) of drained aloe vera into each mould then divide the avocado and cucumber wedges among the remaining moulds. Top with a teaspoon of basil seeds and a scoop of soursop sorbet. Decorate with the green mango, ginger and lemon basil. Serve with 50ml (1/5 cup) of cucumber soup in a jug on the side.

*This simple dessert takes its inspiration from Bali, where mangosteen, native to Indonesia, are full flavoured and succulent. The young coconuts grown on our property at COMO Shambhala Estate are full of meat and abundant in nutrient-rich water.*

Heart Healthy | Gluten-Free | Vegan

# YOUNG COCONUT JELLY WITH MANGOSTEEN SOUP

**SERVES 6**

### YOUNG COCONUT JELLY
2 YOUNG COCONUTS
1 TABLESPOON COCONUT NECTAR
OR AGAVE NECTAR (G)
½ TEASPOON AGAR AGAR

### MANGOSTEEN SOUP
15 LARGE MANGOSTEEN
110G/4OZ (⅓ CUP) COCONUT NECTAR (G)
1 TABLESPOON FRESHLY SQUEEZED LIME JUICE

### TO SERVE
6 MANGOSTEEN, PEELED AND
SEPARATED INTO SEGMENTS
10 RAMBUTANS, PEELED AND FLESH SLICED
OFF TO GIVE 3 'CHEEKS' PER FRUIT
(OR LYCHEES)
12 LONGANS OR LYCHEES, PEELED,
HALVED AND SEEDED

To make the young coconut jelly, cut open the coconuts and drain the coconut water through a sieve into a jug (you will need 400ml/1⅔ cups). Using a large kitchen spoon, scoop out the flesh and cut into strips.

Combine the coconut water, nectar and agar agar in a saucepan. Bring to the boil, whisking well to combine, then strain through a sieve into a bowl. Add the coconut strips and pour the mixture into 125ml (½ cup) capacity dariole moulds. Refrigerate for 4 hours, or until set.

To make the mangosteen soup, peel the mangosteen and remove any seeds (you will need 500g/1lb 1oz flesh). Place in a blender and purée. Pass through a chinois (a fine mesh conical sieve) to yield 300ml (1¼ cups) of purée. Add 50ml (scant ¼ cup) water, coconut nectar and lime juice to the purée and mix well. Store in a glass jar until ready to use.

To serve, unmould the jellies into shallow bowls, and arrange the mangosteen, rambutans and longan around the jellies. Pour 50ml (scant ¼ cup) mangosteen soup into each bowl.

*This dessert is all about mangoes – which are magnificent in aroma and flavour when they come into season in Bali. This dessert also showcases another fantastic Indonesian product, the vanilla bean, with the large, plump pods mainly grown in Java.*

Raw | Gluten-Free | Vegan

# MANGO CARPACCIO
# WITH
# VANILLA BEAN
# AND KAFFIR LIME
# SYRUP

**SERVES 4**

### MANGO SORBET
4 MANGOES
350G/12OZ (1 CUP) AGAVE NECTAR (G)
60ML (¼ CUP) FRESHLY SQUEEZED LIME JUICE

### VANILLA AND LIME SYRUP
125G/4½OZ (⅓ CUP) AGAVE NECTAR (G)
1 VANILLA BEAN (POD), SPLIT LENGTHWISE
2 KAFFIR LIME LEAVES, CRUSHED
1 LIME, ZEST ONLY
2 TABLESPOONS FRESHLY SQUEEZED LIME JUICE

### TO SERVE
4 MANGOES
1 KAFFIR LIME LEAF, VERY THINLY SLICED
4 MANGO LEAVES (OPTIONAL)

To make the mango sorbet, peel the mangoes, cut the flesh from the seed and purée in a blender until smooth (you will need 1 litre/4 cups of mango purée). Add the agave nectar and lime juice to the mango and mix well. Churn in an ice-cream machine until frozen. Transfer to a plastic container and freeze for 2 hours to firm up.

To make the vanilla and lime syrup, place the agave nectar in a bowl, then scrape the seeds from the vanilla bean into the agave nectar. Add the crushed kaffir lime leaves and lime zest, then leave to stand for 15 minutes to allow the flavours to infuse. Add the lime juice, then strain through a fine metal sieve into a glass jar. Refrigerate until ready to use.

To serve, peel the mangoes, cut away the cheeks, place them cut-side down on a board and thinly slice lengthwise. Place 2 whole sliced cheeks in a 12cm/4¾ inch ring mould on a serving plate and gently fan slices around the inside of the mould to create a spiral formation. Drizzle the mango with the vanilla and lime syrup and place a scoop of mango sorbet in the centre. Scatter with kaffir lime leaf. Decorate with a mango leaf for contrast.

*This vibrant gluten- and dairy-free tart is fabulously colourful and flavoursome if you use heirloom varieties of carrot. At COMO Shambhala Estate, we use royal jelly in place of honey, which increases energy levels, helps reduce stress and boosts the immune system.*

Vitamin-Rich | Mineral-Rich | Antioxidant-Rich | Digestive Support | Raw | Gluten-Free

# CARROT, DRIED APRICOT AND COCONUT TART WITH CARROT AND PASSIONFRUIT SORBET

### SERVES 16

### APRICOT TART SHELL
120G/4½OZ (1½ CUPS) FLAKED ALMONDS
75G/3OZ (½ CUP) DRIED APRICOTS, CHOPPED
60ML (¼ CUP) VIRGIN COCONUT OIL
15G/½OZ (¼ CUP) GRATED FRESH COCONUT, TOASTED
1 PINCH SEA SALT

### CARROT AND COCONUT FILLING
150G/5OZ (1 CUP) RAW CASHEWS
5 CARROTS
150G/5OZ (1 CUP) YOUNG COCONUT MEAT
255G/9OZ (¾ CUP) ROYAL JELLY OR RAW HONEY (G)
375ML (1½ CUPS) COCONUT OIL
1 ORANGE, ZEST ONLY, FINELY GRATED
½ NUTMEG, FINELY GRATED
1 PINCH GROUND CINNAMON
¼ TEASPOON SEA SALT

### CARROT AND PASSIONFRUIT SORBET
300G/10½OZ CARROT, CHOPPED
150G/5OZ (1 CUP) YOUNG COCONUT MEAT
500ML (2 CUPS) PASSIONFRUIT JUICE
300G/10½OZ (JUST UNDER 1 CUP) RAW HONEY

### CARROT PURÉE
500G/1LB 1OZ CARROTS
30G/1OZ (1 TABLESPOON PLUS 1 TEASPOON) RAW HONEY

### TO SERVE
340G/12OZ (1 CUP) ROYAL JELLY OR RAW HONEY (G)
250ML (1 CUP) PASSIONFRUIT PULP
6 BABY CARROTS, PREFERABLY HEIRLOOM, PEELED AND SLICED LENGTHWISE ON A MANDOLIN

To make the tart shell, line a 28cm/11 inch tart pan (with a removable base) with clingfilm. Place the almonds in a bowl, cover with water and soak for 1 hour. Drain, rinse and pat dry on a paper towel. Place the almonds and remaining ingredients in a food processor and, using the pulse button, process until it resembles coarse breadcrumbs. Transfer to a bowl, cover with clingfilm and refrigerate for 30 minutes to firm up slightly. Press the mixture over the base and sides of the prepared tin until it is 4mm/¼ inch thick, cover with clingfilm and place in the dehydrator for 3 hours on 48°C/118°F. Alternatively, dry in an oven heated on its lowest setting.

To make the carrot and coconut filling, place the cashews in a bowl, cover with water and soak for 4 hours. Drain and rinse. Push 2 to 3 carrots through a juice extractor and catch the juice in a jug (you will need 250ml/1 cup). Peel and chop the remaining 2 carrots and steam until tender, then transfer to a blender and purée. Add the remaining ingredients to the blender and process until smooth and emulsified. Fill the tart shell and refrigerate until set.

To make the carrot and passionfruit sorbet, steam the carrots until tender, and transfer to a blender. Add the passionfruit juice, young coconut meat and honey and blend until smooth. Pass through a fine sieve, then transfer to an ice-cream machine and churn until frozen. Spoon into a plastic container and freeze to firm up.

To make the carrot purée, chop 300g/10½oz of the carrots and steam until tender. Place in a blender. Push the remaining carrots through a juice extractor and catch the juice in a jug. Add 70ml (⅓ cup) of the strained juice to the blender with the honey and blend to a smooth purée.

To serve, spoon 1 tablespoon of carrot purée onto each of 4 plates, and top the purée with a spoonful of passionfruit pulp. Place a slice of tart over the purée, arrange sliced heirloom carrots over the tart, drizzle with raw honey and serve a scoop of sorbet on the side.

*Most people consider eating chocolate a guilty pleasure. Think of it instead as just pure pleasure by using chocolate or cacao in its raw unadulterated state, which is rich in nutrients and highly beneficial to health. The cacao is packed with antioxidants, as are the grapes, which make this dessert a winner on every level.*

Vitamin-Rich | Mineral-Rich | Gluten-Free | Vegan

# CACAO, COCONUT, RAISIN AND ALMOND TART

### SERVES 16

### ALMOND CACAO TART SHELL

160G/5½OZ (2 CUPS) FLAKED ALMONDS
75G/3OZ (½ CUP) RAISINS
2 TABLESPOONS AGAVE NECTAR (G)
40G/1½OZ (¼ CUP) CACAO BUTTER (G)
1 TABLESPOON ORGANIC PALM SUGAR (G)
1 TABLESPOON RAW CACAO POWDER
1 PINCH SEA SALT

### CACAO AND COCONUT FILLING

125ML (½ CUP) YOUNG COCONUT WATER
2 TABLESPOONS AGAR AGAR
2 VANILLA BEANS (PODS), SPLIT LENGTHWISE AND SEEDS SCRAPED OUT
435G/15OZ (3 CUPS) YOUNG COCONUT MEAT
225G/8OZ (1 CUP) SLICED BANANAS
90G/3OZ (⅓ CUP) AGAVE NECTAR (G)
70G/2½OZ (⅓ CUP) ORGANIC PALM SUGAR (G)
70G/2½OZ (½ CUP) RAW ORGANIC CACAO POWDER
120G/4½OZ (¾ CUP) CACAO BUTTER (G)
125ML (½ CUP) COCONUT OIL

### SEMI-DRIED GRAPE SYRUP

1KG/2¼LB (6 CUPS) SEEDLESS RED GRAPES
150G/5OZ (½ CUP) AGAVE NECTAR (G)

### TO SERVE

165G/6OZ (1 CUP) FRESH RED OR BLACK SEEDLESS GRAPES
160G/5½OZ (1 CUP) SEMI-DRIED GRAPES OR RAISINS
CACAO BEANS, ROUGHLY CHOPPED

To make the almond cacao tart shell, line a 28cm/11 inch tart tin (with a removable base) with clingfilm. Place the almonds in a bowl, cover with water and soak for 1 hour. Drain the almonds and process with the remaining ingredients in a food processor, using the pulse button until the mixture resembles coarse breadcrumbs. Transfer to a bowl, cover and refrigerate for 30 minutes to firm up slightly. Press the mixture into the base and sides of the prepared tart tin until 4mm/¼ inch thick. Dehydrate for 3 hours on 48°C/118°F. Alternatively, dry in an oven heated on its lowest setting.

To make the cacao and coconut filling, combine the young coconut water and agar agar and in a small saucepan and bring to the boil, whisking well. Then transfer to a blender, adding the scraped seeds of vanilla beans. Add the remaining ingredients and blend until the mixture is smooth and emulsified. Fill the tart shell, cover and refrigerate for 4 to 6 hours, or until set.

To make the semi-dried grape syrup, wash the grapes and remove from the stems. Place the grapes on a dehydrator and dry at 48°C/118°F for 18 to 20 hours, or until semi-dried. Combine 160g/5¼oz (1 cup) of semi-dried grapes with the nectar and store in a glass jar. Reserve the extra semi-dried grapes.

To serve, place a slice of the tart on a serving plate, slice the black grapes into rounds and scatter over the tart. Spoon over the semi-dried grape syrup, then top with crushed cacao beans and the extra semi-dried grapes.

These cookies are a staple at COMO Parrot Cay, where the recipe was first devised. They are now featured in many of our COMO properties. Packed full of goodness, they are a great 'sweet treat' snack, and a fun way to get your recommended daily intake of nuts, which contain magnesium, zinc, calcium and iron, and also assist with lowering bad cholesterol.

Heart Healthy | Raw | Gluten-Free

# COMO SHAMBHALA
# POWER COOKIES

### MAKES 30

75G/3OZ (½ CUP) RAW CASHEWS
40G/1½OZ (½ CUP) FLAKED ALMONDS
50G/2OZ (½ CUP) WALNUTS
75G/3OZ (½ CUP) SUNFLOWER SEEDS
100G/3½OZ (½ CUP) PUMPKIN SEEDS
100G/3½OZ (½ CUP) DRIED FIGS
75G/3OZ (½ CUP) DRIED APRICOTS
2 TABLESPOONS RAW HONEY
2 TEASPOONS FRESHLY GRATED COCONUT
SEA SALT, TO TASTE

Place the nuts in a bowl, cover with water and soak for 2 hours. Drain and rinse the nuts. Transfer to a food processor, add the remaining ingredients and season with sea salt. Using the pulse button process until chopped. Check the seasoning and adjust as necessary.

Roll the mixture into 30 even balls and mould into round discs 2.5cm/1 inch in diameter using a small ring mould as a guide. Place the biscuits on a Teflex or non-stick sheet on a dehydrator tray and dry on 48°C/118°F for 12 hours, turning over after 6 hours. Alternatively, dry in an oven heated on its lowest setting. Cool and store in a sealed jar for up to 10 days.

# Beverages

Therapeutic juices are a critical part of COMO Shambhala Cuisine. Each has been developed by our resident nutritionists at our properties to address specific health needs. Some of the ingredients may not read as palatable, but that's where the combinations work. These recipes not only maximise the health benefits, but are also delicious.

Use fresh and organic ingredients wherever possible, and consume the juice soon after making, in order to make the most of those vital nutrients. As to the juicer, we prefer one that gently presses and masticates, without bruising or grinding the ingredients.

The warm beverages are definitely worth a try. The hot cacao (page 260) is simply delicious, while the ginger tea (page 259) is a COMO Shambhala classic. The secret is all in the brewing.

*Liver Flush*

*Vital Veg*

Culture Shock

Liver Flush

Blood of the Earth

Lymph Purifier

This drink is popular with children, as well as those new to juicing. It's great for the skin and can help balance the digestive tract. For busy people, this drink serves well as a breakfast-on-the-run or a mid-afternoon drink to stave off hunger until dinner time. It is quite filling due to the yoghurt and banana content but also refreshing with the passionfruit and orange.

Vitamin-Rich | Mineral-Rich | Heart Healthy | Digestive Support | Smart Carbohydrate | Gluten-Free

# CULTURE SHOCK

**SERVES 1**

1 ORANGE, PEELED AND QUARTERED
150G/5OZ (1¼ CUPS) STRAWBERRIES, HULLED
1 BANANA, PEELED
½ PASSIONFRUIT, PULP ONLY
3 RAMBUTANS, PEELED AND SEEDED
(OR EXTRA BERRIES)
80ML (⅓ CUP) LOW-FAT GREEK-STYLE YOGHURT

Put the orange through a juice extractor, catching the liquid in a jug, and transfer to a blender.

Add the remaining ingredients and blend until well combined. Pour into a glass and serve immediately.

A trio of delicious, 'non-sweet', therapeutic juices. Cranberry Healer supports urinary tract health and is fantastically refreshing with those cooling cucumbers. Green Clean is one of our most popular: balanced and palatable for those not so keen on their greens. Green Clean helps build lean muscles, boosts energy and immunity, and aids detoxification. Liver Flush is one of the most beneficial juices – helping to cleanse the liver and gallbladder, protecting the heart and softening the skin. It's a great way to start the day, and is best consumed on an empty stomach.

Cranberry Healer          Green Clean          Liver Flush

# CRANBERRY HEALER

### SERVES 1

Vitamin-Rich | Mineral-Rich | Antioxidant-Rich | Heart Healthy | Digestive Support
Smart Carbohydrate | Cleansing | Raw | Gluten-Free | Vegan

I LEBANESE CUCUMBER, CUT INTO QUARTERS
I ORANGE, PEELED AND CUT INTO QUARTERS
I LIME, PEELED AND CUT INTO QUARTERS
120G/4½OZ (I CUP) FROZEN CRANBERRIES

Put the cucumber, orange and lime through a juice extractor, using a jug to catch the juice.

Transfer the liquid to a blender, add the frozen cranberries and blend until smooth. Pour into a glass and serve immediately.

# GREEN CLEAN

### SERVES 1

Vitamin-Rich | Mineral-Rich | Antioxidant-Rich | High-Protein | Cleansing
Rejuvenating | Calming | Raw | Gluten-Free | Vegan

2 GREEN APPLES, CUT INTO QUARTERS
½ BABY FENNEL BULB, CUT INTO WEDGES
½ TELEGRAPH CUCUMBER, QUARTERED
50G/2OZ (2 CUPS) ENGLISH SPINACH
½ GREEN BELL PEPPER (CAPSICUM), SEEDED
4 STALKS CELERY, CUT IN HALF
I TEASPOON SPIRULINA POWDER
I TABLESPOON SUNFLOWER SEEDS
I TABLESPOON MACADAMIA NUTS

Put the apples, fennel, cucumber, spinach, pepper and celery through a juice extractor and catch the juice in a jug before transferring to a blender.

Add the spirulina powder and blend to combine. Add the seeds and nuts and blend using the pulse button to achieve a chunky consistency. Pour into a glass and serve immediately.

# LIVER FLUSH

### SERVES 1

Mineral-Rich | Heart Healthy | Raw | Gluten-Free | Vegan

3 ORANGES, PEELED AND CUT INTO QUARTERS
½ LEMON, PEELED AND CUT INTO QUARTERS
I LIME, PEELED AND CUT INTO QUARTERS
3CM/1¼ INCH PIECE GINGER, PEELED AND SLICED
I CLOVE GARLIC, SLICED
3CM/1¼ INCH PIECE FRESH TURMERIC ROOT, PEELED AND SLICED (OR GINGER)
I TABLESPOON FLAXSEED OIL
¼ TEASPOON CAYENNE PEPPER

Put the orange, lemon and lime through a juice extractor, catching the juice in a jug.

Transfer the juice to a blender, add the remaining ingredients and blend until smooth. Pour into a glass and serve immediately.

*Two soothing juices with great texture. Joint Relief strengthens joints and reduces inflammation while Digest benefits digestion and can relieve abdominal bloating.*

# JOINT RELIEF

**SERVES 1**

Vitamin-Rich | Mineral-Rich | Antioxidant-Rich | Heart Healthy | Cleansing | Raw | Gluten-Free | Vegan

½ PINK GRAPEFRUIT, PEELED AND
CUT INTO QUARTERS
1 GUAVA, PEELED AND CUT INTO QUARTERS
1 PEAR, CUT INTO QUARTERS
6 SPRIGS FLAT-LEAF PARSLEY,
LEAVES AND TENDER STEMS
50G/1¾OZ (1 PACKED CUP) SPINACH LEAVES

Put the grapefruit, guava, pear, parsley and spinach through a juice extractor, catching the juice in a jug. Transfer to a glass and serve immediately.

Cranberry Healer

Green Clean

# DIGEST

**SERVES 1**

Vitamin-Rich | Mineral-Rich | Antioxidant-Rich | Heart Healthy | Digestive Support
Smart Carbohydrate | Cleansing | Raw | Gluten-Free | Vegan

1 ORANGE, PEELED AND CUT INTO QUARTERS
150G/5OZ (1 CUP) PINEAPPLE, PEELED
AND CUT INTO SMALL WEDGES
½ BABY FENNEL BULB, CUT INTO WEDGES
150G/5OZ PAPAYA (1 CUP) PEELED, SEEDED AND
CUT INTO WEDGES
10G/⅓OZ (½ CUP) MINT LEAVES

Put the orange, pineapple and fennel through
a juice extractor and catch the liquid in a jug.

Transfer the juice to a blender, add the papaya
and mint. Blend until combined and smooth.
Pour into a glass and serve immediately.

Digest

Blood of the Earth

Liver Flush

Joint Relief

Culture Shock

This earthy-tasting juice is a favourite, and helps the liver to cleanse the blood. Lots of recipes use carrots to soften and sweeten the taste, but here we use apple, which has a lower sugar content.

Vitamin-Rich | Heart Healthy | Raw | Gluten-Free | Vegan

# BLOOD
# OF THE EARTH

### SERVES 1

1 ½ BEETROOT, WASHED, SCRUBBED
AND CUT INTO QUARTERS
2 GREEN APPLES, CUT INTO QUARTERS
1 STALK CELERY, CUT IN HALF
2CM/¾ INCH PIECE GINGER, PEELED AND SLICED

Put the beetroot, apples, celery and ginger through a juice extractor, catching the juice in a jug.

Pour the juice into a glass and serve immediately.

Vital Veg is our version of the classic V8 veg drink, with nine ingredients because of the addition of flaxseed oil. This juice promotes circulation and protects brain and heart functions. As the name implies, Lymph Purifier supports the lymphatic system. Raw broccoli and kale may seem unappealing — even unlikely — ingredients in a juice, but they work brilliantly when balanced by the fennel, ginger and apple.

# VITAL VEG

## SERVES 4

Vitamin-Rich | Mineral-Rich | Antioxidant-Rich | High Protein | Cleansing | Rejuvenating | Raw | Gluten-Free | Vegan

2 VINE-RIPENED TOMATOES, CUT INTO QUARTERS

½ TELEGRAPH CUCUMBER, CUT INTO QUARTERS

2 STALKS CELERY, CUT IN HALF

½ FENNEL BULB, CUT INTO WEDGES

300G/10½OZ PEELED PUMPKIN, SEEDED AND ROUGHLY CHOPPED (OR CARROT)

½ RED BELL PEPPER (CAPSICUM), SEEDED AND CUT INTO QUARTERS

½ LEMON, PEELED AND CUT INTO WEDGES

4 SPRIGS LEMON BASIL OR ITALIAN BASIL, LEAVES AND TENDER STEMS

1 TABLESPOON FLAXSEED OIL

Put all the vegetables, lemon and basil through a juice extractor. Use a jug to transfer the juice to a blender. Add the flaxseed oil and blend until well combined. Pour into a glass and serve immediately

# LYMPH PURIFIER

## SERVES 1

Vitamin-Rich | Mineral-Rich | Antioxidant-Rich | High-Protein | Cleansing | Raw | Gluten-Free | Vegan

½ BABY FENNEL BULB, CUT INTO WEDGES
3 STALKS CELERY, CUT IN HALF
1 SMALL BROCCOLI HEAD, CUT INTO PIECES
2CM/¾ INCH PIECE GINGER, SLICED
1 LEMON, PEELED, CUT INTO QUARTERS
1 GREEN APPLE, CUT INTO QUARTERS
3 BRANCHES KALE, CUT INTO 5CM/2 INCH LENGTHS

Put all the ingredients through a juice extractor and catch the liquid in a jug. Pour into a glass and serve straight away.

*Cranberry Healer*

*Liver Flush*

*Vital Veg*

*Lymph Purifier*

This warming beverage is soothing to coughs and sore throats, colds and flu. It is one of the most popular drinks at COMO Shambhala – and we are asked for the recipe every day. The secret is the timing, with the 2-hour cooking period helping to deepen and soften the pepperiness of the ginger.

Heart Healthy | Gluten-Free

# COMO SHAMBHALA
# GINGER TEA

**SERVES 10**

200G/7OZ PIECE GINGER
100ML (SCANT ½ CUP) LEMON JUICE
290G/10OZ (⅘ CUP) HONEY

Wash the ginger and bruise with a pestle and mortar before placing in a large saucepan with 2 litres (8 cups) water. Bring to the boil, then reduce the heat and simmer gently for 2 hours. Strain through a fine sieve. This ginger water may be kept in the fridge for several days.

To serve, place the ginger water in a saucepan, bring to the boil and remove from the heat. Stir in the lemon and honey, adjusting to taste (though don't reboil once the honey is added). Serve immediately.

Indonesia grows a lot of cacao, so it made sense to feature a raw cacao 'hot chocolate' on our hot beverage menu at COMO Shambhala Estate in Bali. It's important to blend the cacao beans really well with the nut milk; this helps the drink to obtain a good colour.

Mineral-Rich | Gluten-Free | Vegan

## CINNAMON AND CHILLI-SCENTED CACAO

### MAKES 2 CUPS

2 TABLESPOONS CACAO NIBS
500ML (2 CUPS) ALMOND NUT MILK
(SEE BASICS PAGE 267)
1 TEASPOON GROUND CINNAMON
1 PINCH CHILLI POWDER
3 TABLESPOONS COCONUT NECTAR (G)
1 PINCH SEA SALT

Place all the ingredients in a blender and process until combined. Transfer the mixture to a saucepan and heat gently over a low to medium heat until warm, then serve.

*Just the smell of this drink lulls the most overactive mind. As the name suggests it promotes healthy rest, helps balance your mood and soothes a dry throat.*

Mineral-Rich | Heart Healthy | Gluten-Free

## SLEEPY TIME

### SERVES 2

500ML (2 CUPS) ALMOND NUT MILK
(SEE BASICS PAGE 267)
1 TABLESPOON RAW HONEY
¼ TEASPOON NUTMEG, FRESHLY GRATED
¼ TEASPOON GROUND CINNAMON

Combine the almond nut milk, honey and spices in a small saucepan. Heat gently over a low to medium heat until warm. Pour into mugs and serve.

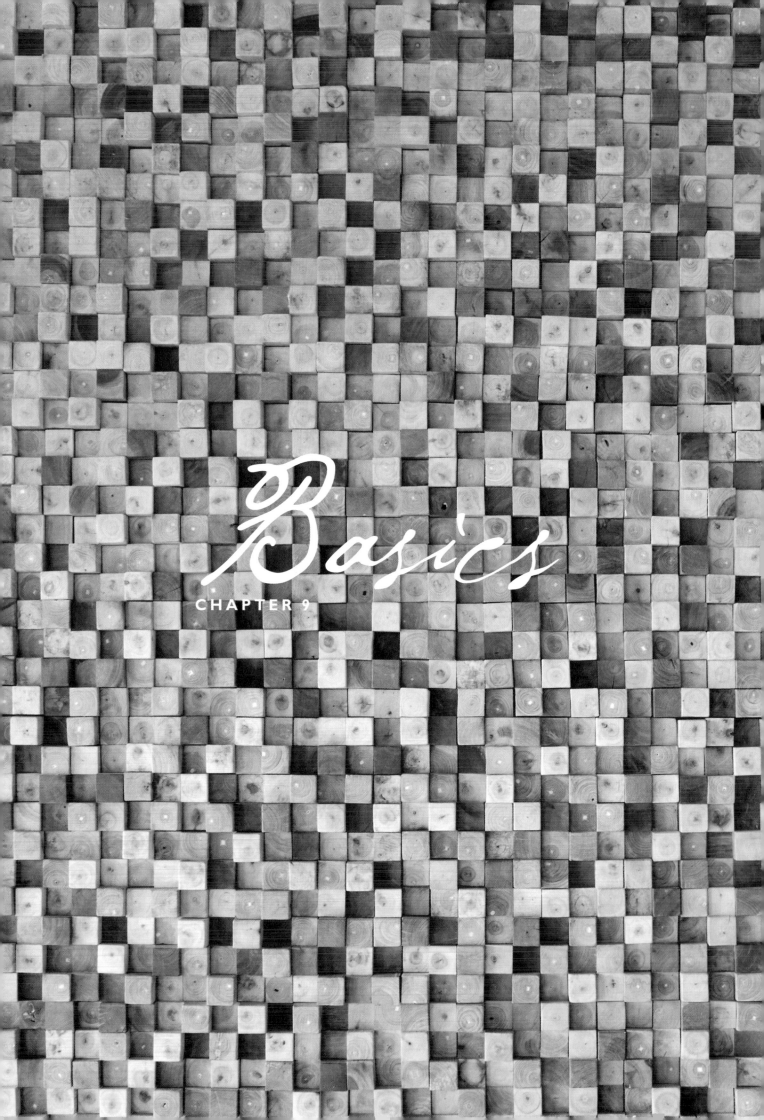

Basics

CHAPTER 9

## COCONUT CREAM AND MILK

**MAKES 1 LITRE/4 CUPS**

2 PANDANUS LEAVES, TIED INTO KNOTS
(IF AVAILABLE) (G)
2 LARGE COCONUTS

Place 750ml (3 cups) water in a saucepan, add the pandanus leaves, and bring to the boil. Remove from the heat. Leave to stand for 15 minutes to cool and let the flavours develop.

Hold the coconut in your hand over a bowl. Using the blunt side of a cleaver or heavy knife, hit the mid-line of the coconut with the cleaver, turning the coconut after every hit until it cracks open and water goes into the bowl. Crack the coconut into smaller pieces, then using a knife, carefully remove the flesh and peel off the outer skin. Grate the flesh and place in a large bowl.

Pour the pandanus water over the grated coconut, and squeeze the coconut for 10 minutes to release the cream from the flesh. Then transfer to a muslin-lined sieve placed over a bowl. Bring the sides of the muslin together and twist to form a ball of coconut, squeezing to extract as much cream as possible from the coconut. Transfer the liquid to a ceramic bowl or jug and refrigerate until ready to use.

For coconut cream, scoop the top layer from the liquid. For coconut milk, stir the contents until they are well combined.

# ALMOND NUT
## MILK

**MAKES 1.1 LITRES/4½ CUPS**

320G/11OZ (2 CUPS) FLAKED ALMONDS
1 TABLESPOON LECITHIN (OPTIONAL)
1 PINCH SEA SALT

Place the almonds in a bowl and cover with 1 litre (4 cups) water. Soak for 4 hours, then drain and rinse.

In a blender, combine the rinsed almonds, 1 litre (4 cups) water and lecithin to emulsify. Add the salt and blend to a fine consistency. Strain through a nut bag or muslin-lined sieve into a ceramic jug. Cover and refrigerate until ready to use.

# *Stocks*

## DASHI STOCK

### MAKES 1.4 LITRES (5½ CUPS)

15G/½OZ KOMBU, 10–16CM/4–6¼ INCH PIECE
20G/¾OZ BONITO FLAKES

Place the kombu and 2 litres (8 cups) water in a large saucepan. Bring to the boil then reduce the heat to a simmer and cook for 5 minutes. Add the bonito flakes and simmer for a further 5 minutes. Remove from the heat and stand for 20 minutes, allowing the flavours to infuse, then put through a fine sieve.

## AROMATIC THAI FISH STOCK

### MAKES 2.8 LITRES (11 CUPS)

1.2KG/2⅔LB WHITE FISH BONES, WASHED AND CLEANED
3 STALKS LEMONGRASS, BRUISED
3 CORIANDER (CILANTRO) ROOTS, CLEANED, SCRAPED AND BRUISED (OR 6 STEMS)
2 ONIONS, SLICED
3 CLOVES GARLIC, BRUISED
4 KAFFIR LIME LEAVES, BRUISED
4 SMALL RED CHILLIES, BRUISED
2 TEASPOONS SEA SALT

Place all the ingredients in a saucepan, add 3 litres (12 cups) water and the sea salt. Cover with a lid and bring to the boil, removing any scum from the surface. Reduce the heat to a simmer and cook for 45 minutes, skimming as required, then strain through a fine sieve into a bowl. When the liquid is cool, refrigerate or freeze.

## CHICKEN STOCK

### MAKES 3 LITRES (12 CUPS)

1KG/2¼LB CHICKEN BONES, INCLUDING WINGS OR LEGS
2CM/¾ INCH PIECE GINGER, SLICED
2 CLOVES GARLIC, BRUISED
2 ONIONS, THICKLY SLICED

Place all the ingredients in a large saucepan and add 4 litres (16 cups) water (or enough to cover the ingredients by 10cm/ 4 inches). Bring to the boil, removing any scum from the surface, then reduce the heat to a simmer and cook, uncovered, for 2 hours. Strain through a fine sieve into a bowl, freezing or refrigerating the liquid when cool.

## VEGETABLE STOCK

**MAKES 3½ LITRES (14 CUPS)**

5 CARROTS, CUT INTO CHUNKS
3 ONIONS, CUT INTO CHUNKS
4 LEEKS, OUTER LAYER
REMOVED, CUT INTO CHUNKS
2 FENNEL BULBS, CUT INTO CHUNKS
2 WHOLE POTATOES, PEELED
AND CUT INTO CHUNKS
4 VINE-RIPENED TOMATOES, CUT IN HALF
6 SPRIGS THYME
6 SPRIGS FLAT-LEAF PARSLEY, CUT IN HALF

Place the carrots, onions, leeks, fennel and potatoes in a large saucepan. Add 4 litres (16 cups) water (or enough to cover the ingredients by 10cm/4 inches) and bring to the boil. Skim any scum from the surface, then reduce heat to a simmer, add the tomatoes and herbs and simmer for 1 hour, or until the stock is fragrant. Strain through a fine sieve into a bowl. When cool, refrigerate or freeze.

## À LA GRECQUE STOCK

**MAKES 600ML (2½ CUPS)**

500ML (2 CUPS) VEGETABLE STOCK (SEE ABOVE)
1 TEASPOON SALT
1 TEASPOON POWDERED COCONUT PALM
SUGAR (OR ORGANIC BROWN SUGAR) (G)
2 TABLESPOONS RAW APPLE CIDER VINEGAR
80ML (⅓ CUP) EXTRA-VIRGIN OLIVE OIL
4 SPRIGS THYME

Combine all the ingredients in a saucepan. Bring to the boil and then remove from the heat. Cool to room temperature then strain.

# Vegetables

## ARTICHOKES
## À LA GRECQUE

**SERVES 8**

8 SMALL GLOBE ARTICHOKES
1 LEMON, CUT IN HALF
1800ML (7 CUPS) À LA GRECQUE STOCK
(SEE BASICS PAGE 269)

To prepare the artichokes, use a sharp knife to cut 1.5cm/ ¾ inch off to the top of the artichoke. Rub the cut surfaces with half a lemon to prevent discoloration.

Pull back and remove the outer leaves of the artichoke until you reach the paler, softer leaves. If the stems are tender, use a small sharp knife to peel away the stringy outer skin, then finish this using a peeler. Submerge in an ice bath until ready to cook.

Place the artichokes in a large saucepan, cover with stock and gently bring to the boil, before reducing the heat and simmering for 15 to 20 minutes, or until the stem is easily pierced with a small sharp knife.

Remove from the liquid and stand the artichoke cut-side down on paper towels, leaving to drain and cool. To prepare for use, cut the artichokes in half and remove the furry choke with a teaspoon, as well as any inner tough leaves.

## AVOCADO CRUSH

**MAKES 250ML (1 CUP) 4 PORTIONS**

2 RIPE AVOCADOS, CUT IN HALF
AND STONED
½ LEMON, JUICED AND STRAINED
¼ TEASPOON SEA SALT, TO TASTE
⅛ TEASPOON FRESHLY GROUND BLACK PEPPER
⅛ TEASPOON TABASCO SAUCE

Scoop the avocado out of its skin using a tablespoon. Place in a bowl and, using a whisk, mash the avocado with the other ingredients until the texture is almost smooth. Transfer to a clean bowl, cover with clingfilm and refrigerate.

# ROASTED BUTTERNUT
# PUMPKIN PURÉE

**MAKES ABOUT 500G (2–2¼ CUPS) PURÉE,
DEPENDING ON THE WATER CONTENT OF THE PUMPKIN**

1KG/2¼LB BUTTERNUT PUMPKIN,
CUT INTO WEDGES AND SEEDED

Preheat the oven to 200°C/400°F. Place the butternut pumpkin wedges on an oven tray lined with baking paper, cover with foil and roast for 50 to 60 minutes, or until the pumpkin is very soft. Leave to cool, then scoop out the flesh and place in a muslin-lined colander and drain for 20 minutes. Pull the sides of the muslin up and twist tightly to squeeze all the excess water from the butternut pumpkin. Transfer to a blender and blend to a fine purée.

# CORN ON THE COB

**MAKES 6 PORTIONS**

6 CORN COBS, HUSKS AND SILKS REMOVED
1 TEASPOON SEA SALT
1 TEASPOON BROWN SUGAR

Place the corn cobs in a saucepan, cover with water and season with the sea salt and sugar. Bring to the boil, reduce the heat and cover with a lid. Cook for 10 to 15 minutes, or until tender, before draining.

# SEMI-DRIED
# CHERRY TOMATOES

**MAKES 4 PORTIONS**

30 CHERRY TOMATOES, CUT IN HALF
1 TABLESPOON RAW APPLE CIDER VINEGAR
1 TABLESPOON RAW HONEY
1 TABLESPOON EXTRA-VIRGIN OLIVE OIL
¼ TEASPOON SEA SALT

Place the cherry tomatoes in a bowl and toss with the vinegar, honey, olive oil and sea salt. Place the tomatoes, cut-side up, on a Teflex or non-stick sheet on a dehydrator tray, and dry at 48°C/118°F for 4 hours. Alternatively, dry in an oven heated on its lowest setting.

# JERUSALEM ARTICHOKE PURÉE

**MAKES ABOUT 200G/7OZ (2 CUPS) 4–6 PORTIONS**

ABOUT 2 TABLESPOONS OLIVE OIL
½ SMALL BROWN ONION, SLICED
1 CLOVE GARLIC, SLICED
SEA SALT AND GROUND WHITE PEPPER, TO TASTE
6 (300G/10½OZ) JERUSALEM ARTICHOKES, PEELED AND CUT INTO 1CM/½ INCH THICK SLICES
500ML (2 CUPS) VEGETABLE STOCK (SEE BASICS PAGE 269)
1 TEASPOON LEMON JUICE

Heat the olive oil in a saucepan, add the onion, garlic and a pinch of sea salt. Cook, stirring occasionally, over a low heat for 8 to 10 minutes until softened but not coloured. Add the sliced artichokes and stock, cover with a cartouche (see Glossary, page 296), and cook for 25 to 30 minutes, or until the liquid has reduced to quarter of the original, and the artichokes are tender. Transfer the artichokes and their liquid to a blender, add lemon juice and blend to a smooth purée. Check the seasoning and adjust as necessary.

# ROAST JERUSALEM ARTICHOKES

**MAKES 4 PORTIONS**

4–6 JERUSALEM ARTICHOKES
SEA SALT AND GROUND WHITE PEPPER, TO TASTE
2 TABLESPOONS OLIVE OIL
4 SPRIGS THYME

Preheat the oven to 160°C/320°F. To roast the Jerusalem artichokes, scrub the artichokes with a clean scourer and cut off any knobs, then cut them in half.

Put the artichokes in an ovenproof tray lined with baking paper, season with sea salt and pepper, then drizzle the olive oil over the artichokes. Lay thyme branches over the artichokes, cover with foil and bake in the hot oven for 20 minutes, then remove the foil and roast for a further 10 minutes, or until the artichokes are soft and golden brown.

# MARINATED SHIITAKE MUSHROOMS

## MAKES 5 PORTIONS

10 LARGE SHIITAKE MUSHROOMS
60ML (¼ CUP) TAMARI SOY
60ML (¼ CUP) LEMON JUICE

Cut the mushrooms into 1½cm/½ inch thick pieces. Combine the tamari, lemon juice and 125ml (½ cup) water in a bowl and add the mushrooms to the liquid. Cover and marinate the mushrooms for at least 40 minutes, or leave the mushrooms in the liquid until ready to use (the mushrooms can be stored for up to a day in this liquid).

# BRAISED SHIITAKE MUSHROOMS

## MAKES 8 MUSHROOMS

8 LARGE DRIED WHOLE SHIITAKE MUSHROOMS
3CM/1¼ INCH PIECE GINGER, PEELED AND SLICED
4 SPRING ONIONS (SCALLIONS), HALVED
3 GARLIC CLOVES, LIGHTLY BRUISED
60ML (¼ CUP) SHAOXING WINE
3 TABLESPOONS POWDERED COCONUT PALM SUGAR (OR ORGANIC BROWN SUGAR) (G)
60ML (¼ CUP) TAMARI SOY
2 TEASPOONS SESAME OIL
2 STAR ANISE
1 CINNAMON
4 STRIPS DRIED ORANGE PEEL

Cover the dried shiitake mushrooms with boiling water and leave to soak for 1 hour, ensuring they are completely submerged. When softened, drain and rinse. Before braising, remove the stems with a pair of scissors.

Place the mushrooms and all the remaining ingredients in a saucepan, cover with water and bring to the boil.

Reduce the heat and simmer for 45 minutes, or until the mushrooms are soft and tender. Allow to cool in the cooking liquid. When cool, remove the mushrooms and strain the stock through a fine sieve into a bowl. Return the mushrooms to the liquid until you are ready to use them.

# ROASTED RED BELL PEPPERS (CAPSICUM)

### MAKES 4–6 PORTIONS

2 LARGE RED BELL PEPPERS (CAPSICUMS)

Preheat the oven to 220°C/450°F. Line a baking tray with foil. Lay the peppers on the baking tray in the oven and roast for 12 to 15 minutes. Remove from the oven and, using tongs, give the peppers a half turn. Return to the oven for a further 12 to 15 minutes.

Check to make sure peppers have fully roasted – the skin should be charred and soft, and the peppers slightly collapsed. If they don't look ready, let them roast for a few more minutes.

Once roasted, place the peppers in a bowl and cover with clingfilm to steam and cool. When cold enough to handle, remove the stalk, central core and seeds, and peel off the charred skin. To retain flavours, this is best done without using water. Cut the roasted peppers into 3cm/1¼ inch strips or as preferred.

# RAINBOW SLAW

### MAKES 4 PORTIONS

160G/5½OZ (2 CUPS) RED CABBAGE, SHREDDED
160G/5½OZ (2 CUPS) WHITE CABBAGE, SHREDDED
120G/4OZ (2 CUPS) BUTTERNUT PUMPKIN, PEELED AND CUT JULIENNE
½ SMALL RED ONION, THINLY SLICED
4G/⅛OZ (¼ CUP) FLAT-LEAF PARSLEY LEAVES
1 RECIPE RAINBOW SLAW DRESSING (SEE BASICS PAGE 278)

Put all the vegetables and parsley in a salad bowl and mix to combine. Then, just before serving, pour the rainbow slaw dressing over the cabbage salad and toss well to lightly coat the vegetables.

# RAW TOMATO SAUCE

### MAKES 500ML (2 CUPS)

350G/12OZ (2 CUPS) SUN-DRIED TOMATOES, SOAKED IN WARM WATER FOR 2 HOURS
1 VINE-RIPENED TOMATO
½ SMALL ONION, CHOPPED
2 TABLESPOONS FRESHLY SQUEEZED LEMON JUICE
60ML (¼ CUP) EXTRA-VIRGIN OLIVE OIL
1 TABLESPOON RAW HONEY
1 PINCH RED CHILLI FLAKES
SEA SALT, TO TASTE

Drain the sun-dried tomatoes and squeeze out all the excess water. Place the sun-dried tomatoes with the remaining ingredients in a blender, season with sea salt and blend until fully combined.

# Dressings

## RAINBOW SLAW DRESSING

**MAKES 180ML (¾ CUP)**

2CM/¾ INCH PIECE GINGER, PEELED AND GRATED
60ML (¼ CUP) RAW APPLE CIDER VINEGAR
1 CLOVE GARLIC, GRATED
1 TEASPOON DIJON MUSTARD
2 TABLESPOONS TAMARI SOY
2 TABLESPOONS RAW HONEY
125ML (½ CUP) EXTRA-VIRGIN OLIVE OIL

Whisk the ginger, vinegar, garlic, Dijon mustard, tamari and honey in a bowl. Gradually whisk in the olive oil until combined.

## LEMON DRESSING

**MAKES 120ML (½ CUP)**

60ML (¼ CUP) FRESHLY SQUEEZED LEMON JUICE
60ML (¼ CUP) EXTRA-VIRGIN OLIVE OIL
SEA SALT AND GROUND WHITE PEPPER, TO TASTE

Whisk the lemon juice and extra-virgin olive oil together in a bowl. Season to taste with sea salt and a grind of white pepper.

# ORANGE BLOSSOM
# DRESSING

**MAKES 180ML (¾ CUP)**

250ML (1 CUP) FRESHLY SQUEEZED
AND STRAINED ORANGE JUICE
1 TABLESPOON COCONUT NECTAR
OR AGAVE NECTAR (G)
60ML (¼ CUP) EXTRA-VIRGIN OLIVE OIL
½ TEASPOON ORANGE BLOSSOM WATER
2 TABLESPOONS RAW APPLE CIDER VINEGAR
SEA SALT AND GROUND WHITE PEPPER, TO TASTE

Combine the orange juice and coconut nectar in a saucepan. Bring to the boil before reducing the heat. Simmer until the liquid is reduced to 125ml (½ cup). Remove from the heat and whisk in the extra-virgin oil, orange blossom water and vinegar. Season with sea salt and a grind of white pepper. Cool before using.

# Spices and Pastes

## VEGETARIAN BALI SPICE PASTE

**MAKES 200ML (SCANT 1 CUP)**

2 TEASPOONS CORIANDER SEEDS
¼ TEASPOON BLACK PEPPERCORNS
2 CLOVES
1 PINCH FRESHLY GRATED NUTMEG
12 RED SHALLOTS, SLICED
6 CLOVES GARLIC, SLICED
5 SMALL RED CHILLIES, SEEDED AND CHOPPED
6 STALKS LEMONGRASS,
TOPS AND OUTER LAYERS REMOVED, SLICED
2CM/¾ INCH PIECE GALANGAL,
PEELED AND CHOPPED
5CM/2 INCH PIECE FRESH TURMERIC ROOT,
PEELED AND CHOPPED
2 CANDLENUTS (G)
100ML (SCANT ½ CUP) CANOLA (RAPESEED) OIL
60G/2½OZ (¼ CUP) POWDERED COCONUT
PALM SUGAR (OR ORGANIC BROWN SUGAR) (G)
2 STALKS LEMONGRASS,
TOPS AND OUTER LAYERS REMOVED, BRUISED
3CM/1¼ INCH PIECE KENCUR OR GINGER,
PEELED AND CHOPPED
6 KAFFIR LIME LEAVES

Dry-fry the coriander seeds in a frying pan over a medium to high heat for 2 to 3 minutes, or until fragrant. Transfer to a mortar or spice grinder and work until the mixture is finely ground. Repeat the dry-frying and grinding process with the black peppercorns and the cloves.

Put all the ground spices, the shallots, garlic, chillies, sliced lemongrass, galangal, turmeric and candlenuts in a blender and blend to a fine paste.

Heat the oil in the frying pan. When hot, add the paste, palm sugar, lemongrass stalks, kencur and lime leaves and cook, stirring frequently, over a low heat for 2 hours, or until fragrant but not bitter.

Leave to cool, discard the lime leaves and lemongrass stalks then store in an airtight container in the fridge for up to a week. Alternatively, divide into portions in airtight containers and freeze for up to 3 months.

## MOROCCAN SPICE MIX

**MAKES 80ML (⅓ CUP)**

1 CINNAMON QUILL
2 STAR ANISE
2 TABLESPOONS CUMIN SEEDS
1 TABLESPOON CORIANDER SEEDS
1 TABLESPOON FENNEL SEEDS

Toast all the spices separately in a hot frying pan for 2 to 3 minutes, or until fragrant. Grind the spices separately in a mortar with the pestle until they are a fine powder, then pass through a sieve to remove any coarse parts. Combine the toasted ground spices in a bowl and mix well.

# HARISSA

**MAKES 500ML (2 CUPS)**

2 TOMATOES
4 RED BELL PEPPERS (CAPSICUMS)
2 TABLESPOONS CUMIN SEEDS
1 TABLESPOON FENNEL SEEDS
2 TABLESPOONS CORIANDER SEEDS
60ML (¼ CUP) OLIVE OIL
3 CLOVES GARLIC, SLICED
1 TEASPOON GROUND CHILLIES
OR CHILLI POWDER
180G/6OZ (½ CUP) RAW HONEY
SEA SALT, TO TASTE

Preheat the oven to 200°C/400°F. Place the tomatoes and peppers on separate oven trays. Cook the tomatoes for 25 to 30 minutes, or until tomatoes are softened and the skins split.

Remove the tomatoes from the oven and peel when cool enough to handle. Cook the peppers for a further 30 minutes, or until the skin is blackened and wrinkled. Place the peppers in a bowl, cover with clingfilm and stand for 20 minutes. Peel them, remove the seeds and cut into 2cm/¾ inch strips.

Toast all the seeds separately in a hot frying pan for 2 to 3 minutes, or until fragrant. Grind the seeds separately in a mortar with the pestle so each is a fine powder, then pass through a sieve to remove any coarse parts.

Heat the oil in a pan over a low to medium heat. When hot, add the sliced peppers and garlic and cook for 30 minutes. Increase the heat to medium, add the seeds and chilli powder and cook for 3 minutes, stirring constantly. Add the honey and cook until lightly caramelised. Add the roasted tomatoes and cook for a further 5 minutes. Then transfer to a blender, season to taste with sea salt, and blend to a fine purée.

Harissa can be stored in a glass jar in the fridge for up to 10 days.

# HARISSA YOGHURT

**MAKES 125ML (½ CUP)**

125ML (½ CUP) LOW-FAT GREEK-STYLE YOGHURT
1 TABLESPOON HARISSA (SEE ABOVE)
2 TEASPOONS FRESHLY SQUEEZED ORANGE JUICE
SEA SALT AND FRESHLY GROUND
WHITE PEPPER, TO TASTE

To make harissa yoghurt, combine the yoghurt and harissa in a bowl. Add orange juice to taste, then season.

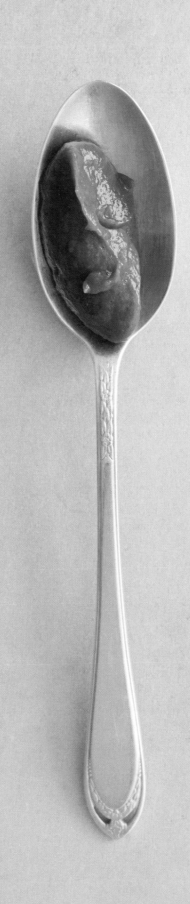

# GARAM MASALA

**MAKES 125ML (½ CUP)**

1 TABLESPOON CARDAMOM SEEDS
3 STAR ANISE
2 TABLESPOONS CORIANDER SEEDS
2 TABLESPOONS WHITE PEPPERCORNS

Toast each spice separately in a hot frying pan for 2 to 3 minutes, or until fragrant. Grind the spices separately in a mortar with the pestle until they are a fine powder, then pass through a sieve to remove any coarse parts. Combine the ground spices in a bowl and mix well.

# CHAAT MASALA

**MAKES 80ML (⅓ CUP)**

3 TEASPOONS CUMIN SEEDS
I TEASPOON CORIANDER SEEDS
½ TEASPOON FENNEL SEEDS
3 TEASPOONS SEA SALT
I TABLESPOON AMCHUR POWDER (G)
(GREEN MANGO POWDER)
½ TEASPOON GROUND BLACK PEPPER
I TEASPOON GARAM MASALA
½ TEASPOON GROUND GINGER
½ TEASPOON AJWAIN
¼ TEASPOON GROUND DRIED MINT
¼ TEASPOON GROUND CHILLIES
¼ TEASPOON PAPRIKA

Toast each seed separately in a hot frying pan for 2 to 3 minutes, or until fragrant. Grind the seeds separately in a mortar with the pestle until they are a fine powder, then pass through a sieve to remove any coarse parts. Pound the sea salt until a fine powder forms. Combine the ground seeds and salt with the remaining ingredients and mix well.

# SZECHUAN
# SALT AND PEPPER

**MAKES 80ML (⅓ CUP)**

30G/1OZ (¼ CUP) FLAKED SEA SALT
I TABLESPOON SZECHUAN PEPPERCORNS

Heat a frying pan, add the salt and cook, stirring occasionally until golden. Toast the peppercorns in a separate hot frying pan for 3 to 4 minutes or until fragrant. When both the salt and peppercorns are cool, pound the ingredients separately in a mortar with the pestle until a fine powder forms. Pass through a sieve to remove any coarse parts then mix them well together to combine.

# Grains

## BROWN JASMINE RICE

**MAKES 400G/14OZ (2⅔ CUPS)**

200G/7OZ (1 CUP) BROWN JASMINE RICE

Place the rice in a sieve and rinse under cold running water until the water runs clear. Place in a saucepan and cover with 500ml (2 cups) water. Bring to the boil, then reduce to the lowest heat. Cover with a tight-fitting lid and cook for 20 to 25 minutes until the water is absorbed and the rice is tender.

Remove from the heat and stand, covered with the lid, for 10 minutes. Fluff with a fork before serving.

## CHICKPEAS

**MAKES 400G/14OZ (2 CUPS)**

200G/7OZ (1 CUP) DRIED CHICKPEAS

Place the chickpeas in a bowl, cover with water, cover with clingfilm and soak in the fridge overnight.

Drain the chickpeas and rinse before placing in a saucepan. Pour in enough water to cover the chickpeas by 5cm/2 inches and bring to the boil, skimming the surface to remove any scum. Reduce the heat to a simmer and cook for 40 to 45 minutes, or until the chickpeas are tender.

Drain the chickpeas and rinse with cold water. The outer casings may be peeled away for a more tender bite.

## QUINOA

**MAKES 320G/11½OZ (2 CUPS)**

200G/7OZ (1 CUP) QUINOA

Place the quinoa in a sieve and rinse under cold running water until the water runs clear. Transfer to a saucepan, add about 1 litre (4 cups) water and bring to the boil. Cover the pan, reduce the heat to a simmer and cook for 12 to 15 minutes, or until the water has been absorbed and the quinoa is tender. Cooked quinoa will be slightly transparent and will sprout a 'tail'.

# RED RICE

**MAKES 260G/9OZ (2 CUPS)**

200G/7OZ (1 CUP) RED RICE

Place the rice in a sieve and rinse under cold running water until the water runs clear. Transfer to a saucepan and cover with 625ml (2½ cups) water. Bring to the boil then reduce to the lowest heat. Cover with a tight-fitting lid and cook for 20 to 25 minutes, or until the water is absorbed and the rice is tender.

Remove from the heat and leave to stand, covered with the lid, for 10 minutes. Fluff with a fork before serving.

# BARLEY AND PEARL BARLEY

**MAKES 360G/12OZ (2 CUPS)**

200G/7OZ (1 CUP) BARLEY*

Place the barley in a sieve and rinse under cold running water until the water runs clear. Place in a saucepan with enough water to cover by 5cm/2 inches. Bring to the boil and cook for 25 minutes, or until tender.

*Pearl barley takes less time to cook (about 15 minutes) until tender.

# BLACK BEANS

**MAKES 360G/12OZ (2 CUPS)**

200G/7OZ (1 CUP) BLACK BEANS

Place the black beans in a bowl, cover with water, cover with clingfilm and soak in the fridge overnight.

After soaking, drain and rinse the beans. Place in a saucepan and add enough water to cover by 5cm/2 inches. Bring to the boil, skim the surface of any scum, then reduce the heat slightly and cook for 30 to 40 minutes, or until the beans are tender. Drain.

### EGG CRÊPE

**MAKES 4 CRÊPES**

2 EGGS
SEA SALT AND GROUND WHITE PEPPER, TO TASTE

Crack the eggs into a bowl and gently whisk with 1 tablespoon of water. Season with salt and pepper.

Heat a non-stick crêpe pan on the stove over a medium to high heat. Wipe over with an oil-soaked piece of paper towel. Ladle enough egg mixture into the crêpe pan to cover the base with a thin layer. Cook until just set (about 30 to 40 seconds), then carefully loosen the egg crêpe from the pan and turn over. Cook the other side for 15 seconds. Turn the crêpe out onto a large plate and repeat with the remaining egg mix. When all the mixture is cooked, roll the egg crêpes into a cigar shape and cut into strips.

### TOMATO JAM

**MAKES 240ML (1 CUP)**

8 VINE-RIPENED TOMATOES
60ML (¼ CUP) OLIVE OIL
2 SMALL BROWN ONIONS, CHOPPED
2 CLOVES GARLIC, CHOPPED
SEA SALT, TO TASTE
55G/2OZ (¼ CUP) RAW SUGAR
2 TABLESPOONS RAW APPLE CIDER VINEGAR

Preheat the oven to 180°C/350°F. Place the tomatoes on an oven tray, drizzle with half the olive oil and roast in the hot oven for 30 minutes. Put the tomatoes through a mouli grater or food mill and set aside.

Heat the remaining olive oil in a saucepan, add the onions, garlic and a pinch of sea salt and cook over a low heat for 8 to 10 minutes, or until soft. Add in the roasted tomatoes, sugar and vinegar, bring to the boil, then reduce the heat to a simmer and cook for about 50 to 60 minutes, or until thickened. Ladle the hot jam into sterilised jars and seal.

# TAMARIND WATER

**MAKES 400ML (1⅔ CUPS)**

250G/9OZ TAMARIND PULP

Place the tamarind pulp in a heatproof bowl. Pour in 325ml/ 1⅓ cups boiling water and soak for at least 30 minutes. Then push through a sieve.

# SEAWEED

## MAKES 80G/3OZ (1 CUP) OF EACH SEAWEED

10G/⅓OZ (½ CUP) WAKAME SEAWEED

15G/½OZ (½ CUP) HIJIKI SEAWEED
OR SEA SPAGHETTI

15G/½OZ (½ CUP) ARAME SEAWEED

Place the seaweeds in separate bowls and cover each with warm water.

Soak the wakame seaweed for 5 minutes, drain, rinse and drain again.

Soak the hijiki and arame seaweed for 10 minutes, or until softened. Drain, rinse and drain again.


# SPICY SEED MIX

## SERVES 6

100G/3½OZ (1 CUP) FLAKED ALMONDS

75G/3OZ (½ CUP) SUNFLOWER SEEDS

75G/3OZ (½ CUP) SUN-DRIED TOMATOES,
SOAKED IN WARM WATER FOR 20 MINUTES,
THEN DRAINED AND CHOPPED

1 TABLESPOON MISO PASTE

1 TEASPOON GROUND CUMIN

½ TEASPOON DRIED CHILLI FLAKES

1 TEASPOON GROUND CORIANDER

1 PINCH CAYENNE PEPPER

1 TABLESPOON OLIVE OIL

1 TABLESPOON COCONUT NECTAR
OR AGAVE NECTAR (G)

½ LONG RED CHILLI, SPLIT LENGTHWISE,
SEEDED AND CHOPPED

3 SPRING ONIONS (SCALLIONS), SLICED

SEA SALT, TO TASTE

Place the almonds and sunflower seeds in a bowl, cover with water and soak for 2 hours. Drain, rinse and drain again.

Place the almonds and sunflower seeds in a food processor with the remaining ingredients, including ½ teaspoon sea salt and 60ml (¼ cup) water. Using the pulse button, process the mixture until it is a coarse consistency. Check the seasoning and adjust as necessary.

Place mounds roughly a teaspoon in size on a Teflex or non-stick sheet on a dehydrator tray and dry at 48°C/118°F for 8 hours. Alternatively, dry in an oven heated on its lowest setting. Store in an airtight container for up to a week.

# SPICED CASHEWS

**MAKES 130G/4½OZ (½ CUP)**

75G/3OZ (½ CUP) RAW CASHEWS
1 TEASPOON CURRY POWDER
2 PINCHES GROUND PAPRIKA
2 TEASPOONS POWDERED COCONUT PALM SUGAR
(OR ORGANIC BROWN SUGAR) (G)
SEA SALT, TO TASTE

Place the cashews in a bowl, cover with water and soak for 2 hours. Drain and rinse.

Toss the drained cashews with the spices, sugar and sea salt. Place the mixture on a Teflex or non-stick sheet on a dehydrator tray and dry at 48°C/118°F for 48 hours, or until crunchy. Alternatively, dry in an oven heated on its lowest setting.

Roughly chop the nuts and store in an airtight container for up to a week.

# WHITE-COOKED CHICKEN

**MAKES 280G/10OZ**

250ML (1 CUP) SHAOXING WINE
1 CLOVE GARLIC, BRUISED
2CM/¾ INCH PIECE GINGER,
PEELED AND SLICED
2 CORIANDER (CILANTRO) ROOTS, BRUISED
(OR 4 STEMS)
2 STAR ANISE
SEA SALT, TO TASTE
1 (640G/1LB 7OZ) DOUBLE CHICKEN BREAST
ON THE BONE, WITH SKIN ON

Place the wine, garlic, ginger, coriander roots and star anise in a stockpot. Add 4½ litres (18 cups) water and season with sea salt. Bring to the boil, then add the chicken, breast side down. Reduce the heat to a simmer and cook for 16 minutes. Remove the stockpot from the heat and leave to stand for a further 16 minutes. Next, remove the chicken from the stock and place in a large bowl of iced water, ensuring it is fully submerged. Leave again for 16 minutes.

Remove the chicken from the ice bath and drain. Remove the skin and the bone from the flesh, then use your fingers to shred the meat.

# PRESERVED LEMONS

**MAKES 5 WHOLE PRESERVED LEMONS / 20 PORTIONS**

10 LEMONS
125G/4½OZ SEA SALT
1 BAY LEAF
2 CINNAMON QUILLS
2 STAR ANISE

Squeeze the juice from 5 lemons and set aside. Cut a cross through the remaining 5 lemons from the top, stopping 2cm/¾ inch from the bottom. Gently prise the lemons apart and fill each with salt before closing again. Place the salt-filled lemons into sterilised jars and add the bay leaf, cinnamon and star anise.

Using a ladle, push down on the lemons to release the juice. Cover with the lemon juice, ensuring the lemons are properly covered. Seal with a lid and place in a cool, dark spot for 1 month to mature. Once the lemons are preserved, store in the fridge.

# GLOSSARY

## INGREDIENTS

**AGAR AGAR** made from a type of seaweed, is a vegetarian substitute for gelatine, and sets liquids into gels. Agar agar is available in sheets, strands or powdered form. Powdered agar agar can be added straight to simmering liquids, but must be cooked for a minimum of 10 minutes to ensure the gelling agents are activated. Once set, agar agar will hold its shape at temperatures up to 32°C/90°F.

**AGAVE NECTAR** is a low-glycaemic natural sweetener made from the sap of the agave plant. Most of the world's agave nectar (syrup) is produced in Mexico and South Africa. It is high in fructose, giving it a much lower glycaemic index than regular sugar, and it is almost one-and-a-half times sweeter than sugar.

**ALOE VERA** is a plant with fleshy leaves with small sharp white teeth. It has been used in herbal medicine for hundreds of years, and nowadays is used in the cosmetic industry in lotions and creams. Aloe vera is renowned for its soothing and healing properties.

**AMCHUR POWDER** is a souring agent made from dried green (unripe) mangoes. The dried mango is ground to a fine powder, which is known as amchur powder. It has an acidic, fruity flavour. Amchur powder is often added to curries as the key souring agent instead of lemon juice or tamarind.

**APPLE EGGPLANT** is a small, round variety of eggplant that comes in a multitude of colours, including green, yellow, orange and purple. Apple eggplants are mainly used in Asian cooking, where they are used fresh in salads or lightly cooked in curries. Choose fresh, smooth skinned, firm apple eggplants, which have a clean and nutty flavour.

**ARAME SEAWEED** is a species of seaweed, used extensively in Japanese cooking, known for its mild and slightly sweet flavour. Dried arame comes in thin dark brown strands. Rehydrate in warm water before using as an ingredient or garnish.

**BARLEY** is a cereal grain high in fibre. It also contains eight essential amino acids. Nutritionally, barley is excellent for keeping the gut regulated with good flora. It contains gluten and is therefore unsuitable for coeliacs and those with a gluten intolerance.

**BASIL SEEDS** are the dried seeds from the Thai basil plant, used in Asian drinks and sweet offerings. The seeds initially have no flavour but when soaked in water they swell and become gelatinous. The soaked seeds are also sometimes used as an appetite suppressant.

**BLACK CHICKEN** is a breed of chicken, also known as the Silkie, with black skin. It is favoured in Asian cooking for its gamey flavour. Black chicken is used in braises and casseroles but its most common use is in soups and stocks. Use regular organic free-range chicken if unavailable, though the flavour will be less intense.

**BLACK WOOD EAR MUSHROOMS** – also known as black fungus, cloud ear fungus, wood fungus or wood ear fungus – grows as a frilly mass on dead wood. It is used in Asian dishes to add a crunchy texture to a meal, rather than flavour. Black wood ear mushrooms are readily available in dried form and are becoming easier to find in their fresh form. The dried fungus needs to be soaked in warm water before use, where it will expand to almost 5 times its dry volume.

**BONITO FLAKES** are one of the two essential ingredients for making dashi stock. The bonito fillets are steamed, smoked, then dried until they are almost as hard as wood. Called katsuobushi in Japanese, these dried fillets can last indefinitely and are shaved as needed on a bladed wooden utensil called a katsuo kezuri-ki.

**CACAO BEANS** are used in the production of chocolate. Cacao beans grow in large leathery pods that hang from the trunks of cacao trees. The pulp and beans are extracted from the pods, after which the beans are dried in the sun for several days. At this stage, the raw beans can be ground into raw cacao powder or cold-pressed for cacao butter. Raw cacao powder and butter are high in antioxidants. The beans can also be roasted and further processed, though roasting does destroy some of the cacao's antioxidant qualities.

**CACAO BUTTER** is the edible vegetable fat from the cacao bean. It can be extracted from the bean in two ways. The most common method is to roast the beans, then hull them before pressing the beans to separate the cacao solids from the cacao butter. The other way is to cold-press the raw beans, extracting the butter from the solids in its raw state. Cacao butter is smooth, creamy white and very stable at room temperature. It has a melting point of about 34°C to 38°C (93°F to 100°F), making it an important ingredient for keeping chocolate solid at room temperature, but enabling it to melt in the mouth when eaten. Cacao butter is used in milk and white chocolates to give the creamy smooth flavour and texture. Also known as cocoa butter.

**CANDLENUTS** are smooth round seeds found in Southeast Asia, the South Pacific and in the tropical rainforests of Northern Australia, encased in a hard shell. Mildly toxic in their raw form, candlenuts must be cooked before eating. The nuts are typically roasted and then shelled to reveal the cream-coloured oily seed. They are used to thicken dishes such as curries and satays. Macadamia and Brazil nuts are suitable substitutes when candlenuts are unavailable.

**CARTOUCHE** is a 'lid' made from baking or parchment paper. It is placed directly on the surface of a cooking mixture in a saucepan to prevent too much evaporation and reduction of the mixture while cooking. To make a cartouche, cut baking or greaseproof paper roughly to the size of the pan you are using. Fold the paper in half, and then in half again. Repeat this twice more to produce a thin, long triangle. Hold the point of the triangle in the centre of pan, then mark where the paper touches the edge of the pan. Cut along this mark in an arc shape, then unfold the paper and it should fit the pan perfectly.

**CHAAT MASALA** is an Indian spice mix used to season potatoes, pulses and curries. It is available commercially but many Indians make their own mix of spices. Chaat masala commonly contains cumin seeds, black salt, amchur powder, black peppercorns, coriander and chilli. The spices are ground and mixed together to form this all-purpose seasoning.

**CHAYOTE** – also known as choko, mango squash and vegetable pear – is a pear-shaped green vegetable that originated in South America but is now also found in Australia, the US and the Caribbean. The flesh of the fruit is bland with little taste and must be cooked before eating. However, it is a very useful ingredient, used as a textural and flavour-carrying element in a dish. The young leaves, shoots and fleshy tuberous root are also edible.

**CHINESE MEDICINE HERBS** are available in pre-measured packets from Asian food stores. Chinese herbs have long been sought after for their medicinal properties and are often used in soups to improve health. The most common pre-mixed herbs are ginseng, wolfberries, angelica root, rhizoma, liquorice root and dried longan.

**COCONUT MEAT** is the white flesh scraped from the inside of a coconut. Young coconut meat is softer and creamier, while mature coconut meat has a nuttier flavour. The amount of meat varies greatly from coconut to coconut, with a single coconut yielding anything from 35g/1½oz (¼ cup) to 150g/5oz (1 cup) of meat. Unused coconut meat can be enjoyed on its own as a healthy snack or frozen for future use. Frozen coconut meat is also sometimes available in the freezer section of some grocery stores.

**COCONUT NECTAR**, produced from coconut palm blossoms, has a low glycaemic index rating and a high content of nutrients and essential amino acids. The sweet neutral flavour can be used for all sweetening needs just like regular sugar or syrup. Agave nectar may be substituted.

**COCONUT PALM SUGAR** is the sugar made from the sap of the coconut palm. It has a low glycaemic index rating of 35, which is half that of table sugar and even lower than agave nectar. It also boasts several different minerals and is a source of protein. Coconut palm sugar is obtained from the sap of the coconut blossom, which is evaporated and crushed to form dry crystals. It has a caramel colour and is a good substitute for regular sugars.

**COCONUT WATER** is the clear liquid found inside a coconut. Young green coconuts are favoured for their coconut water as it is deemed to be the freshest. If buying packaged coconut water, look for unsweetened varieties. A fresh coconut may yield 250ml (1 cup) to 500ml (2 cups) of coconut water, so buy extra coconuts if you are preparing a recipe that calls for specific volumes.

**CHIA SEEDS**, considered a 'superfood', are tiny grey seeds from the Mexican *Salvia hispanica* plant. The seeds are gluten-free and have many nutritional properties including antioxidants, soluble fibre and protein. Chia seeds are high in omega-3 fatty acids.

**DASHI STOCK** is the main stock and seasoning used in Japanese cooking. It is made using bonito flakes and kombu, which is a long dark seaweed. The two items are just brought to the boil, one after the other in the same water, then removed and the liquid is strained. This makes the primary stock, which is used in clear soups. The bonito and kombu are kept and used to make a secondary stock, in which the items are simmered until the liquid has reduced, then more bonito flakes are added. This stock has numerous uses; it is often the base to thick soups and noodle broths.

**DAIKON** is a large white Asian radish, best purchased firm with a tight skin. Common daikons grow to between 35 and 40cm/14 and 16 inches long and are about 4 to 6cm/1½ to 2½ inches in diameter. Daikon is often used in Japanese cooking, either as part of the main dish or finely grated in dipping sauces and dressings. Daikon is believed to help aid digestion.

**DULSE FLAKES** are made from the coarse red seaweed, dulse, found in the north Atlantic and northwest Pacific. The seaweed anchors itself to the rocks in tide pools along the coastline. Dulse is harvested by hand and air-dried on racks, then broken or crushed into flakes. The flakes are high in iron, iodine and many other vitamins and minerals. Dulse flakes – salty in flavour and chewy in texture – are eaten as a snack or used in salads, soups and stews, among other dishes.

**FLAXSEEDS** come from the flax plant, which originates from Africa, Asia and the Mediterranean. Flaxseeds are prized for their high nutritional components and health benefits. They are high in omega-3 fatty acids, essential amino acids and fibre. Flaxseeds are most commonly sold in ground form for easy digestion. They can be used in a multitude of different ways when cooking and are often added to baked goods and smoothies, spooned over cereals or in salads.

**FLAXSEED OIL** comes from the flax plant and is used for its analgesic, laxative and anti-inflammatory properties. It is often used in the treatment of skin issues and digestive problems, but must be used in its raw state (heating destroys its healthful properties). The oil has a mild nutty taste and is suitable for use in salad dressings and as an addition to prepared foods. Keep stored in a dark glass bottle in a cool dark place for up to 3 weeks.

**GALANGAL** is a rhizome grown underground. It has creamy white skin, often tinged with pink. As it ages, the skin turns a golden red colour and becomes thicker. The most common form of galangal in the West is 'kraachai', with a peppery ginger flavour. Galangal is available in fresh, dried and powdered forms.

**HIJIKI SEAWEED** is a brown seaweed found growing on the coasts of Japan, Korea and China. It is harvested, boiled and then dried. The dried form of hijiki looks like little black twigs. It is one of the more textured seaweeds, and is the preferred seaweed for home use in Japan. Hijiki is high in fibre, iron, calcium and magnesium. Some are concerned about reported arsenic levels in hijiki seaweed in particular. Proper soaking, essential for reconstituting, and rinsing reduces the levels. Sea spaghetti, prepared the same way, can be substituted if concerns remain.

**HIBISCUS FLOWERS** are used both in food and drinks. The flower is made into a tea, and is drunk for its health-giving properties – particularly its use as a diuretic. To use hibiscus flowers in cooking, pick just before use, wash and shake dry, then remove and discard the stamen and calyx before separating the petals. The flowers can be used to make syrups for cocktails or ice creams, and they also make beautiful jams.

**JAGGERY** is an unprocessed sugar made from both sugarcane and different palms. It is sold in cylindrical shapes and sometimes balls. Jaggery has a very strong flavour, between dark caramel and molasses. It is used both in sweet and savoury dishes in Southeast Asia.

**JAPANESE MUSTARD POWDER** is a hot, slightly bitter mustard powder often used in dressings, soups, simmered meat and vegetable dishes. Equal parts water and powder are combined to make a paste. Hot English mustard powder can be used as a substitute if Japanese powder is unavailable.

**JICAMA** is a root vegetable native to Mexico, also known as yam bean, Mexican yam or Mexican potato. The Spaniards took jicama to the Philippines, from which it spread to Southeast Asia and China. Its vine can grow to up to 20 metres/20 yards long and the yam bean can grow as large as 20kg/44lb. Jicamas are a bulbous shape with a thin yellowy-brown skin and white crisp flesh, similar to that of a pear or apple. Jicama is mainly used raw in salads and salsas but is also added to soups and stir-fries.

**KAFFIR LIME** is a citrus fruit native to Thailand, Malaysia, Indonesia and Laos, with a bumpy green skin. Both the fruit and the leaves are used in many Southeast Asian dishes. The rind is used in curry pastes and the juice may be used in dressings. Kaffir lime leaves have a very fragrant smell when crushed to release their oils (the fruit can be difficult to find and is often expensive, so the leaves are used instead). The hard vein running through the middle of the leaf from top to bottom needs to be cut out before use.

**KOMBU** is a broad-leafed kelp – olive brown in colour and growing several metres long. When dried, a white powder forms on the leaves; this should be wiped clean and not rinsed, as rinsing will deteriorate the flavour. Scoring the leaves before use helps intensify the flavour when it is simmered. Kombu is one of two main ingredients in dashi stock, along with bonito flakes.

**LIQUID AMINOS** is a liquid protein concentrate derived from certified non-GMO (genetically modified organism) soybeans. It contains 16 essential and non-essential amino acids and is gluten-free. Liquid aminos can be used as a seasoning on most foods, and is a suitable substitute for shoyu and tamari soy. At COMO, we use Bragg's Liquid Aminos.

**MANGOSTEEN** is one of the world's most popular tropical fruits, highly sought after for their white, tangy sweet flesh encased in a thick purple skin. To open a mangosteen, use a small sharp knife to cut and gently prise the skin off one side of the fruit to reveal 6 to 8 segments of mangosteen flesh. This can then be scooped out to be eaten on its own or as an addition to desserts and salads.

**MATSUTAKE MUSHROOMS** are wild mushrooms that grow in the forests of Japan, Korea and Bhutan at the base of pine trees. This variety of mushroom is prized for its spicy, aromatic flavour which, coupled with a very short growing season in autumn, means that it is an expensive ingredient. The mushrooms should be lightly cooked to retain the natural flavour and meaty texture.

**NASTURTIUMS** are a plant with bright umbrella-like flowers, ranging in colour from yellow to orange and red. The flowers and leaves are both edible and are perfect in salads. The flowers can also be used as a decoration for desserts.

**ORANGE BLOSSOM WATER** is used as a flavouring in many Middle Eastern desserts. Also known as orange flower water, the clear liquid is distilled from bitter orange blossoms.

**PALM HEART** is a prized vegetable and delicacy, harvested from the growing stem and inner core of particular palm trees (as some types of palms only grow one stem, the harvesting of the palm results in its death, which is why producers are now growing multi-stemmed palms that continue to live when moderately harvested). Also known as heart of palm and palm cabbage, it is sold fresh, wrapped in clingfilm, and also canned. The fresh product is of superior quality to the canned. The vegetable is used in salads or eaten on its own.

**PALM SUGAR** is a sweet syrup made from the sap extracted from a variety of palm trees, including date, sugar, Palmyra and coconut palms. The sap is harvested daily from a depression cut in the crown of the tree. The sap is caught in a bucket. This sap is then boiled to produce a dark sticky syrup popular in Southeast Asian sweet and savoury dishes. The syrup is sometimes poured into moulds to solidify into little cakes. The cakes may be grated or shaved for easy measurement, and the sugar dissolves easily. Thai palm sugar is usually paler than Indonesian palm sugar, with a lighter flavour.

**PANDANUS LEAF** is a leaf similar in shape to the blade of a palm frond and comes from the screw pine tree. Also known as the pandan leaf, screwpine, ramba or rampe, the leaf has a sweet, almost grassy fragrance and is used both as an aromatic and a colouring agent. The pandanus leaf is bruised and knotted then added to soups and rice dishes.

**PEARL BARLEY** is barley that has been hulled to remove the husk. It is then taken through a further process of steaming to remove the germ before the grain is polished (a process also known as pearling) to produce a smooth white grain. This grain can be further processed to produce barley flour, barley flakes and barley grits. Minimally polished barley is called pot or Scotch barley, and is generally interchangeable (except in desserts).

**POMEGRANATE MOLASSES** is a dark, fruity syrup made from pomegranate seeds. The jewel-like pomegranate seeds are boiled until the liquid is thick and very concentrated. It is traditionally used in Middle Eastern dishes and can be added to tagines, dressings and marinades.

**POMELO** is the largest of the citrus fruit family. The fruit is similar in appearance to a very large grapefruit and has a pale green or yellow skin with white to pink flesh. Pomelos have an extremely thick skin that houses the sweet flesh, which is somewhat drier than other citrus but lacks the bitterness of grapefruit. The segments need to be peeled of their thick membrane before eating. They are popular in Southeast Asian salads with chicken or shellfish.

**PUY LENTILS** or lentils 'verte du Puy' are a particular type of lentil that originated in the region of Le Puy in France. They are very small and slate green in colour. Puy lentils have a slightly peppery flavour. Unlike other lentils, they hold their shape when cooked.

**QUINOA** is the seed from a South American plant. It was used as a staple, like a grain, by the Incas. Quinoa has a high-protein content of 18 per cent, and is considered to be a complete protein. It is also a good source of calcium and dietary fibre and is gluten-free. Similar to rice, it can be cooked by the same method. When cooked, the tiny seeds of quinoa will sprout their spiral germ.

**RAMBUTAN** is a wildly beautiful tropical fruit. It is a bright crimson oval-shaped fruit covered in fleshy hairs. Thick skin protects a semi-transparent whitish flesh, which encloses the seed. The flesh is juicy and sweet, very similar to a lychee. To eat a rambutan, use a small sharp knife to pierce the skin and cut around the middle of the fruit without cutting into the flesh. Remove one half of the skin to reveal the fruit inside.

**RAW APPLE CIDER VINEGAR** is made from organic apples and is not heated, filtered or pasteurised. It contains strand-like enzymes of connected protein molecules, known as the 'mother' of vinegar. Apple cider vinegar promotes good digestion and pH balance, and helps to support a healthy immune system. At COMO, we use Bragg's raw apple cider vinegar. Raw apple cider vinegar is widely available in bigger supermarkets and most health food shops.

**RAW HONEY** is the natural unheated honey produced by bees. Unlike most commercial honeys that are heat-treated to 70°C/158°F to prevent crystallisation, raw honey undergoes a cold extraction and cold filtering process. Because raw honey's enzymes are intact, it imparts greater health benefits than processed versions.

**ROSE APPLES** are a tropical fruit native to India and Malaysia. The pear-shaped fruit is pale green to yellow with a pink tinge when ripe. The fruit has a rose-like aroma and a mild apple flavour. It can be eaten as is or made into conserves and syrups.

**ROSELLA** is the common term for *Hibiscus sabdariffa*. The petals are most often pale yellow to pale pink in colour with a bright crimson calyx. The calyx is used for its deep colour to make food colouring and a purple dye, and added to jams, juices, syrups and jellies.

**ROYAL JELLY** is produced by honey bees to give nutrition to all larvae. Larvae selected to be Queen bees are fed the royal jelly in their hive cells. Royal jelly is packed with nutrition and health-giving benefits. It is believed to improve digestion, increase vitality and improve the condition of hair, nails and skin. Newer discoveries of its benefits include lowering cholesterol, improving liver function and relieving stress. Raw honey can be used as a substitute.

**SALAM LEAVES**, or *Eugenia polyantha*, are an aromatic leaf native to Indonesia and Malaysia. The oils found in the leaves are released when cooked in curries, adding a unique flavour. Fresh curry leaves are a good substitute.

**SEA SALT** is made from evaporated sea water and contains no additives (this is unlike regular table salts, which can contain iodine and other additives). Sea salt features micro-nutrients and trace minerals, including calcium, magnesium and potassium. It is available in flakes or fine crystals.

**SHIITAKE MUSHROOMS** are native to China, Japan and Korea and have been cultivated for over a thousand years. The mushrooms are readily available in dried form but are now available in fresh form. Shiitake mushrooms have brown-coloured caps with a white bloom and creamy gills. They have an earthy flavour that is more pronounced in the reconstituted dried mushroom. Shiitake mushrooms, both fresh and dried, are used in many Chinese, Japanese and Korean dishes.

**SOURSOPS**, sometimes known as prickly custard apples, are a deep green to yellow-green elongated heart-shaped fruit. The skin has short fleshy hooks dotted over the skin. The flesh is tangy and sweet but often quite fibrous. The pulp is used to make smoothies, juices, ice creams and sorbets.

**SPIRULINA** is a microalga and complete protein containing all the vital amino acids, which makes it a good dietary supplement for vegetarians and anyone needing to keep their energy levels high. Spirulina is available in tablet, powder or flake form. In powder and flake form, it can be added to drinks, smoothies and yoghurts, or muesli and salads.

**SUMAC** is an edible berry with a sour but fruity flavour. Sumac trees grow wild in the Mediterranean and the Middle East. The berries are sun-dried for 2 to 3 days after being harvested. They are then crushed to a coarse, deep burgundy powder. Sumac is perfect as an alternative souring agent to lemon or tamarind. Ground sumac is used extensively in Middle Eastern foods —sprinkled over salads, barbecued chicken and roasted meats.

**TAMARI SOY** is a Japanese soy sauce made with little or no wheat. The no-wheat tamari is suitable for coeliacs and those following gluten-free diets.

**TAMARIND PULP** is found inside the long bean pods of the tamarind tree. When the brittle green tamarind pod ripens to a reddish brown colour, the pulp inside becomes rich brown and sweeter while maintaining its acidity. Tamarind pulp is used most often as a souring agent in chutneys, pickles, soups and curries. Tamarind pulp is dried and may be sold with or without seeds. To use tamarind pulp, soak in hot water for 30 minutes to soften, squeeze and knead the pulp to remove the seeds and disperse it through the water, then strain or pass through a mouli. The resulting tamarind water is used.

**TORCH GINGER** is a member of the true ginger family. It has a beautiful flower that can be bright red, pale pink or white. The bud is used in Asian cooking and is important in the making of laksa.

**VIRGIN COCONUT OIL** is pure coconut oil extracted from the coconut meat through cold compression, or from the coconut milk (it is not the same as coconut oil, which is extracted from the dried coconut meat and is often refined, deodorised or bleached). Virgin coconut oil is not heated at any stage of its extraction, which helps the oil to retain its natural coconut taste and aroma. It needs to be warmed slightly to liquefy.

**WAGYU BEEF** is a particular breed of cattle prized for its high proportion of fat marbling throughout the meat. It is valued for its flavour and texture, and is expensive. As an alternative to wagyu, you may use the best beef available.

**WAKAME SEAWEED** is part of the brown algae family. It is most often sold in its dried form. Dried wakame needs to be soaked in water to soften before use. It is highly nutritious and has very few calories. Wakame is most often used in soups and salads.

**YAKS** are long-haired bovine herd animals found in the mountainous regions of central Asia. They may be domesticated or wild, although the wild population of yaks in the world is diminishing. They are valued for both milk and meat.

**YOUNG COCONUTS** are the young fruit of the coconut palm. They are highly prized for their plentiful and nutritious coconut water and tender coconut meat. Young coconuts are sold in their green husk, straight from the tree or with the husk removed revealing a white outer casing. The coconut water is a good source of dietary fibre, proteins, antioxidants, vitamins and minerals. Coconut water also contains more isotonic electrolytes than found in most sports electrolyte drinks. Both the coconut water and jelly-like young coconut meat are used in many different cuisines.

## EQUIPMENT

**BLENDERS** are indispensable for puréeing soups, making beverages, purées and smoothies as well as chopping thick, tough ingredients. The Vita Prep 3 blender is our blender of choice as it has a powerful motor capable of grinding foods to a smooth paste. It makes fine curry pastes and can finely chop nuts quickly without overheating.

**DEHYDRATORS** are used to remove moisture from food at a low temperature. They are important for raw food enthusiasts. The Excalibur Dehydrator is our dehydrator of choice as it is a dehydrator with horizontal air flow, which reduces the amount of flavour mixing between trays when dehydrating different types of food at the same time. It also maintains an even heating between the trays.

**MANDOLINS** allow for fast and even slicing of vegetables. A tooth blade can be attached to create beautiful even julienne of vegetables. The Benriner mandolin, made in Japan from tough ABS and nylon reinforced resin, is our mandolin of choice, with three different-sized teeth allowing for versatility in the cut.

**SLOW JUICERS** cold-press fruits and vegetables. They extract as much as 50 per cent more than regular juicers, which also means more vitamins and antioxidants. We use Hurom juicers.

**TURNING SLICERS** transform vegetables into long strips of vegetable 'spaghetti'. We use the Benriner turning slicer, made in Japan from tough ABS and nylon reinforced resin. It has four different blades for paper-thin slicing, coarse spaghetti, medium spaghetti and superfine spaghetti.

# NUTRITIONAL INDEX

# INGREDIENT INDEX

## DESTINATIONS

# CLEARVIEW

Published by in 2016 by Clearview Books
22 Clarendon Gardens, London W9 1AZ
www.clearviewbooks.com
1st Reprint 2016

By Christina Ong
Text, design and photographs
© COMO Hotels and Resorts (Asia) Private Limited
www.comohotels.com

Compilation copyright © 2016
Clearview Books, London

Managing Editor: Ming Tan
Editor: Sophy Roberts
Contributing Editors: Benjamin Parker,
Kathy Steer and Bronwen Warden
Recipe Consultant and Stylist: Amanda Gale
Nutrition Consultant and Editor:
Eve Persak MS RD CNSC

Creative Director: Rashna Mody Clark
Assistant Art Director: Anna Wiewiora

Photographer: Lisa Linder
Photographer's Assistant: Fiona Kennedy
Producer: Andy Lim

Contributing Photographers:
Martin Morrell: Pages 8-9, 46-47, 60-61,102-103,
132-133, 150, 196-197, 226-227, 262-263
Chris Ryan: Pages 52-53
Keith Levit Photography: Pages 188-189
Francine Fleischer: Page 212

Publisher: Catharine Snow
Production: Simonne Waud

Colour Reproduction XY Digital Ltd, London
Printed in China by Everbest Printing

ISBN 978-1908337-306